Preston Guild 1992
The Official Record

Dr Alan G. Crosby

Carnegie Publishing,
in conjunction with Preston Borough Council, 1993

Preston Guild 1992
The Official Record

Dr Alan G. Crosby

Carnegie Publishing Ltd, 1993

Preston Guild 1992: The Official Record

edited by Dr Alan Crosby

Published by Carnegie Publishing, 18 Maynard St., Preston,
in conjunction with Preston Borough Council

Designed and typeset in 10/12 Old Style Monotype Baskerville by Carnegie Publishing
Printed and bound in the UK by Cambridge University Press

British Library Cataloguing-in-Publication data
Preston Guild, '92: The Official Record
  I. Crosby, Alan
  338.632

  ISBN 0-948789-97-2 (case)
  ISBN 0-948789-99-9 (paper)

Contents

Author's introduction and acknowledgments

SINCE 1882 it has been the custom for Preston Borough Council to produce a permanent official record of the Guild Merchant. This has detailed the events and activities of the Guild itself, and has included extensive reports on the organisation and planning. The books were compiled during the months after the Guild by Town Hall staff, and were usually written or edited by the Town Clerk of the day. These volumes are an invaluable source for Guild historians, and are an attractive and much-prized memento of a magnificent occasion. When I wrote my own history of Preston Guild, between 1988 and 1990, I made full use of the volumes of Guild Records 1882 to 1972—although it must be said that the rather heavy 'official' style, with its rather laboured and ponderous prose, meant that they were not a source to be used for all occasions!

Preston Borough Council has adopted a somewhat different policy towards the production of the official record of the 1992 Guild. Instead of publishing the book itself, it asked Carnegie Publishing of Preston to do this task on its behalf, and I was commissioned to do the writing. My brief was that I might cover all the events and activities of that colourful and exciting year, using as my sources not only the reports and records which the Borough and its officers had produced, but also the historical material available from my work on previous Guilds, and the wealth of eyewitness accounts, newspaper reports and coverage, memories and impressions of the great Guild of 1992.

We have tried to produce an official record which is more approachable, readable and enjoyable than its predecessors, and to take a new approach by including comment, opinion and criticism, as well as the straightforward factual record. Inevitably, since so much happened during Guild Year and since so many hundreds of thousands of people, and hundreds of organisations, firms, schools, voluntary bodies, streets, companies and institutions joined in the celebrations, it has been impossible to mention all by name and to describe everything that went on. I must therefore apologise to all those who have been left out—it was not because you were of no interest or importance, but rather that 100,000 words was far too little space!

This book could not possibly have been written without the assistance of the many people who were involved in the preparations for the Guild, and in organising its huge range of varied events and activities. Some of these were present or former officers of Preston Borough Council, and it is to them that a particular tribute is due. After the Guild was over those who had worked on the projects and events were asked to gather together the information they had accumulated, and to write detailed reports on their role and on the events they had assisted.

These reports were to be used for the preparation of this book, and were also to be filed for reference in the planning of the Guild of 2012. I can testify to the exceptional quality of the reports which they produced, for I have read them all—they are clear, lucid and honest in their assessment of problems and pitfalls as well as successes and triumphs. I am sure that, come 2007, the officers who are charged with the task of organising the next Guild will find the records produced by their predecessors quite invaluable. Other reports, with a similar purpose, were compiled by private individuals who had participated in the planning and organisation, and by the officers of other bodies, such as the County Council. This book draws very heavily on the work of all of them.

In the context of this book I would like to express my particular thanks to Neville Bridge and his colleagues, who not only worked so hard during the long months of the Guild, but who also prepared most of the Borough Council material which has been used in this book. I hope I will be forgiven for not referring to them all by name: they are numerous, and it would be invidious to single out particular individuals. Therefore a collective thanks is due to them all: although the writing and interpretation are mine, I have made the fullest possible use of the records which they made available.

The other major source of information and comment—apart from my own vivid memories of the Guild—has been the *Lancashire Evening Post*, which gave the Guild very full and detailed treatment, and which has been of exceptional importance in providing quotable 'eyewitness' descriptions. In the book quotations have been taken from *L.E.P.* reports, unless otherwise stated. The *Evening Post* also provided extensive photographic coverage of the innumerable events and activities of Guild Year, as well as of Guild Week itself. I have used these pictorial records to supplement my own memories and recollections of Guild Year, and it would be fair to say that without the *Evening Post* this book could not have had its present shape or character.

In conclusion, I would like to express my thanks to Preston Borough Council, not only for asking me to write this book, but also for putting on the greatest Guild in history—the Guild of 1992!

Chapter 1

Historical introduction

I N LATE AUGUST and early September 1992 Preston was—despite the rain—in carnival mood as it celebrated its world-famous Guild, continuing a tradition which certainly dates back to the fourteenth century, and probably for two centuries before that. In its distant origins, several hundred years ago, the celebration was the public and ceremonial meeting of the Guild Burgesses—the members of the Preston Guild Merchant. They gathered together for the transacting of official business, and enjoyed themselves at the same time. As such this event has been an occasion for festivity and civic rejoicing for at least six hundred years.

Many other towns had guilds, and some other towns had festivities comparable to those of the Preston Guild, but almost all of these guilds, and certainly all those which resembled that of Preston, have long since disappeared. The Preston Guild is therefore, more than eight centuries after it was founded, a unique survivor of the Middle Ages, an event which has, quite remarkably, outlived and outlasted all its contemporaries and which shows no sign of fading away or dying. Indeed, quite the opposite is true, for the Preston Guild seems to go from strength to strength, and to adapt with great effectiveness to changes in society, in the world around us, and in Preston itself.

The right to have a Guild Merchant was granted to the town of Preston by King Henry II in his charter of 1179, and this privilege was renewed in the charters granted by later kings and queens. In medieval England most towns of any importance had a guild merchant or comparable body, and similar organisations were found throughout Europe. Guilds were bodies of men who, as the use of the term 'merchant' indicates, were connected in one way or another with the economic life of a town. They had a very powerful and wide-ranging role within the community, and today no single organisation has comparable powers, prestige and status. They can perhaps best be seen as bodies which combined elements of a town council, a chamber of commerce, a trade union, a social club, a religious fraternity and a charitable body. The influence of a guild in the commercial, political, social and cultural life of a town was often pervasive. In many places they became, by the fourteenth century, the dominant force, wielding immense power and exerting a strong control over the inhabitants.

The evidence for our town is limited, because documentary records for Preston and its history are scarce before the early seventeenth century. However, such evidence as does survive suggests that the Preston Guild Merchant was, like its fellow-guilds in other towns of medieval England, a powerful and prestigious organisation. Because a guild was so influential, membership was eagerly sought. To be a member of the Guild Merchant, in Preston as elsewhere, meant that an individual was counted among the leaders of the town, or came within their protection and influence. Commercial interests were the guiding force in the Guild, and were the reason for its creation in the first place. There was seen to be a need—or at least a desire—to foster the economic well-being of Preston itself, against competition from outside. On a more immediate level, the Guild acted in the financial and commercial interests of its individual members. The greatest of all its privileges was carefully and rigorously enforced: the monopoly which it enjoyed over trade within the borough.

This monopoly was an undisguised restrictive practice: anybody who wanted to trade in Preston, whether as a merchant, a craftsman, a market stall holder or in any other capacity, was required to be a member of the Guild Merchant. If he was not a member, and had the temerity to carry on a business or trade in the town, the Guild could take legal action against him, confiscate his goods, and order him to cease trading. This was not an idle threat—it was put into effect regularly, and in this way the Guild remained all-powerful in commercial circles until the early eighteenth century.

Furthermore, its great economic power and influence automatically reinforced the high social position and prestige which the Guild enjoyed in the town: the one depended on the other. For individual traders Guild membership was essential, but once they were in the Guild they would reap important benefits in addition to those directly linked with their business activities. The borough council probably evolved from the Guild, and by the seventeenth century the two bodies were inextricably linked. The Guild could therefore exercise considerable political power. To be a member of the Preston Guild Merchant was indeed a great honour.

Membership of the Guild was hereditary, in the direct male line. New members could be admitted by one of several different criteria, but once they were in the Guild their rights could be passed on to sons and grandsons without question. The possible means of gaining admittance included:

§   the granting by the Guild of gifts of membership: this was a way of honouring distinguished patrons and the local gentry and nobility, and was also given as a reward for services rendered to the Guild;

§   serving an apprenticeship with an existing Guild member gave an almost automatic right to be admitted to the Guild when the apprenticeship was completed;

§   outsiders (that is, people from outside Preston) could buy membership of the Guild, as could inhabitants of the borough who could not claim admittance in any other way: the purchase of membership was based on a sliding scale of fees, according to the wealth of the applicant.

Once anybody had been admitted, by one of these procedures, he could pass on his rights to male descendants. It should be borne in mind that, with minor exceptions which occur in the fourteenth and fifteenth centuries, women were not allowed to be full members of the Guild, although they were allowed to carry on trades which they had inherited from deceased husbands, fathers or brothers.

In effect, the Guild was a male-only organisation for the first 750 years of its existence.

A member of the Guild was called a Guild Burgess (a term usually shortened to 'burgess'). The Guild Burgesses were divided into two categories. The in-burgesses, technically known as 'Inhabitants', were originally, at the very beginning of the Guild's life, those who lived within Preston. The out-burgesses, or 'Foreigners', were those who dwelled beyond the borough boundaries. This did not necessarily mean people living a long distance away, for in the Middle Ages even such places as Ashton, Fishwick and Ribbleton were outside the borough. The out-burgesses, being slightly lower in status, had fewer privileges than in-burgesses. However, since membership was hereditary and at no time was there any restriction on where later generations of in- or out-burgesses should live, the distinction between 'in' and 'out' quickly became blurred. The key point is that by the fifteenth century, because of the hereditary principle and the lack of residence qualification, the members of the Preston Guild Merchant were widely scattered. Many had moved away from the town, and were living in other parts of the country.

The Guild celebrations

All Guilds needed the equivalent of an Annual General Meeting, in order to update their membership lists and to conduct any formal business which might be necessary. Since being a member of the Guild involved the exercise of special privileges, and gave considerable power, it was essential for the Guild officers to know exactly who was a member. The alternative was that individuals might make false claims and take fraudulent advantage of the organisation. Most Guilds, in other towns, met every year or every other year, but these were usually Guilds which either had a residence qualification, or did not have any form of hereditary membership. In the case of Preston such regular meetings were simply not feasible. The membership lived all over the country, and it was quite unrealistic to expect them all to gather for an annual meeting—the time taken in travelling to and from London, for example, might be four weeks in total.

Therefore, at an early date, it seems to have become the custom for the Preston Guild meetings to be held at very infrequent intervals, only once in a generation, unless urgent business of overwhelming importance had to be dealt with. Day-to-day administration would be conducted by smaller or informal meetings of which no record has survived, but once every couple of decades every member would be invited to a great reunion, a gathering of the clans, at which all the business since the last meeting could be formally transacted, membership lists updated, and much feasting and socialising enjoyed.

From the sixteenth century onwards the Guilds were held at intervals of precisely twenty years: before then the interval had been much less regular. The pattern of a strict twenty-year cycle continued without a break until 1942, when, because of the Second World War, the Guild could not be celebrated. The tradition was then resumed in 1952, ten years late, and the twenty-year interval has thus been restored. Beginning with the Guild of 1562 all the celebrations, and the official business, have formally been opened 'on the Monday after the feast of the decollation of St John the Baptist'. This feast day, which honours the patron saint of post-Reformation Preston, falls on 29 August, so that the earliest possible starting date for a Guild is 30 August. This in effect means that the Guild is held during the first week in September.

These great and infrequent meetings, and the attendant celebrations, became known, from an early date, as Preston Guilds. Already by the fourteenth century they seem to have been very special occasions, and their rarity and grandeur meant that by the mid-seventeenth century the Guild had become legendary. The special and unique quality of the Preston Guild was thus well established, and widely famed, at least three hundred years ago. It was this exceptional event, part of a remarkable tradition, which was celebrated with such style and splendour in 1992—despite the torrential rain!

Guild celebrations are recorded in increasing detail from 1500 onwards, in official records and in the more informal sources such as eyewitness accounts and entries in diaries and account books. Preston's first local newspaper appeared in the early 1740s, and thereafter, from the mid-eighteenth century onwards, there is very generous coverage of Guild celebrations in newspapers, journals, and brochures. From this range of documentary and printed sources we can ascertain that the major features of the 1992 Guild—formal and ceremonial civic events, colourful and impressive processions, exciting entertainments, special dramatic events and shows, and large enthusiastic crowds—were already traditional by the time of the 1682 Guild, which was the first to have been described in extensive detail. The 1992 Guild may, to many, have seemed modern, radical and innovative, but it followed faithfully the patterns and structures inherited from more than two dozen previous Guilds dating back as far as the earliest records. It was, without question, both living history and history in the making.

The heart of the Guild celebration is the ceremony in which the Guild burgesses renew their membership of the Guild Merchant. Technically all Guild rights lapse just before the ceremony, and become null and void. All those who wish to be members of the Guild during the ensuing twenty years must then apply either to join for the first time or to be re-admitted. The purpose of this lapse of membership that it proclaimed publicly the fact that Guild members only enjoyed their rights by the grace and favour of the Guild and its officers. Membership was not, in the most technical sense, an automatic right, but one which had to be sought by humble supplication. The requirement that members should seek to renew also emphasised that all of them owed allegiance and duty to the Guild Mayor, and were subservient to him. This applied without exception—even those who, like Lord Derby, were far above the Mayor of Preston in terms of normal social status and precedence were, for Guild purposes, subordinate to him and forced to make a technical submission to his authority. The ceremony of renewal of membership was the central part of the proceedings of the Guild Court, which was itself the heart of the Guild celebrations. It involved the reading out, by the Clerk of the Guild, of the names of applicants: they in turn signified their submission by bowing to the Mayor, and by doing so had their membership renewed for the next twenty years. During the medieval ceremonies this was the focal point, the heart of the matter, and so it was in 1992.

Since 1842 the official celebrations have lasted only a week—always known as Guild Week—but in the seventeenth century, and probably earlier, they went on for no less than six weeks. Nevertheless, most of the ritual procedures of the ancient ceremonies, and the formal events surrounding the ceremonial, have survived unchanged. These include the series of official public proclamations of the Guild, held in the market place; a civic service; various processions through the town; receptions, balls and banquets (though there were no banquets in 1992); and, to conclude the occasion, the formal adjournment of the Guild Court for another twenty years. Around this week of civic events a wide range of attractions soon developed—theatrical, musical and other artistic performances, sporting events, exhibitions and displays, entertainments and firework spectaculars. By 1802 these were as much a part of the Guild as the official programme, and from the mid-nineteenth century they were added to that programme, so that the scope of the Guild became much wider.

The Preston Guild has been celebrated in good times and bad. In 1642 it was held a fortnight before the outbreak of the Civil War, in a town which was riven from top to bottom by social and political dissent and antagonism and which was soon to suffer fierce fighting. We have no eye-witness accounts of what happened at the Guild in the first week of September 1642, but it cannot have been a happy occasion, overshadowed and darkened as it was by the clouds of war between neighbours. The Guild of 1662 is likely to have been in very marked contrast, for it allowed a celebration of the restoration of the old order and of the monarchy, a change which must have appealed to the more conservative citizens of the town and members of the Guild.

During the eighteenth century the old powers of the Guild Merchant gradually ceased to function, as the ideas of monopoly and restrictive practices were replaced by those of free trade. Increasingly the Guild was ignored and snubbed. Although it tried to maintain its powers, and to prosecute those who flouted its regulations, it found its powers waning and ebbing away. The example of flourishing and economically buoyant towns such as Manchester and Bolton, which were thriving even though—or because—they had no ancient guilds or corporations, was not lost on the more enterprising merchants of Preston, and they decided that 'free trade' would henceforth be more advantageous. The Guild thus lost its economic rationale, but the celebrations had attained such an importance, both in terms of their symbolic role and their role as a gigantic carnival, that there was no desire to see them disappear. The commemoration of the Guild every twenty years continued even though the function of the Guild Merchant itself had become purely ceremonial and honorary.

The pace of life in Preston quickened, and soon its lifeblood was manufacturing. In 1802 the Guild was held, in wonderful weather, in a town which was experiencing the first exciting years of large-scale industrialisation. All was new, all was change, all was innovation. Even had the old-fashioned Guild Merchant survived into the early nineteenth century as a force to be reckoned with, it would have crumbled beneath the pressures and challenges of the factory system and the new breed of textile merchants. At the Guild of 1802 John Horrocks, the greatest of Preston's early cotton magnates, lavished huge sums of money to ensure that the textile industries made a dramatic impact in Guild processions. These were, for some at least, the good times, the golden years.

But by the time of the 1842 Guild much had turned sour. In 1835 the Municipal Corporations Act had abolished the old corrupt and undemocratic borough council, and had replaced it with a new and reformed body. The Act, which affected municipal life throughout the country, abolished almost all the privileges inherited from previous centuries, and many local people believed that it had also swept away the Guild. These people also felt that the Guild, having long since ceased to be anything but a nominal body, was no longer needed, and that the celebrations themselves had long outlived their usefulness. Undeterred, others in the town pressed for the Guild to continue, and they eventually won the argument: the 1842 Guild went ahead as planned. But Preston was then in the midst of a trade depression, and there was violent and bloody civil unrest in the town. Only two weeks before the start of the Guild five people were shot dead by troops in Lune Street, and many of the gentry and nobility stayed away from Preston, fearful that the revolution which had been much talked about was going to break out in the town.

In spite of all this fear and distress, the Guild of 1842 was held, was celebrated with great enthusiasm, and was judged by almost all to be a success. The immediate threat of revolution—always a mirage in any case—soon faded away, but the civil unrest, very poor labour relations and extreme social problems which characterised mid-nineteenth-century Preston proved to be much more persistent. When the 1862 Guild came round Preston had once more been plunged into the depths of economic distress. The great Cotton Famine was at its most severe, people were starving in the streets, and over a quarter of the population of the town was officially classed as destitute. The Guild was held against a background of fierce opposition from those who felt that the extravagance and ostentatious magnificence were entirely inappropriate—a view echoed by many of the newspaper reporters who came to the town from London. But not even the Cotton Famine could break the strong thread of that historic tradition. In 1882 and 1902 the Guild was a glorious celebration of a town in the full flush of late-Victorian prosperity, secure—it was thought—on the foundation of cotton which had utterly transformed Preston and the lives of its people in the previous hundred years. The Guilds of these years were magnificent occasions, and in keeping with the times there was lavish decorating of the streets, immense patriotic displays of banners and flags, and—in 1882—royal patronage for the first time. The 'golden age' continued after the First World War—in many ways the Guild of 1922 was the last of the Victorian Guilds, as cotton still reigned supreme, Preston enjoyed what were to be the last years of its confident economic buoyancy, and the pageantry and ceremony of the Guild were eclipsed by the splendour of the seemingly endless textile industries procession.

Yet again the times changed, fortunes changed, the world changed around us. In 1942 Hitler succeeded in doing what no other had done: Preston Guild was cancelled because of the war, and many people suggested that this meant that no more Guilds would be held in the future. After the war there was much talk of abandoning the eight hundred year old tradition, and holding industrial exhibitions instead. Who, it was asked, was interested in processions, regalia and the old, outdated trappings of the past? Preston was a go-ahead progressive town, and all that historical nonsense gave quite the wrong impression!

Other, wiser, counsels prevailed. In 1952 the Guild was held, ten years later than scheduled, and it was judged a triumph. The people of Preston showed their own enthusiasm for history, tradition and their town's special and unique celebration by attending in larger numbers than ever before—and by holding a highly successful industrial exhibition as well! The Guild tradition continued, through the mini-skirts, platform soles and long hair of 1972, and on to the 1992 Guild. The success of the post-war Guilds, held in dramatically different circumstances from their predecessors, in a town which had undergone radical and profound social, political, economic and visual change, shows the strength of the eight centuries-old tradition. Floreat Gilda Mercatoria Prestoniensis!

The Clerk of the Guild, Antony Owens, delivering the third Guild proclamation. (Preston B. C.)

Chapter 2

Planning the 1992 Guild

W E KNOW NOTHING at all about the planning and organisation of Guilds before 1500, and very little about those before 1682. For the medieval Guilds there are no documentary records which give any detail, apart from the Guild Rolls which list the names of members and Guild officers. What went on at the Guild celebrations, and how the officers of the Guild planned and organised the formal proceedings, will never be known. We can, however, make some assumptions based on a few fragmentary references in documents from the sixteenth century, and on the invaluable eye-witness account of the 1682 Guild, written by the great Preston antiquary Richard Kuerden and first published in 1819. Kuerden, who not only watched but participated in the Guild of 1682, fully appreciated the antiquity and importance of what he saw. It is clear from his report that many of the events and traditions at the Guild celebration, and all of the formal civic ceremonies, were already several centuries old.

He tells us that preparations for the celebrations in 1682 began around Easter time, when the Town Clerk issued invitations to those Guild Burgesses whose whereabouts were known. At this time, too, he and the other officers made a start on the detailed planning of events, began to assess catering requirements, and looked at older records to see how the order of ceremonies had proceeded in previous Guilds. Then, as now, the experience of people who had been present at the last Guild would have been invaluable—not only to explain how things were done, but also to warn about possible pitfalls. In 1682, therefore, it took about five months to plan the Guild from start to finish.

By the standards of the day this was a comparatively leisurely pace, for the later records suggest that most of the preparation for seventeenth- and eighteenth-century Guilds occupied only a few weeks. Nevertheless, there was some longer-term planning, as building projects and improvements were put in hand for forthcoming Guilds: in 1760, for example, the Corporation was engaged in major reconstruction and alteration work at the Guildhall in readiness for the 1762 Guild. Since the Guild was a great and eagerly anticipated event, major projects such as these could be organised well ahead—although in both 1762 and 1782 urgent building work was required because the Town Hall and Guild Hall were in serious danger of collapse!

The 1842 Guild, which almost did not take place, was not even discussed until the February of that year, and it was not until the end of June that the Corporation agreed to hold the celebrations. All the planning and preparation work was therefore undertaken in less than eight weeks, a quite outstanding achievement on the part of the Corporation's officials. By 1862, perhaps anxious to avoid the intense pressure which this very limited span had produced, detailed planning was already in progress a year in advance of the Guild, and separate committees were established to deal with the organisation. By 1952 the preparation time had extended to two years, and for the 1992 Guild the Borough Council began serious discussion of the Guild during 1987, five years ahead of the event itself. The complexity, cost and sophistication of the modern Guilds means that a long timespan is required for all the intricate organisation involved.

The Guild Committees and Sub-Committees

For the Guild of 1992 the first step in the planning was the preparation by the Town Clerk/Chief Executive of a preliminary report, which was presented to the Policy and Resources Committee of Preston Borough Council in July 1987. It gave a summary of the origins and purpose of the Guild Merchant, explained some of the possibilities for the forthcoming Guild, and was intended to be the basis for more detailed discussion of the administrative arrangements which would be needed. An event of this magnitude and importance cannot be held without careful consideration, very detailed planning, staff of the highest calibre and an efficient organisational structure. A second report, in February 1988, suggested the establishment of a Guild Committee and referred to the possible appointment of consultants who could co-ordinate Guild activities. The management of the Guild by a separate committee had been a practice followed since the nineteenth century: the first was that created for the Guild of 1862, and this seems to have worked well—although a surprising amount of space in its minutes is devoted to reports on the tasting of wine, sherry, port, champagne and other spirituous liquors.

In its deliberations the Borough Council was guided by the example and experience of what had gone before, and especially by the planning and organisation of the Guild of 1972. This time it was particularly fortunate that a number of those who had been closely involved in the previous Guild, including several leading councillors, were still available to give advice and the benefit of their knowledge. Of great importance, too, was the fact that the borough officers in 1972 had kept extensive and detailed records of how they had carried out their tasks, the arrangements which had been made, and the problems they encountered.

At the 1988 Annual Meeting of the Council a full Guild Committee was appointed: originally there were sixteen members, but this figure was shortly afterwards increased to eighteen, and to twenty in 1990. A complete list of councillors who served on the Guild Committee between 1988 and 1993 is given in Appendix 1. In 1990 three sub-committees were established to deal with specific issues: Events; Civics; and Public Relations, Marketing and Sponsorship. Members of the Council who were not on the Guild Committee were permitted to serve on sub-committees, but it was soon found—as indeed it had been in 1972—that the use of such sub-committees was unsatisfactory, because the division of responsibility between them and the full Guild Committee was unclear. There was considerable confusion over which should deal with what business, and therefore in April 1991 the sub-committees were dissolved and all work was returned to the direct control of the Guild Committee.

The Committee met very frequently during 1991 and 1992 as planning progressed, and there were two meetings after the Guild celebrations to receive reports on the various events, to resolve outstanding matters, and to finalise the Guild accounts. The last meeting of the Guild Committee was held on 20 January 1993. A list of the members of the Preston Borough Council during the administrative year 1992–3 is given in Appendix 2. In accordance with the usual custom of the Borough Council during the preparations for the Guild, the formal resolutions that a Guild should be advertised and held were not passed until the spring of Guild Year—this procedure gave official recognition and authorisation to a process which had, of course, been in progress for three years already! The texts of the formal resolutions is given in Appendix 3.

The Guild Office

The Guild Officers' Working Party. (Preston B. C.)

Once the Borough Council had established its Guild Committee, it was possible to set up the necessary administrative and staffing arrangements and to begin

detailed preparation work. Early in 1990 the Council's Director of Personnel and Management Services, Neville Bridge, was seconded as Senior Guild Co-ordinator, and it was on his capable shoulders that much of the responsibility for Guild organisation was laid. He was ably assisted by Colin Ryding, seconded from his usual post as Urban Programme Manager, and Harry Walker, the Senior Personnel Officer, who were designated Deputy Senior Guild Co-ordinator and Guild Administrator respectively. They were not new to their tasks, for until the formal appointments as full-time Guild officials were made they had undertaken a good deal of work on a less formal and part-time basis.

These three Guild officials made the headquarters of their operations an office on the top floor of the Town Hall, and it was here, in the Guild Office, that the elaborate and complex planning of the 1992 Guild was masterminded. This was the nerve centre of the entire campaign. The scale and variety of the task meant that a great deal of additional help was needed, with special assistance in particular issues being supplied as required. The small Guild team was therefore supported by the other officers of the Borough Council, who in addition to their normal duties spent time on relevant Guild matters. Thus members of the Town Clerk and Chief Executive's Department assisted with the arrangements for the civic and ceremonial functions; the Leisure Services Department with sporting, leisure and arts; and the Finance Department with all the funding arrangements and accounting.

The making of all major decisions, and the continuous process of developing the detailed arrangements for all the many aspects of the Guild, was made a great deal easier by the formation of a Guild Working Party, which consisted of the Town Clerk/Chief Executive (who was retitled Clerk of the Guild at the start of Guild Year), the three senior Guild officers, the Director of Leisure Services, the Assistant Directors of Development (Engineering) and Finance, and the Principal Administrative Officer. Initially this body met at four-week intervals, but the frequency increased as the Guild approached. The Working Party was expanded whenever necessary, to include representatives of other interested parties such as the Lancashire Constabulary.

One of the leading features of all Guilds since 1842 has been the role played by the schoolchildren of the borough, and the prominent part given to the schools in the Guild events. The children's pageants and processions have, for almost a century and a half, drawn enthusiastic crowds and a particularly warm response, and there was never any question that they would also be crucial to the success of the 1992 Guild.

Right from the start it was agreed by all concerned that the children's events were of outstanding importance. They therefore needed particularly careful and detailed management, and that became even more apparent when it was realised that the officers of the Borough Council would be the planners and designers of the children's events. Whereas it was soon decided that many of the processions and other events would be managed by outside committees, this was not so for the Schools' Pageant.

Late in 1989 arrangements were made for John Cotterall, the recently retired District Education Officer, to assist in a part-time capacity with this vital aspect of the planning of the Guild. His particular responsibility was to co-ordinate the activities of all the many schools which would be participating in the Pageant.

He was joined by another part-time officer, Frank Hartley, who had been a senior drama teacher. He had been very closely involved with the 1972 Guild Schools Pageant, and so was the ideal candidate to take charge of the planning for the 1992 Pageant; because of the scale of this work he was assisted by Fred Green and Brian Berry, a retired headteacher and retired teacher respectively, who joined the team in 1991. These four men were kept busy throughout their period with the Guild team, and it was thanks to their efforts that the Pageant of 1992—despite very considerable difficulties—was as great a success as any of its predecessors.

During 1991 a number of other staff were appointed to deal with specific aspects of Guild preparation. In May George Hoare, the recently retired Dock and Marine Officer, undertook responsibility for the many events which were scheduled to take place at the dock and in the area of the Riversway development. Although ill-health sadly forced his resignation later in the year, he had done invaluable groundwork, and was ably succeeded in the job by Alison Young, seconded from the Council's Personnel Department. Jim Allen, recently retired from the Works Department, gave essential technical advice and assistance. Between January and July 1992 Palmira Stafford co-ordinated the planning for a number of big events in various parts of the town, including the Heineken Big Top (one of the outstanding attractions of Guild year), while from March 1992 Christine Hurford took responsibility for the activities planned for Avenham Park—the logistical organisation of these was one of the most complex parts of the entire preparation for the Guild.

The Guild officers were valiantly, indeed heroically, assisted by the clerical and administrative staff within the Guild Office and elsewhere in the Borough Council organisation. Colin Ryding wrote afterwards that 'There were days when no-one could possibly imagine that the chaos experienced could ever be converted into a well planned and programmed Guild. The sheer volume of enquiries, particularly as the main Guild Week approached, threatened to overwhelm the office at times, but the staff coped admirably, albeit occasionally on their nerve-ends, and the office proved to be an excellent information centre for all Guild matters … The variety of involvement was quite immense, and required a great deal of commitment and patience in order to ensure that assistance and advice was always available to all sectors of the community.'

And after the Guild was over? The work was not finished, for there were post-Guild events to oversee, and numerous administrative tasks to complete. Accounts and financial arrangements had to be checked and finalised, the video record of the Guild had to be produced, and all documents, reports, working papers and photographs filed and arranged so that the organisers of the Guild of 2012 would have a library of information about what to do, and what not to do, ready to hand. Last, but not least, was the task of writing detailed reports of every aspect of the Guild for use in the compiling of this, the official 1992 Guild Record. Without the work of the officers who undertook that task this book would have been impossible.

The Guild Mayoralty

When the Preston Guild Merchant was founded, in the second half of the twelfth century, there was no borough council and therefore no mayor. We do not know who was the head of the Guild at this time, and neither do we know what his ceremonial duties might have been. Did he have robes and regalia? Did he have a formal title? We simply do not know. The office of mayor, as the chief spokesman of the town (the 'maior' or 'greatest' person), probably evolved during the thirteenth century. Not until 1327 is there any record of the name of a mayor of Preston, but this is certainly not the first year in which there was a mayoralty—rather, the lack of surviving documentary sources means we cannot know about his predecessors. At about the same time as the mayoralty was becoming established the infant borough council was developing. It is quite probable that this body grew out of the Guild, and that its officers were also Guild officials: that was frequently the case in other towns.

By the time of the earliest surviving Guild records, which date from the late 1320s, it is clear that the mayor of Preston was also the chief officer of the Guild, and presided over its meetings. From this point onwards the mayoralty in Guild Year has been an office of exceptional symbolic importance, and the Guild Mayor—as he seems to have been known since the Middle Ages—has occupied a central position in the celebrations. His role was always one of public prominence and dignity: he had to preside over ceremonial occasions, to be present at public events and walk in processions, to sign Guild proclamations and other official documents, to receive distinguished visitors to the town, and to entertain them in a style which befitted their rank and the dignity of the borough. The choosing of the Guild Mayor has therefore always been a matter for particular care and weighty deliberation, and to be selected to fill this office is, perhaps, the greatest honour which the town of Preston can bestow.

Until 1974, when local government reforms abolished the office, the aldermen of the borough of Preston also played an important role in the ceremonial and civic business of the Guild, and the three most senior aldermen were usually granted the honour of being appointed Stewards of the Guild. In 1992 this honour fell to the five senior members of the Council (see Appendix 3). The Stewards of the Guild supported the Guild Mayor throughout Guild Year, and the borough councillors, in traditional robes of office, also supported him at the formal Guild events.

However, the most important figure was, as it always has been, that of the Guild Mayor. In June 1991 it was decided that an informal meeting of the Council should be held to select the mayor for Guild Year, 1992–3, and this took place on 18 July 1991. Councillor Ian Whyte Hall proposed, and Councillor Joseph Hood seconded, that Councillor Harold Parker be requested to allow himself to be nominated as Guild Mayor. Harold Parker, the manager of a local golf club, was then the leader of the Council, and was one of its longest-serving members— he had been a councillor for twenty-seven years, and had served as Mayor of

The magnificent mayoral chain which was added to the borough regalia in 1892. (Preston B. C.)

Preston in 1976–7. Councillor Parker accepted the nomination and thanked the members warmly for the honour which they intended to confer upon him. He said that he would endeavour to carry out the onerous duties of Guild Mayor to the best of his ability. On 21 May 1992, therefore, Councillor Harold Parker was formally elected as Guild Mayor, signed the necessary declaration, and was ceremonially installed into office. Earlier in the evening he had, with Councillors Hood and Hall, been made an honorary freeman of the Borough.

In the address which he then made he thanked his colleagues on the Borough Council for electing him to this high office, which is known to have been held by only twenty-six other people in the past six hundred years: 'To be elected as Guild Mayor and Mayoress is an honour and a privilege to my wife and me, particularly since both of us were born and have lived in Preston all our lives. We know the importance of the Guild to Preston people, and what we offer you is total commitment during the Guild year. We pledge ourselves to do all we can to ensure that Preston Guild is a great success. The Guild, of course, is a celebration for the people of the town … The Mayor and Mayoress [are] simply the pivot around which the Guild revolves, and we look forward to playing that part.'

'The Guild', he continued, 'is [also] a time for enjoyment, the pleasures of meeting old friends and making new ones, the re- uniting of family and friends from home and abroad. The Guild has been described as England's greatest carnival. We should enjoy it with enthusiasm and style, but in doing so, and I ask this pledge from the caring people of Preston, do everything you can to ensure that others also enjoy it. The elderly, the young, the deprived, they too are Prestonians. It is their birthright also to enjoy the Guild … Let this be the year when we all pull together for the good of the town, and let history record that the Guild celebration of 1992 was the finest ever held.'

Guild patrons

Traditionally, the Guild Mayor invited 'the Nobility and Gentry of the town and country' to be patrons of the Guild. It is likely that in earlier centuries these patrons were expected to provide some financial assistance towards the cost of the Guild celebrations, but their main purpose—certainly in more recent times—was to give additional dignity and social prestige to the event. Many would attend the Guild in person, and they would walk in the processions and be present at banquets and balls. That they did so gave a cachet to the events, and so raised the tone of the proceedings. After 1842 the role of the patron was purely honorary, and simply implied a benevolent interest in the proceedings, although many still came to the Guild in person. The number of patrons gradually increased, and included a wide range of local and county people—magistrates, judges, clergymen, leaders of other local authorities—as well as the nobility and gentry. During the twentieth century the numbers grew at each Guild, so that in 1972 the list included no fewer than 144 names.

As the planning of the 1992 Guild began, it became clear that the position of the Borough Council in relation to patronage was very different from that in previous Guilds. On the one hand it was now thought to be particularly important that there was full recognition of the vital role played by the various firms and commercial concerns which would be helping to fund the Guild through sponsorship. On the other, there was a feeling that some form of traditional 'list of patrons' was needed to give the necessary status to the Guild.

In April 1991, therefore, the Guild Committee decided that the list of patrons for the Guild of 1992 would be divided into two parts. The title of 'patron' would be restricted, and was to be given only to enterprises which had contributed £20,000 or more, in cash or in kind, to the Guild fund. This recognition of 'corporate patronage' was seen to be desirable as an acknowledgment of the important part played by these bodies, and was also considered as more in keeping with the spirit of the times. Since the extensive but nominal personal patronage of previous Guilds was less favoured than before, it was agreed that the other list should be for 'honorary patrons', and would be confined to a very carefully chosen group of individuals who would be asked to give their names in this way. The list was thereby reduced dramatically, to a select twelve, who included the leaders of the three political parties and of the churches. The names of the patrons are given in Appendix 4: the Borough was honoured to have at the head of the list Her Majesty the Queen, who in late October 1991 signified her agreement to become an honorary patron. She had been a patron in 1972, but the only previous monarch to have this title was Queen Victoria, in 1882. In welcoming this news, the Chairman of the Guild Committee, Councillor Richard Atkinson, said that he was 'sure that people in Preston are proud and honoured that the Queen has given her name to the Guild', while the Leader of the Conservative Group on the Borough Council, Councillor Joseph Hood, felt that 'it does something for the Guild and it proves that Preston is a town of some standing in the country'.

The question of women burgesses

With very few exceptions, all of which dated from before 1582, women played no official part in the Guild until the middle of the twentieth century. Many of the formal Guild events were only for men, and women, if allowed to attend (which was by no means invariably the case), only came as spectators. In the late eighteenth century, however, a change of attitude seems to have taken place. The wives and daughters of Guild officers and distinguished visitors probably expressed the wish—unofficially and behind-the-scenes—to take a more prominent role in the proceedings. As a result of their wishes, a Ladies' Procession (the forerunner of the modern Guild Mayoress' Procession) was instituted, involving a short walk around the town centre followed by a civic service. Although this did give some women—from the higher levels of town and county society—a chance to participate in a public event, it was only granted as a concession, and was not yet part of the full programme of civic and ceremonial events. Above all, women were still ineligible to become members of the Guild.

In the years after the First World War the centuries-old policy of excluding women came under ever increasing pressure. This was particularly the case after women began to be elected as borough councillors and, in due course, to be chosen as aldermen. Since all members of the Borough Council had to participate in the formal civic events of the Guild, and since leading and senior councillors and aldermen were given the titles of Guild officers, it became impossible to prevent women from participating. At the 1952 Guild, therefore, Alderman Mrs Avice Margaret Pimblett was a Guild Steward, and thus was second only to the Guild Mayor in seniority. A further problem was created by the tradition of granting Guild Burgess-ship to ex-Mayors of the Borough and to leading councillors. In 1972 this meant that Doris Dewhurst, Florrie Hoskin, Rita Lytton and Catherine Sharples were made Guild Burgesses, and their hereditary rights and title could pass to their sons. Despite this, women were still unable themselves to become Guild Burgesses by hereditary right, as daughters of burgesses, and these creations remained quite exceptional.

Twenty years later, as the planning for the 1992 Guild was in progress, it was clear that this exclusion of all but a tiny number of carefully selected women would be a policy difficult to sustain and much opposed. Nationally, the climate of opinion, and the legislative background, had moved very strongly in favour of admitting women to areas where they had previously been excluded, and so not only would a continued policy of male exclusiveness have provoked sizeable and strong opposition locally, but it might even have been of doubtful legality. In January 1989 the Town Clerk was asked to investigate the possibility of admitting to the Guild Roll of Burgesses the female heirs of current burgesses. He concluded that there would be no legal bar to such a move, as since 1957 'heirs and successors', the term used in the Guild orders and charters, had legally meant daughters as well as sons.

The Guild Committee therefore resolved that daughters of current Guild members could be added to the Guild Roll at the 1992 Guild, and that they would in turn be able to transmit their hereditary rights of membership to their own sons and daughters: in other words, that male and female members of the Guild would in future have equal rights. At the 1992 Guild, in consequence of the removal of this restriction, 274 women were admitted as Guild burgesses. A full list of all the 1992 Guild Burgesses is given in Appendix 5.

With the minor exceptions in the fifteenth and sixteenth centuries, and in the Guilds of 1952 and 1972, this is the first time in its history of over eight centuries that the Guild Merchant of Preston has admitted women as Burgesses. The implications of this for future administration, and its impact on the numbers of Guild members at celebrations to come, are considerable. Although this was their first Guild, 34 per cent of those who renewed membership or were admitted as new members were women—in other words, there was an increase in total membership of about 50 per cent as a result. This means that in future the number of burgesses is likely to be significantly higher than in the past few Guilds, and so the ceremonies may well take longer. In administrative terms a particular problem will be the identification of the membership: hitherto this has been simple, since a hereditary male-only system has been able to rely on the straightforward use of surnames. In future, with the change of surname of married women, and the subsequent additional changes in successive generations

§ preparing reports to be presented to the officers, in the areas of public relations and publicity;

§ researching, writing and distributing press releases;

§ writing leaflets, articles, letters and other literature as required;

§ liaising with tourist and information bodies, including the various tourist boards in the North West;

§ managing a wide range of publicity events;

§ providing an information service to local media;

§ providing the publicity and support for special publications such as schools' packs.

In promoting the Guild, and the town, the tourist authorities were extremely supportive, as were Lancashire County Council and the other district councils in the area: the boroughs of Blackpool, Fylde and Wyre were especially helpful in this respect, while the Lancashire County Council tourist bus provided an excellent means of publicising the Guild by means of its nationwide tours. The help and support of other authorities, and the interest which was shown by Preston's neighbours, was a particularly encouraging feature of the 1992 Guild.

The initial publicity drive, carried out during the second half of 1990, seemed to produce satisfactory results, with general notice of the forthcoming Guild being provided locally, regionally and, in some cases, nationally. Local enthusiasm was particularly encouraging, with much interest coming from industry, voluntary organisations and the commercial sector, and this promised to be a valuable asset as 1992 approached. During 1991 the effort was stepped up, with the publicity being targeted towards specific outlets. The Guild Office was represented at a number of important exhibitions and tourist events, and many pre-Guild talks and lectures were given throughout the county.

It was hoped that one of the key features of the publicity would be the development of a 'Guild image', with the extensive employment of a special logo. This was to be used on a very wide range of souvenirs and 'Guildiana', as well as on literature, publicity material and stationery. The consultants, Heckford Associates and Glasgows, produced an abstract design for the 1992 Guild logo, with a series of pale blue 'wave' shapes divided by a green wave. Although symbolic associations and representations of the River Ribble and aspirations towards a greener and ecologically harmonious environment were claimed by some, there was in fact no deep underlying message—the logo was simply a straightforward and pleasing shape! All Guild stationery and publicity carried the message 'A celebration of Preston Past, Present and Future', echoing the 'retrospective and prospective' theme of the 1972 Guild. The Lamb and Flag badge of Preston was also used on all stationery and literature.

In spite of the encouraging results of the first part of the publicity drive, as Guild year got under way the Council felt that its efforts were not having the desired results—people away from Preston, it was felt, did not fully appreciate either what the Guild was, or what would be happening in late August and early September 1992. When events were held, and it was possible to test whether the campaigns had indeed been effective, there was certainly some evidence to suggest that the message of the Guild had not been conveyed satisfactorily. Despite renewed work during the remainder of the run-up to the Guild the overall impression, after the close of the celebrations, was that the publicity had not been a total success—'Tried hard: could have done better' was the verdict.

The consultants had fulfilled all that was required of them in terms of the original contract, and its subsequent renewals, but there was little indication that, for example, any significant national or international interest had been attracted except from those who were, historically, linked to Preston by ties of ancestry or former residence. Likewise, there were many communities in areas within easy travelling distance of Preston which remained unaware of the Guild, its associated events and its significance and interest. Television coverage was extremely sparse—less than in 1972—although local radio gave extensive attention to the Guild, and the local press, particularly the *Lancashire Evening Post*, was very supportive.

The consultants' original proposals had calculated the net cost of the Guild at approximately £1.5 million, and had suggested that it would be 'one of the most cost-effective marketing exercises ever undertaken by the borough'. The final accounts reveal that the cost was actually significantly less than the original estimates had implied: truly, therefore, it could be said that it was a 'cost effective' Guild.

In retrospect it is clear that at least some of the factors which led to disappointments were completely outside the control of the Guild organisers and planners. The worldwide recession, and the very severe economic difficulties of the United Kingdom, must have played a significant, although unquantifiable, part in reducing the tourist response, and in discouraging international travel. On a more immediate, and more local, level, the appalling weather during the first half of Guild week was undoubtedly responsible for deterring many visitors.

The local response, as was to be expected, was quite superb, and the Guild generated as much enthusiasm and excitement within Preston as any of its predecessors had done—witness the holding of street parties where people thoroughly enjoyed themselves in spite of howling winds and driving rain—but the attendance at some 'fringe' events, and those held in advance of the Guild was undoubtedly a disappointment. The weather, the allegedly high prices, and the phenomenon, recognised in both 1952 and 1972, that interest does not peak until August, just before the Guild, may be partial explanations of a rather poor attendance at some pre-Guild events. Another, perhaps, is that there can be too much of a good thing, and that a full year of Guild events is, for many people, excessive.

The involvement of the private sector

At an early date the Council determined that the support of local industry and commerce would be fundamental to the success of the Guild. Such a decision was sound in terms of Guild finances, since the resources of the Borough Council were already hard-pressed and sponsorship offered a means of supplementing the public purse. It would also be very valuable in developing the publicity for the Guild and would be important as a means of making the forthcoming celebrations as truly representative of the town, its work and its people as was possible. The close involvement of the private sector, in the form of trade, industry and commerce, was also in keeping with the spirit of the original Guild, founded more than eight centuries earlier as a body devoted to protecting and developing the commercial strength of Preston.

Because of the very specialised nature of sponsorship schemes it was essential to appoint experts to manage this aspect of the Guild preparations, and in 1989 B.W.P. Consultants were selected to carry out the task under the personal responsibility of their locally based director Hugh Pennant-Williams. As the first phase of his work he evaluated all the events scheduled for Guild Year, and then developed a strategy which assessed the likely costs and the probable commercial advantages which a sponsor would derive from each event. It was recognised that although straightforward cash support would be very valuable, sponsorship in kind would also represent a major opportunity both for the Borough Council and for the companies involved. As a number of local and regional firms had already expressed an interest in being involved in Guild events there was a ready-made basis upon which the consultants could work.

One problem which immediately became apparent was that some firms had already been approached for sponsorship by the organisers of privately promoted 'Guild' events, involving voluntary and charitable organisations. This raised difficulties, because although the Borough Council welcomed such interest in the forthcoming Guild it did not intend that all of these activities would necessarily be included on the official Guild programme. It was also felt, very strongly, that all the Guild events and their publicity should be properly co-ordinated by the Guild organisers, to avoid the Guild Year programme—and Guild publicity and advertising—becoming incoherent and piecemeal. The Council therefore directed that all requests for funding or sponsorship involving events to be included in the official programme should be channelled through the Guild Office. The firms involved would therefore be negotiating only with officers or their appointed consultants, and the officers and organisers would be fully aware of all events which were being planned within the Borough.

After much discussion a number of key areas for sponsorship were identified:

§ indoor events at the Guild Hall, such as receptions and concerts;

§ exhibitions and other attractions at the Harris Museum and Art Gallery—these would, in some cases, run through the whole of Guild Year;

§ family events in Moor Park and Avenham Park;

§ special-interest events within the parks and at Riversway;

§ certain of the official—but not the ceremonial—Guild functions;

§ the major cultural events in Avenham Park;

§ sporting events;

§ ethnic and community events.

The sponsorship would, it was hoped, allow the firms to demonstrate their commitment to the town, their staff and their customers; draw the attention of potential investors and of the public to Preston and the opportunities which it offers; and produce specific marketing benefits. Special recognition would be given to sponsors in Borough Council publicity, in addition to the usual promotion of the sponsors at the events themselves, and, as noted above, the major sponsors would be given the status of Guild patrons.

The sponsorship initiative was launched during a ceremony held at the Harris Museum in January 1991, and the organisers were particularly pleased that the National Westminster Bank took the lead as founder sponsor. Although the nationwide recession was by this time well advanced, the response to the initiative was very warm, and new deals were agreed almost up to the Guild week itself. A complete list of the sponsors for the 1992 Guild is given in Appendix 6 of this book.

After the end of the Guild a report was prepared to assess the effectiveness and scale of the sponsorship initiative. It considered that the efforts of the Borough and its consultants had been amply rewarded, for 'the interest shown ... was quite remarkable, and the Consultants, on behalf of the Council, finalised many valuable contracts ... the end result in each case was of benefit to all concerned [and] the total value of sponsorship received by the end of Guild year to support all the various events was in excess of £800,000, in cash and in kind. This was a magnificent sum which clearly demonstrated the commitment of local industry and commerce not only to the Guild itself but also to the community of Preston ... An added benefit was that many community events were specifically aimed at certain charities, providing much needed funds to these organisations.'

Souvenirs and publicity

The earliest known record of a Preston Guild souvenir occurs in 1742 when, in various Lancashire newspapers, advertisements appeared offering engravings of the mayoral procession. It was claimed that the pictures would be drawn from life, and the cost was to be 2s. 6d. each—an enormous sum in mid-eighteenth-century terms. No copies of these engravings have been traced—it is possible that they were never in fact produced—but it is certain that at all subsequent Guilds the marketing of souvenirs, memorabilia and special commemorative items was an important and very popular feature—and often a very lucrative one as well. By the early nineteenth century a wide range of cheap souvenirs was available at each Guild, and from 1842 onwards official medals were struck for presentation to schoolchildren in the Borough. Special ranges of commemorative china and glassware have been well received for over two hundred years, and at the Guilds of 1952 and 1972 numerous plastic items appeared, including pens, umbrellas, carrier bags and pennants.

In 1991 the Consultants recommended that the sale of souvenirs and commemorative material for the 1992 Guild should be heavily promoted, but that, as in previous Guilds, a very strict control should be exercised over the use of the official Guild logo and the town's badge and crest. The Guild Committee agreed that there should be three types of merchandise—those marketed solely by the

Council; those marketed jointly by the Council and other organisations; and those marketed only by outside organisations, who would use the Guild logo or Preston crest and would make a royalty-type payment to the Council for the right to do so.

The Council commissioned two exclusive and specialist pieces of china—a beautiful bowl and a plate produced by Spode with a decorative border design based on one of Preston's treasures, the Mayoral Chain which was commissioned to mark the Golden Jubilee of Queen Victoria and which was delivered in 1892. The bowl and the plate were produced in fine bone china, and printed in six colours and 22 carat gold. They depict the lamb of Preston and the motto *Privilegio Possessio Pro Populo*, signifying that the liberties and freedoms of Preston are 'held for the benefit of the people'. Each was a limited edition: 1,000 plates and 500 bowls were made.

The majority of souvenirs were jointly marketed with the *Lancashire Evening Post*. There was a wide range of items, from pens, pencils and key-rings, through tea towels and mugs, to commemorative china and crystal. *The Official Guild '92 Brochure*, published and marketed with the *L.E.P.*, was very successful, as was the Souvenir Calendar jointly produced with Heckford Creative Advertising and showing scenes from previous Guilds. The sale of items which used the official logo or Council crest, but which were not produced under the auspices of the Council, eventually involved over twenty organisations and firms, and included goods as varied as silver tea caddies, wine, postcards, umbrellas, balloons and, suggesting that the Guild had an all-over appeal, lingerie.

All these items sold extremely well, particularly at the Tourist Information Centre, the Harris Museum, the Town Hall and *Lancashire Evening Post* premises. Large sales of souvenirs began in November 1991, in anticipation of Christmas, for many made excellent presents, and during the period after Easter 1992 the Tourist Information Centre in the Guildhall Arcade had to recruit extra staff to cope with the ever-increasing demand for goods and information. In Guild Week itself no less than £35,000-worth of stock was sold at the Information Centre alone, and between January and September 1992 its turnover was £750,000 compared with £40,000 during the same period in 1991.

As in 1972, the Guild Committee decided that it would be appropriate to produce a special commemorative postal cover. This was designed and produced by Dawn Cover Productions of Stockport, and a special cancellation was used. The stamps chosen were the set of five which commemorated the fortieth anniversary of the accession of Her Majesty Queen Elizabeth II, the chief honorary patron of the 1992 Preston Guild. The cover was stamp cancelled on 31 August, the date of the official opening of the 1992 Guild, and was extremely popular: the entire stock of 1,000 was sold out within ten days of issue. Postal publicity of a different kind was provided by a special Guild advertising frank, which was used on all mail passing through the Preston Mechanised Letter Office. The Borough Council bought franking dies for use during a twenty-week period from 1 April, at the bargain price of only £705. For this small sum an estimated 2.7 million items were franked with the Guild advertisement. This was generally regarded as a very valuable and cost-effective form of publicity.

As a souvenir for the future, and as a record of the Guild of 1992, the consultants employed by the Borough Council were requested to arrange for the production of a video which would show the Guild in all its splendour and variety. By March 1992 the plan had not been finalised, so the Council took over responsibility, and negotiated with Gatehouse TV Ltd of Whalley for the production of the video and 2,000 boxed tapes. Filming took place from April onwards, and major problems were encountered because of the appalling weather at some of the events. The heavy rain and high winds meant that some of the proposed filming had to be abandoned, but despite this a superb video was prepared, which fully demonstrates and records the colourful traditions, pageantry and wonderful community spirit of the Guild.

The video was launched in November 1992, when almost 2,000 advance orders had been taken. The response was generally excellent, and many people ordered extra copies for family and friends overseas. There were a few criticisms regarding the omission of certain events, but clearly it was impossible to fit all that happened over six action-packed months into a single 90-minute tape. A version compatible with North American video systems was also produced, and proved to be especially popular with the Canadian market. The project can be counted a great success, and one important benefit is that there is now a comprehensive visual record of many Guild events to help with the design and planning of the next Guild, in 2012.

The work of the police

Ever since the establishment of a proper force in Preston, after 1836, the police have been closely involved in planning successive Guilds. The immense size of the crowds, the potential dangers to public order and public safety which they brought, and the major increase in petty crime (especially pickpocketing) which had been seen in previous Guilds all contributed to their concern. In 1842 there was even the fear that armed insurrection or revolution might break out during the Guild, and the military were called in to supplement the small contingent of Borough police. Ever since then the organisers have consulted with the police about the routes of processions, the best methods of crowd control, and the most effective way of ensuring that the great events passed off safely.

The police planning for the 1992 Guild began two years earlier, with preliminary discussion about the best routes for the processions. There was considerable difference of opinion about this between the police, the Guild Office, the organisers of the various processions, and the residents and traders of the areas through which the routes might pass, but after some months of proposal and counter-proposal an agreement was reached. The police set up a planning office, which eventually had a staff of seven, and this liaised very closely with the Guild Office, the organisers of events, and public representatives. The office had studied details of the policing of the 1972 Guild, but the Police Guild Co-ordinator, Superintendent Gary Price, decided at an early stage that, because so many major changes in the town and in society had taken place in the intervening twenty years, the task had to be completely reassessed.

He identified several particularly important ways in which the circumstances of the Guild had altered: terrorism had increased dramatically since 1972, and Preston had recently been the scene of two terrorist incidents, including the bomb explosion in Fishergate; traffic levels had risen very sharply, and the potential congestion and disruption were much greater than at the previous Guild; the road layout had altered significantly, and the pedestrianisation of many side roads and shopping streets had affected potential routes and access points; and public attitudes and behaviour had also changed, with a startling rise in crime during the previous two decades, and the tendency towards public disorder which had been seen since the early 1980s.

He defined the aims of the police as ensuring that there was:

A good-humoured and friendly police presence was a hallmark of the 1992 Guild. (Lancashire Constabulary)

§ a safe environment in which events could be enjoyed by all;

§ the preservation of order by firm, fair and friendly policing;

§ the maintenance of free movement of traffic and the prevention of congestion;

§ the provision of a planned and immediate response to any criminal, disorderly or offensive conduct;

§ the provision of high-profile, informative support to the public.

It was pointed out early in the planning process that, because in 1992 there would be public events and celebrations spread over an entire year, the organisation would have to cover a longer period and be considerably more complex than had been the case in previous Guilds. The new pattern required extra policing at a number of weekend and Bank Holiday events, and this was met by officers from the Central Division of the county force, assisted by members of the Special Constabulary. No major difficulties were experienced at these events, but it was recognised that the scale of policing during Guild Week itself would be quite different.

During that week up to 900 officers per day, drawn from all parts of the county, were drafted into Preston, and special accommodation and transport arrangements were made. Preston College in St Vincent's Road was used for the reception, feeding and briefing of the officers, while in the town centre two buildings were taken over for use as rest and refreshment sites. Temporary police stations were erected at Avenham Park, Moor Park and Preston Dock, and the whole exercise was co-ordinated from the Guild Control Room at the Divisional Police Headquarters in Lawson Street, using twelve radio channels and over forty telephone lines. Closed circuit TV was installed at strategic locations to monitor traffic flow, and in addition a police helicopter transmitted TV pictures to the control room—the helicopter achieved some extra local fame when, during Guild Week, it was used to chase a stolen car which was being driven at very high speeds along the M55. The fire and ambulance services co-ordinated their planning with that of the police, and their representatives were in the Guild Control Room to ensure that in the event of emergencies the three services would produce a very effective response.

To maintain free traffic movement—as far as this was possible—the police liaised with the Borough Engineer and the other emergency services in working out details of road closures and diversions, and ensuring that access routes for emergency vehicles were clear at all times. The diversion programme involved extensive signposting, and the provision of teams of officers to enforce the new arrangements. To deal with the sixty-seven closures 124 officers were employed, together with forty-four motorcyclists who maintained traffic flow and supervised the processional routes. The police also helped with the procedures for the marshalling and dispatch of the processions at Tom Benson Way, and for their dispersal at Moor Lane. In order to ensure that the processional route was clear 141 side streets had to be closed to traffic from one hour before each of the processions began, parking in these areas had to prevented, and arrangements to allow access for residents and business users were also required.

At the Guilds of 1842 onwards the railways played a dominant role in bringing visitors. Indeed, the coming of the railway, and the availability of cheap excursions and bargain tickets, made possible the transformation of the Guild from a relatively local event, drawing its visitors mainly from Lancashire, to a festival which attracted people from all over northern England. In the late nineteenth century hundreds of thousands of people arrived at Preston railway station each day during the Guild, and this remained the case up to 1922. In 1952 the numbers reduced, as many people came by motor coach and some by private car, but the decline of railway transport and the rise of private motoring in the two decades after 1952 was such that in 1972 only 12,500 extra railway passengers were thought to have travelled to Preston for the Guild. In 1992 so parlous was the financial state of British Rail that although both the County and Borough Councils asked for extra train services to be provided, the shortage of rolling stock meant that this was impossible and the request was turned down.

Car parking was the subject of extensive discussions between the police, the Borough Council, and the owners of potential temporary parking areas. It was decided that the Council should try to cater for a visitor traffic flow of about 60,000 vehicles per day, and that as far as possible park-and-ride parking schemes would be operated. After negotiation a series of car parks was designated, ranging in size from eight different sites on the Riversway estate, with a total capacity of 6,000 cars, and Ashton Park with a capacity of 5,400, to the small site at Corpus Christi school, St Vincent's Road, with 300 spaces.

In the event the number of vehicles using the temporary car parks fell far short of expectations. The capacity was 26,400 spaces per day, but the total number of cars parked during the whole of Guild Week was only 4,734. A similar phenomenon had been noted in 1972, when some of the car parks provided remained virtually unused. Possible explanations for the shortfall in 1992 were that the weather kept many potential visitors away, especially in the first half of the week; that public transport—and particularly the bus services—were used to a greater extent than anticipated; that local people walked into town rather than using cars; and that motorists found unofficial parking space outside the central area, or used permanent public and private car parks to which they could still gain access.

From the police point of view, by far the largest single event was the great Torchlight Procession and firework spectacular on the Saturday night at the end of Guild Week. The appalling weather in the earlier part of the week had to some extent reduced crowd size, but it was quite different on the Saturday night. An hour before the start the numbers were so great that movement within the town centre was almost impossible, and it is estimated that about half a million people were present along the procession route for this event. After the procession a huge crowd—perhaps 250,000 strong—headed for Avenham Park to see the firework display. Many thousands of these had to be turned away from the park, which accommodated about 200,000 people. Despite the immense difficulties in controlling this event, and the potential for danger in the presence of so many people in the unlit, muddy and sloping park, all was achieved without incident—a remarkable tribute to the skill of the police operation and to the good behaviour and commonsense of the crowds.

The organisers and the police themselves were delighted with the effectiveness of the policing work during the Guild. Much credit must go to the 'Guild spirit', and to feeling of co-operation and friendliness which it involved. That an event of such a size, spread over so long, could take place with the absolute minimum of incident is a very praiseworthy and commendable achievement, of which Preston can be proud. The Lancashire Constabulary has, since the Guild, received many letters acknowledging the efficient planning of the event, the friendliness and helpfulness of the police officers, and the great value which was placed upon their role in the Guild of 1992.

First Aid planning and organisation

For the major events of Guild Year the provision of First Aid was the joint responsibility of the St John Ambulance and the British Red Cross Society. Late in 1991 the Borough Council submitted a request to the two organisations, asking them to provide the necessary cover, and this was agreed. A joint working group was established, made up of senior officers from both organisations, and this met monthly at first, with the frequency of meetings increasing to weekly as the year became busier.

The planning focused on four main areas. Firstly, it was essential to avoid duplication of effort and resources, and so a central reporting system was set up to channel all requests for assistance and to allow a duty officer to assess the level of help required. Secondly, contacts were established with all three emergency services and with the Royal Preston Hospital. The most important links were with the ambulance service, which shared information and which was informed when the two First Aid organisations received requests for assistance. In conjunction with the three services an emergency plan was agreed, to be implemented if a serious crisis developed.

Thirdly, there was liaison with the local organisers of processions, concerts and shows, and with Preston Borough Council, to ensure that the First Aid services were fully informed about the nature and scale of each event. The numbers likely to attend and the particular hazards involved were identified by consultation with Guild and event organisers, though in practice the attendance was often considerably lower than had been anticipated. Fourthly, and following on from all these, the planning identified the resources which might be required—these were eventually assessed in total as 120 personnel, six ambulances, up to eight mobile first aid units, and equipment and communications vehicles. Some of these had to be brought from outside the county.

During Guild Week, the busiest time of the entire year of celebrations, the two organisations dealt with numerous incidents, ranging from minor cuts and grazes to sudden collapse and a road accident. There were no serious problems in the organisation of cover, and the careful planning and preparation bore fruit in an efficient and effective first aid service, which operated very successfully in its cooperation with the emergency services. The only period with a potentially high danger risk was during and after the Torchlight Procession on 5 September, when the huge crowds in Avenham Park meant that finding casualties was very difficult, and taking them to be treated was often even harder—fortunately there were no serious problems as a result of these difficulties. In Guild Week over 5,000 duty hours were served, by about 450 personnel, with 42 ambulances and 30 first aid units. They treated 107 casualties during the week, and took sixteen of these to hospital in their own ambulances.

Planning the processions

Processions have been a central feature of the Guild celebrations for at least five hundred years, and 1992 was no exception. Although always focused on the town centre, the routes had varied over the centuries, the biggest changes coming in 1842 and 1862 when, because of the growth of Preston and the development of new residential areas east of the old centre, the route was extended. For the 1972 Guild, and indeed at several before that, the processions had marshalled in New Hall Lane, with many of the side streets in the area being used to gather different groups before they joined the main body of the parade.

In 1992 this was no longer possible. Environmental improvement works undertaken in the twenty years since 1972 had meant that many of the side streets in the vicinity of New Hall Lane were now closed to vehicular access, and blocked off with trees and bollards. Floats could therefore not be marshalled there, and in consequence the organisers had to rethink not only the starting and finishing points of the processions, but also the processional routes themselves. The main requirements were a large area of open ground for marshalling pedestrians and a long stretch of road for the vehicles, these two being reasonably close together and not too far from the town centre.

During 1990 the officers considered various options, and eventually decided that Tom Benson Way, the new Ingol distributor road, would be the most suitable marshalling area for vehicles. Pedestrians were to assemble at the University of Central Lancashire's Adelphi Street car parking area, and the two groups would then combine in Fylde Road before proceeding in strict order to the town centre. The original plan, put forward by the Guild officers, was that they would process via Corporation Street, Fishergate, Church Street, Tithebarn Street, Lancaster Road, Harris Street and Friargate to Moor Lane. The Guild Committee, after considering this plan, wanted additionally to include Ringway and North Road in the route.

The police, however, objected strongly to that proposal. Their overriding concern was that traffic flow around the centre should be maintained for the longest period without disruption, and to ensure that there was always adequate access to any part of the town centre for emergency vehicles. It was thought that blocking North Road would result in excessive disruption. Eventually, after no less than eight months of patient negotiation, a route was agreed: it went from Corporation Street, via Lancaster Road, Birley Street, Friargate, Ringway, North Road and Walker Street, to the dispersal point in Moor Lane. This route was used for all the processions during Guild Week, with the exception of the Mayoral

Processions, although on the Saturday the Torchlight Procession dispersed at Ringway rather than Moor Lane.

The proposal to merge the vehicular and pedestrian components *en route* had previously given rise to much concern. It was felt by many that it would cause a good deal of confusion, and make proper co-ordination very difficult. Other criticisms were directed at the choice of route, which was inevitably the subject of lengthy debate because it represented a radical departure from the pattern at previous Guilds during this century. Nevertheless, when the time came the organisation proceeded very smoothly. Most of the processions started approximately on time, and there were few problems resulting from the combining of the pedestrians and vehicles.

That the new arrangements were so successful was a considerable achievement, due in large part to very thorough and careful planning for many months in advance. The implementation of the plan was the responsibility of Bob Cunningham, the Council's Safety Officer, who was designated Chief Marshal, and he, with the assistance of his staff, ensured that the merging of the two parts of each procession was orderly and efficient. In addition to the Council's marshals, each procession entrant was requested to provide a steward. The marshals and stewards were fully briefed in advance during a series of meetings in the Town Hall, chaired by Guild Co-ordinator Martin Haworth. All were

The route of the processions through the town centre was the subject of very detailed discussions.
(Preston B. C.)

identified with armbands, and issued with personal radio units with which to keep in touch: these were held to be a particularly important contribution to the efficiency of the operation.

Very precise instructions were issued to each participant, and the planning was meticulous. Tom Benson Way was divided into numbered sections, each vehicle was given a corresponding reference number, and special arrangements, involving assembly at Maudland Bank, were made for the exceptionally heavy or horse-drawn vehicles which would move too slowly if coming from Ingol. This ensured that the processions followed the prescribed order (and, as far as possible, that which was printed in the programmes). Pedestrians were likewise assembled in order and then directed to the meeting point by the marshals. It was estimated that the total number of pedestrians involved in the five days of processions was 13,000, and very careful arrangements were made to ensure that all of them assembled in the correct order and at the correct location.

In preparing for an orderly departure the main aim of the marshals was to build up the front of each procession in Fylde Road, so that there was no delay once departure had been authorised. Accordingly, the first vehicles moved from Tom Benson Way down to Fylde Road at least 45 minutes before the start of the procession, and there the head of the procession was merged with its appropriate pedestrian element. After this, and once the movement had started, a smooth

A superb view, taken from the police helicopter, of the merging of vehicles and pedestrians in Fylde Road, adjacent to the university, during the Community Procession. (Lancashire Constabulary)

flow of pedestrians and vehicles could be maintained. Marshals at selected points *en route* helped to assist larger or more cumbersome vehicles at difficult corners and turns, and marshals in Moor Lane, from Cragg's Row to Garstang Road, supervised the dispersal of pedestrians and those travelling on floats.

The provision of grandstand seating along the processional route presented some difficulties, since sites were not readily available because the route passed along many streets which are continuously lined by buildings, and where there was no spare pavement space for grandstands. The most obvious sites were those in the centre of the town, where the Flag Market and other open space gave more room. Eventually a total of 6,537 seats was made available at eleven different sites. Of these 3,822 were in the town centre, 2,076 in the Ringway/ Walker Street area, and 742 seats in Corporation Street. Designated areas were reserved for the disabled and other groups with special access needs. It was notable that every seat was sold for both the Trades and the Torchlight Processions.

Marching bands

In the planning of the Guild, and especially of the processions, the importance of bands was at once recognised. Accounts of Guilds as long ago as the seventeenth century refer to troops of pipers, drummers and fiddlers, and there are references to Guild musicians in the records of the sixteenth century. In the Guilds of the past hundred years military and other bands have played a

As always, marching bands were prominent in the processions—this exchange of views took place just before the Guild Mayoress' procession on 4 September. (Preston Citizen)

prominent role, marching in the processions and providing appropriate music and fanfares at events. In August 1990, therefore, the Guild Committee asked the Town Clerk to compile a list of bands which might participate, and this was undertaken in conjunction with the North Western Area Bands Association and local military band secretaries. A list of thirty-five bands was produced, and this was made available to the organisers of the processions.

The Lancashire Constabulary held an International Police Tattoo at its headquarters at Hutton on 30 August 1992, as part of its celebrations for the Guild, and this brought top-quality police bands to Preston from several European countries. Some of these were involved in major Guild events, notably the Third Proclamation Ceremony, and their performances were received with special enthusiasm by the crowds. Their presence in Preston was a bonus, and added much colour and excitement to the pageantry of the Guild.

Because band hire was expensive, particularly in the case of those bands where members had to take time off work, the Borough Council agreed to give financial support, which eventually totalled £10,408, to the organisers of the religious and community processions. Most of this sum was given to assist the Ecumenical Procession, since in the case of the Community Procession it proved possible to negotiate sponsorship. The bands which attended as part of the International Police Tattoo were not a charge upon the Guild account, but in recognition of the very great deal of work and expenditure committed by the Lancashire Constabulary in presenting these bands the Borough Council made a contribution of £3,750 towards the costs involved.

Decorations and illuminations

Old photographs of Guilds—and, from even further back, eighteenth- and early nineteenth-century engravings—show that street decorations and elaborate displays of flags, buntings and ornamental features have long been seen as essential to the success of the celebrations, and have been important in the long build-up of excitement during Guild Year. Watching the streets being decorated, and seeing the town gradually being transformed, has for many people been the sign that all the talk of the Guild is at last being turned into action, and that it really is going to happen.

In previous Guilds some of the decorations were exceptionally large, elaborate and costly. In 1992, though, there were problems. Money was not freely available, and some of the highly ambitious and spectacular effects which had been attempted earlier in the century would not have been financially feasible or realistic. Since 1972 there had been major changes to health and safety regulations which limited the scope of what could be done—some of the impressive arches seen in earlier Guilds would have given nightmares to present-day inspectors! For example, the design and building of triumphal arches over traffic routes is now governed by safety considerations which were of no concern to our Victorian predecessors. Some of the initial ideas which the Guild organisers considered therefore had to be abandoned.

The decoration of town centre streets gave Preston a festive air throughout 1992: (right) Fishergate and (below) outside the Miller Arcade.
(Preston B. C.)

Four simple archways were erected on the approach roads to the town, at Brockholes Brow, London Road near Walton Bridge, Garstang Road near the M55 roundabout, and Blackpool Road in Lea. The traffic requirements meant that other possible sites were not suitable, and the construction and appearance of these arches, of plywood cladding on a scaffold tower held down by concrete ballast blocks, was much less ornate than in previous Guilds. They were painted with the message 'Preston Celebrates Guild Merchant 1992', and the total cost of installation and removal was £36,100.

The illuminated decorations were only in the town centre, because the cost of installing suitable power supplies to other districts would have been prohibitive. Illuminated decorations are themselves costly, and it was decided that the Christmas display should be adapted for the Guild. The 1991 Christmas lights therefore included a lamb of Preston and the words 'Guild '92'. From February 1992 the Christmas elements of the display were removed; additional Guild elements, including specially designed features produced after a competition among children in local schools, were then installed. The Guild decorations remained until the end of the year.

Red, white and blue bunting was hung from wires attached to the lighting columns along the whole length of the processional route, and additionally in the town centre red garlands were draped across the road. Guild banners were erected outside the Town Hall entrances, and on the main approaches to the town, as well as in the outer parishes of the Borough of Preston. The Town Hall entrances also had very large red, white and blue canopies. The pillars of the Harris Museum building, which as the setting for the official proclamations and other public events had a prominent place in the celebrations, were decorated with huge vertical Guild banners.

Chapter 3

Before the Guild: events and activities, January to August

U NTIL 1922 most of the events which made up the Preston Guild celebrations were held during Guild Week itself. A few took place during the last week in August, just before the start of the official proceedings, and there was a limited number of post-Guild activities, but in general all was concentrated in the first week of September. The only important exceptions were private, not public, ceremonies—notably the election and installation of the Guild Mayor, which took place in May. This short but very busy period of Guild celebration was characteristic of all Guilds during the previous hundred years, although in the eighteenth century and before the duration of the Guild festival was up to six weeks. The main reason for this seems to have been that if people were spending several days each way travelling to and from Preston to be present at the Guild, they wanted to make their journeys worthwhile and so stayed in the town for a considerable time.

In 1952 the first concessions to the 'modern age' were made. Guild events were spread over a rather longer period, even though the great majority were still concentrated in Guild Week itself. The 1972 Guild saw a major expansion of Guild activities, with official and semi-official events held throughout the summer and into the depths of winter. The idea that the phrase 'Guild Year' would not simply mean 'the year in which the Guild was held' but would refer to 'The Year of Guild Events' had taken hold, and it was almost inevitable that in 1992 the process would be carried much further.

The Guild Committee decided that its policy would be to spread events widely during the year, and that once the weather began to improve (or at least might reasonably be expected to improve) and once the days grew longer and lighter, the celebrations could begin. Thus, the build-up to Guild Week proper began around Easter 1992, and there were five months of events and activities, shows and festivals, before the official Guild Week and the formal civic ceremonies. Guild Week would be the heart of the celebrations, as it always has been, but the people of Preston could enjoy an unprecedented range and variety of pre-Guild entertainments. This chapter looks in detail at just some of the main events which took place in the eight months between the beginning of Guild Year and the official opening of the Guild. There were many other activities in progress: some of those are considered in the next chapter, and others are recorded in the Guild Year calendar which forms Appendix 7 of this book.

Welcome to Guild Year

The excitement began on the Flag Market on New Year's Eve, with a spectacular open-air event to welcome Guild Year 1992 in a most memorable fashion. From 7 p.m. onwards people were gathering in the market place as the Red Rose Road Show provided musical entertainment. Great firework displays lit up the sky at 8 p.m. and 10 p.m., and during the evening circus performers, including a traditional Lancashire New Year's dancing Hobby Hoss, amused and entertained the crowds. Preston's new and already very popular Town Crier, Sergeant-Major Mike Chapman from the Army Recruiting Centre, was in fine voice on the first day of his very arduous Guild Year duties. There were performances on stage from Martini's Magic, well-known local magicians, while 'a cavalcade of entertainers kept everyone in good cheer, and included ... professional fool Dave Fowkes [who] kept up a medieval tradition as the Lord of Misrule ensuring everyone was having fun'.

Just before midnight the Mayor of Preston, Councillor Miss Mary Rawcliffe, left a New Year Dance and addressed the massive crowd from the steps of the Harris Museum, promising the people of the town a Guild Year to remember. Immediately after the Mayor's speech 'party-goers young and old counted down to the stroke of midnight with the sounds of Big Ben relayed from London, and a rousing chorus of 'Auld Lang Syne' was sung'. This was immediately followed by a final breathtaking firework display, which turned the sky into a blaze of glorious colour. Guild Year was well and truly launched!

The Guild Emblem and Scrolls of Friendship

Technically, however, the activities of Guild Year were already under way, for one of the traditional Guild scrolls of friendship had embarked upon its long journey around the world a week previously. The sending of Guild scrolls is a recent, but deeply symbolic and highly effective, Guild custom. In 1902 and 1922 the organisers of the Guild made special efforts to remind Prestonians of their fellow-citizens who had gone to live overseas, and to bring the Guild to the attention of those exiles in Canada, the United States, Australasia, Southern Africa and elsewhere. For the Guild of 1922 over 300 former Prestonians made the long trip from overseas, and this dedication and enthusiasm captured the imaginations of local people and of the newspaper reporters. The renewal of ties with people overseas, long-lost friends and relatives not seen for many a year, was a new Guild theme, and it saw further development in 1952. After the war, and all the attendant upheaval, and after the traumatic economic circumstances which Preston had experienced as the cotton industry collapsed, the renewing of old connections of family and kinship seemed especially important.

The Town Hall, that magnificent and much-loved symbol of Victorian Preston, had burned down in 1947. The Guild organisers in 1952 hit upon the imaginative idea of making emblems in the shape of the old Town Hall clock tower, carved from wood which had been retrieved from the remains of the building. These emblems were sent on tours to several countries in the New World and the Southern Hemisphere, accompanied by scrolls of friendship on which exiled Prestonians or their descendants could sign their names as a reaffirmation of past associations and affectionate attachment. The exercise not only appealed to sentiment but also provided extremely good publicity, and was very well received at home and abroad. It was repeated in 1972, and there was much support for the sending of emblems and scrolls as part of the 1992 Guild celebrations.

The planning was carried out by Preston Rotary and Preston Lions, in conjunction with the Guild Committee. Routes were worked out taking in twenty two major centres in Canada and the United States, to be organised by Rotary, and fourteen centres in Australia and New Zealand in the charge of the Lions. In addition, special scrolls were prepared for circulation to Preston's twin towns in Europe. Between July and December 1991 the Mayor of Preston, Councillor Miss Mary Rawcliffe, sent letters of greeting to the major cities and towns on the two routes, to give advance notice of the arrival of the emblems, and the organisers contacted local Rotary and Lions Clubs in the thirty-six cities, to ensure the smooth operation of the complex exercise.

The emblems were officially dispatched at the end of the year. On 23 December the Mayor and the Guild-Mayor Elect handed the North American scrolls and emblem to Roy Beaumont and Bill Oldcorn, of Preston Rotary Club, while on 7 January the Australasian emblem was presented to Norman Leigh and other officers of Preston Lions, and given a civic send-off with a vintage fire engine. As a result of appeals in the local press early in 1991 the Guild Office had compiled a list of the names and addresses of many Prestonians and their families living overseas. Individual scrolls of friendship were subsequently sent to as many as possible of these who did not live on or near the routes of the two emblems. In January 1992 Karen Fowler, Miss Preston Guild 1972, took scrolls of friendship to Durban, Cape Town and Johannesburg as part of a private holiday visit to South Africa.

The Australasian emblem returned safely on 29 August 1992, and was presented to the Guild Mayor, Councillor Harold Parker, on the occasion of the Third Proclamation of the Guild. The scrolls from Preston's twin towns in Europe were handed over ceremonially on the same occasion by the Mayor of Almelo, Mr H. G. J. van Roekel; the Deputy Mayor of Nimes, Madame V. Bombal; the Mayor of Recklinghausen, Herr J. Welt; and the Presidente of Kalisz, Mr W. Bachor.

The North American emblem was almost lost *en route*! It disappeared for several days somewhere between Boston and Quebec, and was eventually tracked down to a Canadian customs post. The delay meant some alterations to its journey, and it did not arrive back at Manchester Airport until the afternoon of 28 August. At 8.00 a.m. on the 29th it was given a civic send-off on the steps of Manchester Town Hall by the city's Deputy Lord Mayor, and then a team of runners from the Preston Harriers and Athletic Club, all wearing Preston Guild shirts, brought it along the A6 to Preston. Led by police outriders, June Butter-field, carrying the emblem, and Rick Curwen and Mike Barton carrying Ameri-can and Canadian flags, arrived precisely on time in the Market Square. They climbed the steps to the podium of the Harris Museum and, to thunderous applause and cheers, handed over the emblem to the Guild Mayor.

There is no doubt that the organisers of the 1952 Guild, in introducing the idea of the emblems and scrolls, were making an instant tradition, a piece of inspired and effective theatre which combines meticulous planning, large-scale organisation and much flair. The emblems and scrolls appeal to the sentiments of all those who recognise the Guild as a celebration of Preston, and the renewal and reaffirmation of old links and associations is thereby encouraged and devel-oped. The 1992 Guild showed, in the numbers of overseas visitors and the success of the emblem tours, that those feelings are as strong as ever.

Managing Avenham Park

Avenham Park is part of one of the finest urban open spaces in northern England and is an outstanding feature of the townscape of central Preston. With the river alongside, and views into open countryside, it is an extremely popular amenity. Not the least of its advantages is that it forms a superb natural amphitheatre or arena, and this feature has been recognised by the organisers of Guilds ever since 1862, when the park was not yet finished. In that year the massed gathering of schoolchildren—the largest event ever held at a Guild up to that date—took place in the Park.

In 1922 the famous Children's Pageant was held there, an event still remem-bered by many who were participants, and this—perhaps the single most popular event which has ever been held in any Guild—confirmed the place of Avenham Park as an ideal venue for very large Guild shows. The 1992 Guild was no exception—indeed, the range and overall scale of the activities in the Park during Guild Year 1992 were probably greater than at any previous Guild. The use of the Park culminated in the intensive programme of eight major events during Guild Week itself. All these plans posed particular problems for the organisers—how to ensure crowd safety and security, what to do about wet weather and the threat of the arena becoming waterlogged (as often happens in prolonged wet periods), how to minimise damage to the park itself, and how to manage and provide for the vast crowds which might be expected.

An officer, Christine Hurford, was appointed in March 1992 to supervise and co-ordinate the facilities for the eight Guild Week events. The programme meant that the Park would be in use on every day during that week. The priority was to ensure that the necessary equipment was identified and booked as soon as possible, since August Bank Holiday weekend, which coincided with the start of the Guild, is a very popular time for outdoor events. The equipment and staff needed included temporary toilets to cater for crowds of up to 10,000 people; marquees to serve as changing rooms and refreshment areas; cleaning and security staff; kitchen facilities; security equipment; temporary roads and path-

Making Avenham Park ready for a long succession of major events was a crucial part of the Guild preparations.
(Preston B. C.)

ways; programmes, tickets and notices; fencing and furniture. Every requirement, from portable site offices to bars of soap, had to be identified and ordered.

An intricate and detailed programme of planning was put into effect during August, with careful co-ordination of the arrival and installation of equipment and facilities. There were innumerable meetings between the organisers and managers of events, the contractors, representatives of the Guild Committee, and the Guild Event Co-ordinators, to ensure that everything went as smoothly as possible. Officials from the Borough Council's Development Department and the Council Safety Officer gave technical support and advice, and their specialised knowledge and enthusiastic participation were of immense help—their efforts, which far exceeded the original brief for the job, were much appreciated.

The large-scale construction work began on 17 August, and was completed in time for the first full dress rehearsal of the Schools Pageant on 27 August. The threat of waterlogging, and the fear that the whole arena bottom might, if there was heavy rain, turn into an impassable quagmire, remained, although the weather in mid-August had been comparatively good. Professional advisers from the contractors had recommended the use of temporary steel roadways and loading areas so that the large container trucks and low loaders would not wreck the ground surface (and would not sink into the mud!). This procedure allowed work to continue without interruption when the weather did, as feared, begin to deteriorate towards the end of the month. It was decided that, in addition to the steel surfaces, rubber matting should be laid to form pathways across the Park and to make some aisles between seats. This proved to be a wise move, because during Guild Week itself, when the weather was particularly bad, the roadway and walkways remained in good condition and stood the test of extremely heavy use, without the ground turning into the dreaded sea of mud—although it was perilously close to doing so.

The promotion of the Avenham Park events was undertaken by the Guild Office, with the advice of Performing Arts Management Ltd., who presented the various concerts. A total of 100,000 leaflets and 500 posters was produced, and distributed throughout the North West. Advance ticket sales were handled by the Guildhall Box Office, and a temporary office was provided at the Park for sales 'on the day'. Up to seventy stewards and ten cashiers were required at each event to deal with security, public safety, advice and ticket checking. Catering for construction and operations staff was provided in a large marquee served by a mobile kitchen: it is calculated that between 17 August and 10 September 1,563 full meals and countless cups of coffee and orange squash were served.

After the Guild Week events were over the site had to be cleared. This work began on 4 September, to make space for the firework display on 5 September, which ended the official and formal programme of events. The clearance work was carried out with exceptional efficiency, so that the last equipment and the security fence were removed on 11 September. The ground was then cleared of any remaining litter and debris, and some restoration work carried out, before the arena and the Park itself were left to recover … until the next time!

The advance planning for the musical events of the Guild began in 1990, and in the early days a wide range of names and possible attractions were mentioned as candidates for Guild stardom. The organisers hoped that singers, groups and musicians of international reputation could be attracted to the town for Guild concerts. In September 1990, for example, there was extensive publicity for the suggestion that the giant Italian operatic giant, Luciano Pavarotti, might—in the words of the *Evening Post*—'lend his massive musical weight' to a spectacular concert in Avenham Park. Other names mentioned during 1990 included a series of celebrated rock groups and artists—among them, Phil Collins, Queen and Dire Straits. There was some adverse comment about this optimistic sprinkling of famous names: it was said that the Guild organisers were being unrealistic and that their plans were 'just pie in the sky'. This was, of course, firmly denied, but ultimately the musical attractions of the Guild, although by no means unimpressive, were not of the very top-rank calibre which had been hinted. Some of the original criticism therefore proved to be accurate.

The Guild Steam Rally (2–4 May)

The major events of Guild Year began after Easter, the first 'spectacular' being the Guild Steam Rally which was held at Riversway during the Mayday Bank Holiday weekend. The event was designed to attract enthusiasts for all types of steam power and traction, and to have—it was hoped—a national appeal. It was organised by the Rotary Club of Preston South, with some assistance from the Guild Office staff. The 1992 President of Preston South Rotary was Alan Atkinson, a keen steam enthusiast, and the event was partly his inspiration: the organisation undertaken by the Rotarians was crowned by outstanding success, and was a magnificent achievement. Generous sponsorship was secured from GEC Alsthom. It was estimated that over 11,500 people attended the three-day event, and the overall profit was a quite exceptional £16,000, which was distributed to local charities.

There were over 250 exhibitors, and machinery on show included steam traction engines, rollers, wagons, farm machinery and vintage vehicles. The oldest machine on view was an 1880 Shand Mason horse-drawn fire appliance, formerly owned by Fulwood Urban District council, and another major attraction was a superb traction engine, built by Burrells of Thetford and first displayed during the 1902 Guild celebrations. Traditional merry-go-rounds, stalls and side-shows added to the excitement, while music from several steam organs—including the 140-key Dutch 'Centenary Organ', the world's largest fairground organ—added to the carnival atmosphere.

It was suggested to the Steamport Museum at Southport that a steam passenger service should be run along the dock railway, which is owned by the Council. Since the line is used only for freight it was necessary to make some improvements to the track and to ensure that this and the temporary platforms met the standards of the British Railways Inspectorate. This was done, and in late April the inspector, Major Oliver, authorised the running of a passenger service.

Temporary platforms were erected at the junction of Navigation Way and Port Way, using the signal cabin from the old sidings as a ticket booth, and at the engine shed at the western end of the line. Two steam locomotives were provided—'Agecroft' No. 2 from Steamport, and No. 22 'Defiant' from the

*The Guild Steam Rally in May
saw traction engines and steam
trains, among other attractions.
(Preston B. C.)*

Yorkshire Dales Railway at Embsay near Skipton. They were coupled to each end of a rake of two passenger coaches. A total of 2,875 people travelled on the service, and many thousands of others watched the splendid sight of the steam trains along the dock railway during the weekend. From many surrounding vantage points the sight, sound and smell of steam trains provided an unforgettably nostalgic experience.

During the following Bank Holiday, 23–25 May, a 'Thomas the Tank Engine' Weekend was organised. This was a last-minute addition to the Guild programme, but thanks to extensive and effective advertising it was also a great success. The same steam passenger service was operated, both locomotives being embellished with a face—one was changed into 'Thomas' and the other into 'Henry'. At the western end of the line the sidings housed static exhibits, including Bertie the Bus, Trevor the Traction Engine, Terence the Tractor and Evil Diesel (which was another and more malevolent incarnation of the Council's own diesel locomotive, normally used on the dock railway). The Fat Controller made surprise visits during the day, and during the weekend a total of 2,709 passengers used the steam service.

The naming of a locomotive and the Guild Steam Train (16 May)

Preston has strong historic connections with the railway industry, and it remains a railway centre of national importance. Its first railway was opened in 1838, the last scheduled steam-operated train on British Railways ran from Preston in 1968,

Naming Class 86 locomotive No. 86212 'Preston Guild 1328–1992', on 16 May.
(Preston B. C.)

and in 1975 British Rail named a Class 86 electric locomotive 'Preston Guild'. An event with a railway theme was thus very appropriate for the 1992 Guild, and in fact two such events were ultimately arranged. Steamport was asked if it would like to organise a steam visit, but this offer was declined for technical reasons— although, as noted above, Steamport did participate in the Steam Rally held in early May at Riversway. Approaches were also made to British Rail with a view to naming a locomotive to commemorate the Guild.

In the autumn of 1991 British Rail agreed to allow the naming of a locomotive, and also suggested that Flying Scotsman Services Ltd might be interested in operating a steam special from Preston during Guild Year. The negotiations resulted in agreement for a circular trip whereby the special train was diesel-hauled to Blackburn, then steam-hauled via Hellifield and the scenic Settle and Carlisle line to Carlisle, and then back to Blackburn, for a change to diesel traction to take the train on to Preston. Efforts to persuade British Rail head-quarters to allow steam haulage out of Preston itself were unsuccessful, despite personal appeals from the Mayor to the Chairman of British Rail.

The trip, which had 460 places at £15 per head, was quickly sold out. Class 86 locomotive No. 86212, which in 1975 had been named 'Preston Guild', was rededicated 'Preston Guild 1328–1992' during a special ceremony on 16 May at Preston railway station, just before the trip to Carlisle. The naming was performed by the Mayor, Councillor Miss Mary Rawcliffe, and Ivor Warburton, Director of Inter-City West Coast. The Longridge Silver Band entertained the guests before the departure of the train. At Carlisle the City Council provided a civic lunch for the distinguished guests. Special souvenir mugs and memorabilia were sold on board the train, and for both the Borough Council and the sponsors of the event, the *Lancashire Evening Post*, the trip was profitable.

The commemorative headboard carried by Flying Scotsman was raffled for £250, in aid of the Guild Mayor's Charities. British Rail had cast four nameplates for No. 86212. Two are still borne by the locomotive, one was presented to the town and is now in the Harris Museum, and the fourth was offered for sale in a postal auction, which raised a further £862.12 for the mayoral charities.

Aerial Spectacular at Ashton Park (16–17 May)

In the original report prepared by the consultants there had been a proposal for a large-scale air show during Guild Year. However, subsequent investigations showed that not only would the cost be in the region of £200,000, but that there was insufficient time available to plan such an extensive and technically challenging event. There were some local enthusiast groups willing to be involved in a less ambitious show, with 'air travel and transport' as its theme, but none was able to organise it. In December 1991 the Council agreed to take over management of an event of this type, to be held on Ashton Park, and to underwrite the costs: attempts to attract sponsorship were, unfortunately, largely unsuccessful.

The event thus got off to a somewhat uncertain start, and it was troubled with a number of additional minor difficulties. The use of Ashton Park posed problems of security, so a temporary fence was erected around the park for the weekend of the event: this, in turn, gave rise to some objections from local residents who felt that they were being denied access to a public amenity. There were some incidents of vandalism at night, and security staff had to be employed to safeguard the equipment. A park-and-ride car park at Riversway, opened specifically for the Aerial Spectacular weekend, was almost unused—probably because of the additional expense which it involved—and with the benefit of hindsight the organisers felt that a combined 'admission plus free parking' procedure would have been more popular and more straightforward.

Nonetheless, the event itself was very successful. The weather was excellent, and approximately 4,500 adults and 2,500 children came—as well as an unknown number of children under three, who were admitted free. Total attendance was probably about 10,000. The show was divided into three main sections. An aerial enthusiasts' area featured past, present and future air transport. There were hot air balloons, microlights, a flight simulator, and a Space Adventure Zone—run by Barnardos—which included samples of moon rock supplied by NASA. A kite-flying competition, supported by earlier workshop sessions at local schools and sponsored by Preston Bus, was very popular. The family entertainments section included a fun fair, Punch and Judy, crafts, laser-clay pigeon shooting, go-karting and, as described below, on the Sunday a vintage motorcycle tour of

The Aerial Spectacular at Ashton Park, 16–17 May 1992. (Preston B. C.)

the perimeter of Lancashire finished with a rally at Ashton Park. In the arena there was an impressive and exciting programme of events during both after-noons, with an aerial escapologist, the Royal Marines, a parachute display team, unarmed combat demonstrations, and falconry and working gundogs displays.

Vintage Motorcycle Club Guild Rally (16–17 May)

The Vintage Motorcycle Club, with over 12,000 members, is a nationwide organisation and caters for the owners of, and enthusiasts for, machines over 25 years old. At its meeting held in late 1991 the North Western Section agreed to hold an event to commemorate the 1992 Guild, and after much discussion it was decided that a rally should be held. It was planned so that it would begin and end in Preston and would follow, as closely as possible, the boundary of Lanca-shire. The event was christened 'The Once Every Preston Guild Rally', and sponsorship was sought to aid the Derian House Appeal, a charity dedicated to providing and operating a hospice for the terminally ill children of the Preston area.

Commercial sponsorship was obtained from Carole Nash Insurance of Man-chester, which specialises in insuring vintage and classic motorcycles, while British Aerospace agreed to provide medals, vehicle support and T-shirts, and to match all monies raised by the Club and distribute this sum to its own nominated charities. At 9.30 a.m. the forty competitors were flagged away from the Market Square by the Deputy Mayor, Councillor Albert Richardson, and on the Sunday afternoon they arrived back at Ashton Park, after a 300-mile trip with an overnight stop at the Melling Hall Hotel near Lancaster.

The machines were displayed for the rest of the afternoon, and over the next few weeks the sponsorship money was collected: £3,837 was given to Derian House, £686 to other local and national charities, and a further £4,523 came from British Aerospace as part of its 'Charity Challenge'. The total donations to charity, of some £11,000, was a superb achievement, and meant that this event was one of the largest charitable fundraisers of Guild Year. No less important was the fact that the rally, an innovation on the part of the organisers, was extremely popular with members and public alike, and as a result it is hoped that a similar event can be held in Preston long before the Guild comes round again!

Preston Guild Town Criers' Competition (23 May)

The voice of the newly appointed Preston Town Crier, Mike Chapman, was a particularly noticeable feature of many events during Guild Year, and it was fitting that there should be a national competition for town criers as part of the Guild programme. On Saturday 23 May the Guild Mayor welcomed all the competitors to Preston at a civic reception, held at the Guild Hall, and then the

The Preston Town Crier, Sergeant-Major Mike Chapman, in all his splendour.
Preston B. C.)

criers paraded in procession to the Flag Market, led by the Corps of Drums of the Army Cadet Force under the leadership of Captain Mann.

Mike Chapman acted as host and Master of Ceremonies for the competition. This involved the calling of special cries from each town crier, followed by a final massed cry from all the competitors. The judges awarded the winner's prize to Paul Gough, Town Crier of Nuneaton & Bedworth, and the prize for the best-dressed Town Crier went to David Peters, of Guildford. Several hundred people attended this unusual, but very popular and well-received event, which was sponsored by Daniel Thwaites plc, the *Lancashire Evening Post*, Alan Bleazard PA and the Guild Committee. It is hoped that it might be repeated in future years.

Guild Folk Fiesta (30 May 1992)

The Preston Folk Dance Club, a member of the English Dance & Folk Song Society, had spent more than two years planning the Guild Folk Fiesta, which was held at the end of May in the Guild Hall and at other venues in the town centre. It was a great success, although marred by poor weather in the later part of the day, and was almost certainly the largest such event ever held in Preston.

The Fiesta day began at 10 a.m. with folk dancing in Harris Street by the Preston Folk Dance Club, and then continued as over 150 children from Longridge, Leyland St James, Leyland Seven Stars, Harris, St Ignatius, Ingol and Deepdale primary schools, and Moor Park High School, performed in a two-hour dancing display in the Grand Hall of the Guild Hall, to the music of the Scallywags Band.

There were outdoor dance demonstrations and indoor workshop sessions for much of the day, with good audiences until heavy rain descended in mid-afternoon and curtailed the outdoor programme. The celebrated Britannia Coconut Dancers showed great ingenuity and cunning in choosing to carry on their performance inside Yates' Wine Lodge, and the management reported, with considerable satisfaction, that the Wine Lodge did 'a roaring trade' as a result. As well as the Coconutters, teams taking part in the outside demonstrations and evening fiesta were Folk North West (American Square), North Lancashire District Dancers, Dawnswyr-y-Fedwen Fair (from Conway), Preston Folk Dance Club, Preston Scottish Dancers, Shamrock Dancers, Leyland Morris, O'Brian Irish Dancers, Ossie Cloggers, St Mary's Penwortham Handbell Ringers, and

The Guild Folk Fiesta, 30 May.
(Preston B. C.)

the Tatlers (Longridge folk singers). The evening fiesta was held in the Grand Hall of the Guild Hall, and was attended by 616 people. A total of £651 was raised on behalf of Cecil Sharp House, the headquarters of the English Dance & Folk Song Society, for the upkeep of the building and its Vaughan Williams Library.

Return of the Vikings (13–14 June)

Among the most dramatic of all the Guild events was the 'Return of the Vikings', which was held on Avenham Park in June. It was enacted by Regia Anglorum, a group of professionals and enthusiasts which specialises in the re-enactment of Viking-period events. The organisation of the marauding and pillaging was undertaken by representatives of four local charity groups—St Catherine's Hospice, Heartbeat, the Preston Lions, and the Red Rose Radio Community Trust. A particularly interesting feature, which attracted a great deal of public attention, was the authentic reconstruction of a Viking village. It faithfully recreated the daily life, work and environment which might have characterised a Viking settlement in Lancashire a thousand years ago, and, by special arrangement with individual schools in the Preston area, was visited by many groups of local schoolchildren.

The highlight of the 'Return of the Vikings' was a full-scale battle, performed on both days and demonstrating the weapons and battle strategies of the period. A further attraction was the display of replica longboats moored on the Ribble alongside the park. These boats were subsequently used for charity-sponsored

Above:
The Vikings occupy Avenham Park,
13–14 June. (Preston B. C.)

Right:
Viking invaders converse with the
natives in friendly fashion.
(Preston B. C.)

races at the Dock, under the supervision of members of Regia Anglorum. The battle and displays at the Park were supported by side shows and other events, including the Royal Marines display unit, pipe bands, tug-of-war, falconry and dog displays and other family entertainment. Despite a level of attendance which was somewhat lower than had been predicted, the weekend was a great success, helped by good weather—not always a feature of this 1992 Guild Year!

Guild Hobbies Fair (20–21 June)

A hobbies fair was held at Tulketh High School during the weekend of 20–21 June, on the initiative of Paul Gaywood. Twenty-four non-commercial organisations and societies with a hobby interest—all from the Preston area—were represented, and attendance was between 800 and 900. This was thought to be a reasonable figure, in view of the excellent weather which meant that many people wanted to be out of doors. There were several other major events in and around the town during the weekend, and it was thought that these may well have further reduced the attendance. A profit of £184 was made, and divided between the school fund and the Guild Mayor's Charity.

The Countryside Comes to Town (27–28 June)

Since it is one of the declared policies of Preston Borough Council to support and encourage conservation, and environmental protection and improvement, it was felt that an event which encompassed these themes ought to form a major feature of the Guild celebrations. It would reflect that policy, and would also provide an unusual family show which would be of wide popular appeal. A firm of environmental consultants was retained to advise upon a plan for the two-day event, which was christened 'The Countryside Comes to Town'. The organisation was undertaken by a steering committee which comprised representatives of the Country Landowners Association, the Countryside Commission, English Nature, Lancashire County Council, the National Farmers Union, Preston Borough Council, and the Rural Development Commission, as well as the major sponsor of the event, National Westminster Bank. The Guild Mayor, Councillor Harold Parker, and the Rt. Hon. Lord Shuttleworth acted as President and Patron of the event respectively.

The show, held on Moor Park, was advertised as a festival of rural life, and it demonstrated the wealth of activity, culture and heritage flourishing in the rural areas—including the rural areas to the north and east of Preston which come within the borough. Its aim was to create increased public awareness of rural life in its entirety, and it was hoped that this would be achieved by providing a family show of enjoyment and education. There was a number of specific themes: food and farming; wildlife; working with the countryside; living in the countryside;

sports and recreation; heritage; industry and the environment; making the most of the countryside; youth in the countryside; the country market.

Each theme was represented by static and moving displays and models, demonstrations of skills, and information and promotional material, but at all times the emphasis was on 'fact finding through fun'. The standard of exhibits was extremely high, and there was an immense amount of interest and enter-

The Countryside Came to Town on 7–28 June, when Moor Park was bathed in sunshine.
(Preston B. C.)

tainment in the show. Arenas were used to provide supporting events, such as brass band performances, morris dancing and Shire horse-racing, and there were numerous additional side shows and stalls.

Yet, despite the excellent weather which was enjoyed throughout the weekend, the attendance was very poor and in that sense the show was a major disappointment. Although the conditions seemed right, the expected crowds did not materialise, and apparently the publicity was not sufficiently effective. Comment in the local press, and other feedback, suggested that the possible reason was that the ticket prices were considered by many people to be excessive: entrance fees of £5 per adult and £3 per child, or £10 for a family ticket purchased in advance, were levied. Nevertheless, the organisers claimed that the aims and objectives of the project had been achieved, and that the success of the planning and the high standard of the displays were very creditable. It was, however, an inescapable disappointment that attendance was poor.

Preston Multi-Cultural Arts Festival (11 July)

Since the Second World War Preston has become a multi-ethnic and multi-cultural community, with people from many and diverse geographical backgrounds making up its population. The Ukrainian community was first represented in the 1952 Guild, and the Asian population in that of 1972, and it was hoped that in 1992 the participation of the ethnic communities would be much greater, to reflect their important part in the life of the town. However, ahead of the Guild there was a widespread feeling within the ethnic communities that they might be under-represented in Guild events. That there was such a deficiency is probably the case, but to some extent this was because there was no response to invitations to participate which were issued by the Guild Office to many organisations representing the ethnic communities—a lack of response which caused considerable disappointment. To counter the apparent under-representation Preston College chose to stage an ethnic minority arts festival as its own contribution to the Guild.

The Multi-Cultural Arts Festival, a title chosen because it is positive and recognises the diversity of the theme and the participants, was scheduled to take place at the college's Winckley Square annex. This was a venue which, because of its town-centre location, would have attracted Saturday crowds. Unfortunately the organisers failed to obtain a public performance licence, and did not realise the omission until it was too late. Consequently the venue was shifted to the college's Open Air Theatre on its St Vincent's Road site in Fulwood. The theatre is a very fine setting for such performances and events. However, on this occasion it proved to be less than ideal—on the day it poured with rain, an inevitable hazard of drama in the open air in England! Most of the events had to be moved indoors into classrooms and the drama studio.

The Festival organisers, PRESCAP (Preston Community Arts Project), aimed to develop 'out of school' arts activities among young people; to support cultural equity in Preston; to encourage an awareness among the wider community of the variety and nature of ethnic minority arts within the town; and to increase the representation of the ethnic minority communities in Preston's Guild Year celebrations. Financial support was received from Preston Borough Council, Lancashire County Council, North West Arts and The Prince's Trust.

There were workshops (all of which produced plenty of audience participation) in contemporary African dance, by Raven Dance; Ghanaian culture, including history, geography, music, dancing and story-telling, by Miso'shi; the variety and range of Indian music, by Manju Varma; hip hop and rap music, by First Generation; and Indian classical dance, by Mrittika Arts. In the middle of the day all the participants—audience as well as performers—had a meal together, with Caribbean food provided by Cayso and Asian food by the Gujurati Hindu Society. In the afternoon there were special performances of different arts by the O'Brian School of Irish Dancing; their own poems read by Agbara, a group of African and Caribbean women; the Gujurati Hindu Society Boys' Band, Sangam Arts, performing Asian film music; quadrille, calypso and hip hop dancing by Raven Dance; a rap presentation, by First Generation; folk dances from India performed by Mrittika Arts, with explanation in Bengali, Tamil, Malayalam and Sanskrit; and a local Bhangra band, Josh, performing Bhangra music with a guest appearance by Manju Varma.

It was particularly disappointing that the overall attendance was less than had been hoped, partly because of the very bad weather during the day, partly as a result of inadequate publicity, and—most significantly, it was felt—because of the move from the town-centre location to Fulwood. Nevetheless, the Festival was a very exciting and innovative project, and there was a great deal of enthusiasm and enjoyment among the artists who took part and among those who watched or came to join in. It is hoped that the experience will provide the basis for a regular festival on these lines, so that by the time of the next Guild, in 2012, there will be a ready-made organisation which can participate fully in the celebrations.

Heineken Music Big Top (23–26 July)

The brewers, Whitbread, have sponsored the Heineken Music Big Top, a highly successful touring music festival, each summer since 1990. The Guild Sponsorship Consultant, Hugh Pennant-Williams, approached them with a view to including Preston in their tour for 1992, and the promoters proved to be very enthusiastic about the idea. The possibility of a music festival or similar event fitted in well with the ideas of the Senior Guild Co-ordinator, Neville Bridge, who was anxious to fill in a gap which had been apparent in the provisional Guild programme—there was, so far, little which was aimed at the 18–35 age group. The promoters were very impressed by Avenham Park as a possible venue, and after discussion chose this in preference to the original suggestion of Moor Park.

The Heineken Music Big Top event, which was free of charge, ran from Thursday 23 July to Sunday 26 July, and was an outstanding success—one of the best attended and best received of all the many and varied events in Guild Year. It began at 7 p.m. and finished at 11 p.m. each day, with the exception of Sunday,

when the entertainment began at 1 p.m. and continued through the afternoon and evening. The featured bands were:

Thursday ('Blues-n-Fireworks')

The Blues Band
Paul Lamb and the Kingsnakes
The Stargazers
The Harpbreakers

Friday

Steve Harley and Cockney Rebel
Liberty Cage
Gary Hall and the Stormkeepers

Saturday ('Preston Guild's Party in the Park')

Edwin Starr
Darts II
Sounds of the Blues Brothers
Brilliant Wish

The Heineken Big Top musical event, on Avenham Park in July— such a success that it is set to become an annual feature. (Preston B. C.)

Sunday ('Roots Music')

Kirsty MacColl
King Masco
Edward II
Tansads
Citizen Swing
Skin the Peeler
Plunkett Club

On the Thursday evening a magnificent firework display, lasting twenty minutes, provided a spectacular finale to the performances. During the four days of the event an estimated 30,000 people visited Avenham Park. The promoters, Square One Events, later wrote that they were 'delighted with the results ... and could not have asked for a better response from the Preston crowds or the newspaper publicity'. Indeed, the event was so successful that the organisers intend to add Preston to their list of venues for future summer tours.

Final of the 'Young Musician of the Guild' Competition (25 July)

From 1989 onwards the members of the Harris Charity, which funds and sponsors educational and cultural projects which are intended to help Lancashire residents aged 25 or under, had been organising a competitive Guild musical event aimed at young people. A committee under the chairmanship of Arthur Dawson was formed in April 1990, and in conjunction with the Guild Office and the National Westminster Bank, the main sponsor of the 1992 Guild, the project took shape. The eventual plan involved a series of heats in which musicians would perform on their chosen instruments, on the lines of the very popular BBC series 'Young Musician of the Year'. Invaluable advice was given by Roy Tipping, the producer of the BBC's 'Young Musician', and by Sandra Parr, the concert manager of the Royal Liverpool Philharmonic Orchestra. Building Design Partnership were generous in the provision of premises and offering facilities for printing.

The Lancashire Students' Symphony Orchestra agreed to accompany the finalists, and with the help of Lady Grenfell-Baines and Mrs Margaret Birtle, members of the Committee, the organisers were fortunate in obtaining the services of Lady Barbirolli as chairman of the panel of judges: the original chairman-designate, Sir Charles Groves, most unfortunately died before the event. The competition was open to anyone under 21 who was born in Lancashire or had been living in Lancashire for the two previous years, and by October 1991 over forty entries had been received. Preliminary rounds were held during November and December 1991, and the second rounds during February 1992. The semi-finals took place during the weekend of 11–12 April, and the organisers were greatly encouraged by the considerable numbers of people who bought tickets to attend.

Rehearsals for the final of the 'Young Musician of the Guild' competition began in late June 1992, under the conductor Malcolm Doley (a Lancashire

County Music Adviser), and the event was held at the Guild Hall on 25 July. The four finalists were:

Tim Jackson (brass)	Horn Concerto No. 1 in E flat (op. 11) (Richard Strauss)
Catherine Bullock (strings)	Violin Concerto No. 1 in E minor (op. 26) (Bruch)
Jason Ridgeway (piano)	Piano Concerto No. 2 in A (Liszt)
Zoe Cran (flute)	Allegro Andante—Allegro Sherzando for Flute Concerto (Ibert)

The winner, the 'Young Musician of the Guild', was Jason Ridgeway from Fulwood, who received a prize of £1,000, and the other three finalists were awarded £250 each.

The Canal and Vintage Festival (8–9 August)

Guild Year, 1992, was also the 200th anniversary of the passing of the Act of Parliament which authorised the construction of the Lancaster Canal. Since this had been such an important event in the history of Preston, and because recent years have seen growing pressure for the construction of a link between the north end of the canal and the River Ribble, to allow through navigation to the rest of the inland waterway network, it was felt that a Guild Festival based on the canal would be particularly appropriate.

The members of the organising committee of the Canal and Vintage Festival were drawn from the Young Farmers; Fylde Vintage and Steam; canal boats clubs; the Inland Waterways Association; and the Association of Cruising Enthusiasts, Lancaster Canal. The last-named group initiated the idea in a letter to the Town Clerk in November 1989, and within the Guild Co-ordinating Team the festival was the responsibility of Alison Young.

The northern end of the canal (Preston to Tewitfield) is physically separate from any other canal or river navigation, and as many of the craft involved would be coming from elsewhere it was necessary to arrange for their transfer by road. Chris Miller Crane Hire, a section of Preston's oldest company, provided a low loader and crane which transported boats from the Leeds & Liverpool Canal at Botany Bay, Chorley, and from Preston Dock, and every opportunity was taken to promote and publicise the scheme for a link canal, the absence of which had necessitated these arrangements.

There was general agreement that the most appropriate location for the Festival would be the stretch of canal which runs alongside Haslam Park, and planning proceeded during 1991, approval in principle having been given in October 1990. Problems to be overcome included the difficulty of access to the park, the possibility of traffic congestion on Blackpool Road, access to the canal bank, and financial questions associated with car parking, stewarding and provision of services. The Borough Council agreed to underwrite a substantial

The Canal and Vintage Festival (8–9 August)—this view shows boats on the Lancaster Canal at Ashton.
(Preston B. C.)

proportion of the costs which might be incurred, a decision which was based on estimates suggesting that up to 300 boats would be present, with perhaps 20,000 visitors. A profit of £15,000 was projected, and it was decided that this would be given to charities.

The Festival was publicised as one of the largest of its kind ever held in northern England, and it was emphasised that as well as canal boats it would include other types of vintage transport, traction and steam engines, fairground organs and farm machinery among the 440 exhibits. Brass bands, bouncy castles, side shows and craft stalls were planned, with runs of the historic Norwich Union mail coach carrying representatives of the Council and the Festival Committee.

The event was very well planned, and after the initial problems had been resolved the preparations went very smoothly. Unfortunately, the organisers—like all the other organisers of events in a very wet Guild Year—could not plan for the weather. On the first day of the weekend event, 7 August, torrential rain fell from midday onwards, and almost all the open-air activities had to be cancelled. Attendance by the public was, in consequence, minimal. The weather on Sunday 8 August was much better, and attendance was very good, but the disastrous weather on the Saturday meant that overall the Festival made a loss of £7,687—a most unhappy result after so many people had put in so much hard work and planning for what would have been a very successful event.

The Storming of Preston (15–16 August)

Having been attacked by Viking raiders in June, Preston—and Avenham Park in particular—experienced another bout of savage warfare in mid-August. One event in the run-up to the Guild which will be particularly remembered by posterity is the re-enactment of the 'Storming of Preston' by some 3,000 members of the Sealed Knot, the society which specialises in Civil War battles, demonstrations and displays. Guild Year, by happy coincidence, was the 350th anniversary of this dramatic episode in the history of the town. The participants came from all over the country, and in addition to recreating the colour, clamour and spectacle of the struggle between royalist and parliamentarian forces, they built a reconstruction of a seventeenth-century village to add further realism. The event included demonstrations of archery, street theatre, and cameo scenes, culminating in a two-hour battle, complete with cavalry charges, cannon volleys and other artillery effects, on both afternoons.

Despite bad weather on the Saturday the event was well supported, and the charity organisers, Barnardos (North West) benefited from the proceeds. Before the weekend many local schools had taken part in projects and exhibitions connected with the Civil War and its local associations, and the event therefore had a valuable educational role as well as being excellent entertainment.

The presence in the town of so many uniformed military servicemen from a previous age was put to additional good use. On the morning of 15 August a detachment of the Sealed Knot marched along Friargate to the Flag Market, where they demonstrated weapons drill. Following this members lined the Harris Museum steps and formed a guard of honour for the Civic Party which had assembled to hear the reading of the First Proclamation of the Guild. The 'Storming of Preston' was principally sponsored by the Royal Mail and the Iron Trades Insurance Group, to whom the organisers were extremely grateful.

Historic Commercial Vehicle Spectacular (23 August)

At an early stage in the planning of the Guild the organisers were approached by the North West Area Branch of the Historic Commercial Vehicle Society, which offered to hold a major event as part of the celebrations. The intention was to reflect the important contribution which the commercial vehicle industry had made to the Preston area during the twentieth century, with firms such as Atkinsons, Leyland Motors and Vulcan having played a prominent role.

The Guild Committee was very enthusiastic about this proposal, and although it did not wish to become involved in the detailed arrangements it offered to give full assistance in overseeing and co-ordinating the plans. Generous sponsorship was obtained from Leyland/DAF, a particularly appropriate source of finance in view of the company's central position in the history and economy of the district. Lanfina Bitumen, which is based on the Riversway Dock estate where the main displays took place, also provided sponsorship, and many other local operators and firms, especially those in the road transport sector, provided valuable assistance.

The late morning of Saturday 22 August saw the reading of the Second Proclamation of the Guild, from the steps of the Harris Museum. A parade of historic vehicles, representing local companies, took part in the civic procession

*rowds gathered at Riversway on
2–23 August for the Historic
Commercial Vehicle Spectacular.
Preston B. C.)*

on this occasion. The Guild Mayor and Mayoress and other dignitaries were
invited to ride on some of the vehicles, which ranged from a 1908 Leyland
X-Type lorry, via a 1921 Burrell steam traction engine, to a 1970 Atkinson
Viewline Artic unit. The eight vehicles then remained on display in Harris Street
for the afternoon.

On the following day a great rally was held at Riversway, based on the British
Aerospace car park in Channel Way. The morning was occupied by a spectacular procession of vehicles which left the site in parade order and travelled via
Ashton, Blackpool Road, the town centre, Walton-le-Dale and Bamber Bridge
to Leyland, where they visited the British Commercial Vehicle Museum. The
return journey was via Lostock Hall and Lower Penwortham. During the
afternoon 114 vehicles were displayed at the exhibition site, and these were visited
and inspected by large crowds. The exhibits included light trucks, heavy articu-
lated units, cranes, breakdown vehicles, fire appliances, military vehicles,
coaches, double-deckers and buses. Particular interest was shown in those which
had been manufactured locally: in this respect a vehicle built by the Todkills
Company of Marsh Lane, and a Ranger van produced by Bond Cars of
Ribbleton, were outstanding.

The weather was good, the visitors very numerous, and the nostalgia abun-
dant. The air rang with the sound of whistles and horns, and clouds of steam

Heavy rain assisted the task of the firemen during the 'Firefighting through the Ages' display on the Flag Market (27 August). (Preston B. C.)

and smoke from traction engines and steam lorries were visible from long distances, the particular smell evoking many memories of times long past. Even the relatively recent 1950s' double-decker buses, once ubiquitous but now museum pieces, were a powerful reminder of how designs have changed.

'Fire-fighting through the Ages' (27 August)

The Lancashire County Fire Brigade was established in 1948 upon the amalgamation of many small brigades from individual towns and villages across the county: among these were the Preston Borough and Fulwood Urban District brigades. The headquarters of the County Brigade is in Preston, and it has always had close links with the town. For these reasons, therefore, it was anxious to be involved in the Guild celebrations. The contribution which was proposed, and which was eagerly accepted by the Guild Committee, involved an exhibition of equipment and fire engines from the past 150 years, and a demonstration of fire-fighting techniques over the centuries. The event took place on the Flag Market during the afternoon of 27 August, in pouring rain—cynics in the audience suggested that they did not need firemen to put out fires that day! Despite the weather the event was well attended and very well received.

The vintage and historic fire engines were in immaculate condition, with shining red, black and gold paint and superbly polished brasswork, and they made a splendid sight as they lined up outside the Sessions House and the Harris Museum. The fire-fighting demonstrations began with the slave gangs of the Roman period, and proceeded via the bucket chains and hooks of the seventeenth century, the manual pumps of the eighteenth, and the magnificent steam engines of the nineteenth, to the sophisticated techniques of the present day. As with the Historic Commercial Vehicle event held the previous weekend, much nostalgia was induced by the sight of engines which, though only thirty years old, seemed extraordinarily 'old-fashioned'. There were practical demonstrations of how to deal with chip-pan fires, accidents and other emergencies, and the public participation in some of these provoked particular entertainment and light-heartedness.

Police Band Spectacular and Tattoo (28 and 30 August)

The Lancashire Constabulary hosted the International Police Tattoo at its Hutton headquarters on 30 August. As a special contribution to the Guild it offered to arrange a Police Band Spectacular two days earlier, at the Guild Hall. The programme featured bands from Antwerp, Cologne, Maastricht, Moscow and Rome, as well as the Fanfare Trumpeters and the Band of the Lancashire Constabulary itself. All the tickets were sold out well in advance of the event, and the bands provided an outstanding evening of entertainment.

The International Police Band Spectacular and Tattoo at Hutton (28–29 August) drew large crowds: (above) the Rome Carabinieri band and (below) two visitors enjoying the occasion, Rachel Duffy, 10, and her sister Sarah, 8, from New Longton.
(Lancashire Evening Post)

There were marching and stationary musical performances, with each band playing international music as well as themes traditional to its own country or region. The audience was particularly appreciative of the folk tunes played by the Russian band. The co-ordination, both musically and while marching, was very impressive, and the splendid uniforms and polished instruments likewise. The bands themselves were enthusiastic about the event, and seemed to enjoy themselves very much. As a finale, all the bands joined together in a display which symbolised the new spirit of friendship prevailing between Eastern and Western Europe.

The concert involved two full days of rehearsal, and was a credit to the Lancashire Constabulary members involved in its planning—not least because preparation and rehearsals with six different languages involved was far from easy. Although arranged and promoted by Lancashire Constabulary, the event was also given generous sponsorship by many organisations: particular help was given by the Citizen Newspaper Group, NORWEB, British Aerospace, Preston Borough Council, Group 4 Securities, National Westminster Bank and Group Sonitrol Security Systems.

The International Police Tattoo at the Hutton Park headquarters of the County Constabulary was held on Sunday 30 August. It therefore enjoyed the same terrible weather which forced the cancellation of many of the events at the Riversway Festival, and which tested the endurance of worshippers gathered on Avenham Park for the Ecumenical Service. Nevertheless, the turnout for the tattoo was excellent, and huge crowds gathered to watch one of the largest events which the Lancashire police had ever held. There were many police bands from all over the world, and these treated the spectators to a feast of marching and music.

There were demonstrations by the Royal Air Force Police Dog Team, the Metropolitan Police Motorcycle Precision Team, and the Royal Marines Commando display team. The Lancashire police gave displays of dog-handling and equestrian skills, and the tattoo ground housed a wide range of other events, exhibits and attractions. The police were delighted by the enthusiastic response from the crowds, and the day was judged a triumphant success in its own right—as well as a great triumph over the foul weather.

'Little Miss Guild' contest (Saturday 29 August)

As part of the run-up to the Guild the *Lancashire Evening Post* held a 'Little Miss Guild' competition. Some 620 little girls were entered for the event, and their photographs were published in a special supplement to the newspaper on 18 August. Readers were asked to send in their postal vote for the contestants, and their views were taken into account when the judges selected thirty finalists. The

*Three-year-old Rachel Burke was crowned Little Miss Guild 1992 in the popular Lancashire Evening Post competition.
(Lancashire Evening Post)*

judging was done by the 1972 Miss Preston Guild, Karen Mortensen Fowler; the 1992 Miss Preston Guild, Hazel Taylor; the Editor of the *Evening Post*, Philip Welsh; Helen Neuhaus of Adams Childrenswear; and Sue Travis of Children's World.

The final of the contest was held on Saturday 29 August, at the Proud Preston Exhibition on Moor Park. The winner was three-year-old Rachael Burke of New Hall Lane, who attended St Joseph's Nursery School. Rachael said that she liked swimming and dancing, and the judges were impressed by 'her delightful smile and bubbling personality'. The runner-up was Laura Cowell, aged seven, of Goosnargh, and in third place Joanne Tracey, aged five, of Ingol—who told the judges that she liked dancing and music but hated salads and sausages!

Miss Preston Guild 1992 was Hazel Taylor, seen here riding in style during the Community Procession.
(Preston B. C.)

Sporting events before Guild Week

Traditionally, many and varied sporting events have been arranged for the Guild, with special competitions for Guild trophies and prizes. The sporting highlight of Guild Week before 1842 was the horse-racing, which took place on Preston

Moor (now Moor Park) until 1822, and which involved very large and valuable prizes. During the 1830s the racecourse was removed, as the landscaping of the future park began, and in 1842 the races were staged on Penwortham Holme, the large flat island between two channels of the Ribble where the bridge at the foot of Fishergate Hill bridge is today. In 1842, too, there were special wrestling matches, including Cumberland wrestling; cricket matches; and rowing and sailing regattas on the Ribble. In 1992 the range and variety of the sporting events was, perhaps, not quite as large as in the Guilds of 1972 and 1952—but there was still plenty to see.

One of the highlights of the Guild Year sporting calendar was the 1992 Milk Race, the 35th consecutive year of Britain's biggest cycle-racing event. This involved 108 riders who followed a gruelling and challenging route, and was held between 24 May and 6 June. Preston was chosen to host the finish of Stage 7 of the race, on 30 May. This stage covered the 73 miles from Southport, via Chorley, Bolton, Blackburn and Darwen, to Preston, and then as an exciting conclusion the competitors had to complete eight laps of a town-centre circuit of 2 miles, which incorporated Avenham and Miller Parks and finished in Church Street adjacent to the parish church.

The weather was excellent and a crowd of several thousand people gathered to watch the finish. They were entertained in Church Street by a Road Show and clowns, while the Milk Race organisers distributed quantities of free gifts. The conditions for cycling were perfect, and the first group of riders arrived some 40 minutes ahead of the scheduled time. After a magnificent sprint finish the joint first place, with a time of 2: 42: 57, was awarded to Lars Michaelsen (Denmark), Neils Bogard (Holland) and Shane Sutton (Banana-Met). Willy Willens (Coll-strop-Histor, Belgium) held on to the coveted yellow jersey as he came in with the main field 1 minute 25 seconds behind the leaders.

Stage 7 of the Milk Race was sponsored by the Guild Committee and Leyland/DAF. The arrangements had been the subject of careful planning, involving the Borough and County Councils, the Lancashire Constabulary and Preston Bus, and the race organisers later agreed that this preparation had been very effective and successful. The event, which attracts extensive national and international coverage, was watched by thousands of people in the streets of Preston, and can be considered one of the sporting highlights of Guild Year.

Preston Golf Club celebrated its centenary in Guild Year, and the Guild '92 Golf Trophy Competition was held at its Fulwood course on 5 July. It was played on a '4-ball-better-ball' stableford basis, and was open to all golfers with a recognised Club handicap not exceeding eighteen. The competition was heavily over-subscribed, and the entrants were drawn from all over the North West—the majority were from outside Preston. The weather was warm and sunny, the competition excellent, and—perhaps appropriately—the winners were members of the Club itself.

On Tuesday 7 July West View Leisure Centre was the venue for a day of sporting entertainment for over 1,000 schoolchildren from the Borough of Preston. With financial assistance from the Guild Committee the Centre, in conjunction with the Preston Schools Sports Council, staged the Preston Schools Guild Adventure Challenge. Thirty primary schools, each represented by one class, went through a series of sporting challenges, as children from all walks of

life and of varying sporting abilities assembled to face challenges and to participate in demanding and rewarding activities.

The range of pursuits was wide, and included many which in normal circumstances would only have been available to older children or adults. There was
an 'exercise to music' aerobics session, the latest fitness equipment including
rowing machines, treadmills of a non-penal variety, a climbing wall, a special
six-metre high training wall brought in for the occasion, and an aeroball court.
The swimming pool was taken over by a large slippery inflatable, which formed
part of an obstacle course and adventure course at the end of a very energetic,
very tiring and very memorable day.

The Ramblers Association (Mid-Lancashire Area) took the opportunity to
celebrate Guild Year by publishing, with the co-operation of the Borough
Council, a new edition of its very successful booklet on the 'Round Preston Walk'.
New signposting was erected at several places on the route, and a commemorative walk was held on 20 June 1992 after the booklet was launched in the presence
of the Guild Mayor in Avenham Park.

A walk of a very different magnitude—although not in Preston at all—was
held three weeks later, when thirty-six young people, aged between eleven and
fourteen, set off from St Bees in Cumbria to walk to Robin Hoods Bay in North
Yorkshire. This two hundred mile walk, which lasted two weeks, was promoted

*Stage 7 of the 1992 Milk Race
finished with eight exciting laps
around a 2½-mile circuit of Preston
town centre.
(Preston B. C.)*

by the Preston Police Schools team, a group dedicated to helping young people experience outdoor pursuits outside school hours. It was planned in 1990 as a special walk to celebrate the 1992 Guild, and it received the additional support of the Army Youth Team and the Racial Equality Council in Preston. The local business community raised £8,500 to cover the cost of food, equipment and other expenses, and extensive training was undertaken as preparation for the walk.

As part of the event the organisers arranged for celebrities to meet, or send off, the walkers each day, and some even walked part of the way with them. Thirty-four of the walkers completed the course, and they raised over £3,000 in sponsorship money. This was presented to the Guild Mayor at a small ceremony later in the year, and was used to benefit Guild charities. Chief Inspector John Waring of Preston Police Community Affairs Department congratulated the participants on their great achievement, and on their determination, enthusiasm and spirit during the long walk itself, and during the many hours of training undertaken over the previous months.

The Preston and District Blind Bowling Club, which was formed in 1982, decided to commemorate Guild Year by holding a national tournament. Teams from six bowling clubs for the visually handicapped were invited to attend: Metro (London), Oldham, Cheltenham, Greenwich, Gateshead and Pennine (Todmorden), with Preston providing two teams to make a total of eight. The competition was held on Saturday and Sunday 22–23 August, and on the Saturday evening the visitors and local members were given a superb buffet dinner at Howick House, Penwortham, followed by a convivial evening at the County Hall Staff Club.

The tournament was held at the flat bowling green in Moor Park, by courtesy of Preston Borough Council, which also assisted with sponsorship. Other financial help was received from M. Foley & Co. Insurance, Whitbreads Brewery, Heritage Covers of Preston, A. S. Facer (Veterinary Chemists of Longton), B.T.R. of Lostock Hall, Eavesbrook Housing, British Aerospace, Baxi Heating, and Tote Credit of Wigan. The winning team was Greenwich, with runners up Metro, while a play-off among the teams which failed to reach the final stages was won by Cheltenham, with Oldham as runners-up. Prizes of Guild commemorative plates and other Guild china were presented by the Guild Mayor and Mayoress, and the whole weekend was judged an outstanding success.

Firework and Laser Symphony Concert (29 August)

All of the long and careful preparation of the arena in Avenham Park was finally put to the test on the evening of Saturday 29 August, when, just before the official start of Guild Week, the town was treated to a splendid firework display which accompanied a sensational and dramatic concert. Fireworks, music and laser concerts have throughout the country in recent times been among the most fashionable and popular 'crowd' events, and they make the fullest use of the latest technology to produce an extremely effective and often breathtaking display of sound, light and colour. The advance publicity, and the nature of the event itself, ensured that the concert in Avenham Park was a sell-out: all 10,255 tickets were snapped up well before the concert.

The morning of Saturday 29 August began with rain, and there were intermittent heavy showers throughout the day: fortunately the evening remained fine until just after the end of the concert, but there were many anxious faces as the more pessimistic among the organisers foresaw damp squibs instead of spectacular fireworks. Eager queues built up over half an hour before the gates were due to open, and the box office staff, who did not have to sell tickets as there was none left to sell, instead distributed specially designed plastic poly-ponchos, printed with the distinctive Guild design, free of charge to each ticket-holder.

The programme was as follows:

8.00 p.m. Popular Classics (Royal Philharmonic Pops Orchestra)
Conductor: Nicholas Smith

Shostakovich	Festival Overture (with RM Band)
Bizet	Suite from Carmen
Strauss	Blue Danube Waltz
Dvorak	Slavonic Dance
Gershwin	Rhapsody in Blue
Elgar	Pomp and Circumstance March No. 1

Interval

9.00 p.m. The Band of HM Royal Marines, Commandos
Conductor: Captain D.C. Cole

Meacham arr. Gray	American Patrol
Trad. arr. Finegan	Little Brown Jug
Waterworth arr. Gibson	Penelope
Barnet	Skyliner
Mangione arr.	Kerchner El Gatotriste
Fain/Webster arr. Baker	Love is a Many Splendored Thing
Zawinal	Birdland

Interval

10.00 p.m. Fireworks and Laser Symphony Concert
Conductor: Nicholas Smith

Mussorgsky	Great Gate of Kiev (with RM Band)
Dukas	Sorcerer's Apprentice
Holst	Mars
Mascagni	Intermezzo from Cavalleria Rusticana
Khatchaturian	Sabre Dance
Tchaikovsky	1812 Overture (with RM Band)

During the first part of the concert Nicholas Smith, 'suitably attired in dress suit and green wellies', encouraged audience participation. Many people were able to waltz to the 'Blue Danube' and it was noted that the rest of the audience, unable to dance because of the seating arrangements, 'swayed in time to the music': the reporter from the *Lancashire Evening Post* noted that 'as each row tilted from side to side covered in their all-white Preston Guild waterproof ponchos, it looked like the bizarre ritual of some strange religious cult'. The Royal Marines proved themselves to be excellent quick change artistes, having played in white dinner jackets for their 'big band' section and then returned only twenty minutes later in military uniform.

The climax of the evening, the magical display of superb fireworks, dramatic laser effects and excellent music, had the whole audience spellbound for an hour. There were gasps of amazement interspersed with stunned silence and rapturous applause, while the grand finale, Tchaikovsky's 1812, met with an enthusiastic ovation. The sense of occasion was enhanced by the illumination of the tree-lined perimeter of the arena by a multitude of coloured spot lamps, and the Chinese Water Garden was highlighted by a multi-coloured animated light display. Just before 11 p.m. a bank of giant skytracker spotlights burst into life and criss-crossed the sky with sixteen immense beams of light, which were visible for several miles.

It was all summed up in the *Evening Post*: 'Mix the Last Night of the Proms with the most breathtaking bonfire night party ever seen, add an astounding array of Star Wars-style special effects, and what have you got? A recipe for magic'. The concert ended ... the audience began to disperse ... the rain began to fall slowly but steadily. Guild Week was about to start!

The Firework and Laser concert in Avenham Park on 29 August was a sensational start to the events of Guild Week.
(Preston B. C.)

A highlight of Guild Year for many was the mammoth party for elderly Prestonians, held in the Covered Market in June.(Preston B. C.)

Chapter 4

Community activities
before the Guild

SINCE 1842 the Guild festivities, and the Guild itself, have been generally seen as a celebration of Preston as a community. This was not so before that time. Until 1822, when the town saw its last Guild before the reform of the Corporation in 1835–6, these had been essentially elitist events. The Guild Merchant, in its distant origins, operated a restrictive practice whereby the traders of the town formed an exclusive body with a monopoly over Preston's commercial life. Strenuous efforts were made—and for almost six hundred years were made with great success—to keep outsiders away, and to prevent non-members from trading in Preston. The meetings of the Guild members, and its infrequent and grand celebrations, were therefore also 'elitist'. For example, the processions, now such a popular communal feature of the Guild, were in origin quite the opposite—they were public parades and demonstrations designed to emphasise the power and grandeur of the leading groups in Preston's commercial, social and political life, and to impress upon the ordinary folk who stood watching that they were looking at their superiors and betters. Likewise, the social events—the balls and banquets, receptions and feasts, horse races and theatrical performances—were exclusive affairs, in which the 'ordinary' people had no place.

In 1842 all this changed. The participants in the Guild included, for the first time, schoolchildren and church representatives, and the process began which has over the ensuing 150 years led to the present character of the Guild as 'a celebration of Preston, past, present and future'. In this way the community as a whole has become closely involved in the planning, organisation and staging of the Guild, and the celebrations themselves are now a communal affair. Thus, Guild Year 1992 saw a great deal of activity on the part of voluntary groups, local organisations and individuals, who contributed in many vital ways to the success of the Guild. There were social, environmental and educational projects, plays, musical programmes and competitions, exhibitions and new publications. All combined to make 1992 a year to remember—even before the Guild began!

Publications, lectures and recordings

Well before the start of Guild Year several major projects aimed at the publication of local history and Guild history were under way, and during the period of the Guild itself the recording of sights and sounds went ahead apace. There is a long history of Guild publishing, which ranges from the ephemeral souvenirs and booklets which are produced in the tens of thousands, to substantial works on the history of the town and the Guild. In the nineteenth century substantial town histories—not always of the highest quality—were published by Hardwick, Hewitson and Whittle, while Abram, and Dobson and Harland produced important accounts of the origins and development of the Preston Guild Merchant.

However, since 1912, when William Clemesha produced what is perhaps the finest of the earlier histories of the town, nothing substantial had appeared. In 1972 Hewitson's history (1883) was reprinted, and Abram's *Memorials of Preston Guild* (1882) also reappeared: both sold well, but they were almost a century old, and a great deal of new research and analysis had been undertaken since then. A new history of Preston Guild, and a new history of the town itself, were therefore long overdue, and when the Borough Council and County Council were considering what might be done to mark the 1992 Guild the possibility of commissioning major new works on these subjects was raised at an early date. In the event two definitive books were produced in advance of the Guild, and another important volume appeared at the end of the year.

The Lancashire County Library Service was asked by the Harris Free Public Library and Museum Endowment Trust if it would be willing to undertake a joint publishing venture to commemorate the Guild. The Library Service was enthusiastic, and as a result the two bodies commissioned the research and writing of Dr Alan Crosby's book, *The History of Preston Guild*. This was published in September 1991 by Lancashire County Books, an imprint of the County Council. It was the first comprehensive history of the Guild to appear for more than a century and, unlike all its predecessors, it looked at the Guild in its wider context, with full consideration of the ceremonial and official aspects but also detailed coverage of the fringe activities, the carnival and entertainment, the balls and banquets, the social impact and the planning and preparation. It also broke away from the previous pattern of writing about the Guild in a chronological sequence, and instead divided the eight centuries of Guild history into four major periods, and discussed these thematically. The research for the book was funded by the Harris Trustees and the production by Lancashire County Books. The preparation of *The History of Preston Guild* was greatly assisted by the co-operation of the Borough Council, which allowed free access to the archives which were then held in the muniment room of the Town Hall. The book was very well received and sales were extremely good.

Preston Borough Council chose to make its contribution to historical research and writing for the Guild by giving generous financial and practical support to a project, suggested by Carnegie Publishing of Preston, for a completely new and authoritative history of the town. Support was also received from the National Westminster Bank plc, and the assistance of the bank and the Council made it possible to publish a substantial and lavishly illustrated volume, *A History of Preston*, at a price which was highly attractive and affordable. The book, written by the Preston-born historian Dr David Hunt, who is a supporter of Preston North End and custodian of South Ribble Museum, is packed with previously unpublished photographs and other illustrations, and is the result of extensive new research into the history of the town. Sales of this book have also been excellent, and it has become the standard work on the subject. A photographic record of the town, *Preston: A Pictorial History*, was published at the end of 1992 by Phillimore & Co. It was compiled and written by Dr Geoff Timmins, senior lecturer in history at the University of Central Lancashire, and made excellent use of the photographic resources of the Harris Museum.

'The Old Lamb and Flag' was a dramatic musical presentation which told the story of Preston, its rich and varied past and its notable, notorious or simply ordinary people. Tom Walsh and Gregg Butler put together a programme of music and songs, based on research in original sources, and this was performed during Guild Year by their Jolly Fine Company Company [sic]. A commemorative book with words, music and detailed notes woven into a historical account was published, together with a CD and tape. The reviewer from the *Lancashire Evening Post* described the opening night's performance: 'exciting history as recorded by the folk in their own music of the day. Songs ranged from sad ballads like 'Flodden Field' to the rousing 'The King Enjoys His Own Again' ... had the group presented their show in an amateur way it would still have been a magical evening. But their enthusiasm was matched by their professionalism and they received a tremendous ovation ... Let's hope this Jolly Fine Company is around in 20 years' time when they can add another chapter and verse to the Guild.'

Christine Sbresni, who lives in Buckinghamshire but was educated in Preston, and is a collector of china, wrote and produced a short booklet entitled *Commemorative China for Preston Guild 1822–1992*. It had numerous black and white pictures, and was a comprehensive guide to this very important and popular form of Guild souvenir. The Fulwood and Broughton Committee of the NSPCC compiled *Memories of Preston Guilds*, as a fund-raising venture. The booklet included, among other items, contributions by Miss Preston Guild 1972 and by people who had watched or joined in the Guilds of 1952 and 1922. As a result of excellent sales more than £1,600 was raised for the NSPCC. Ten elderly residents of Preston were interviewed during 1989 by Frank Hartley and John Cotterall of the Guild Office, and were asked about their memories of the town, and its Guilds, in years long past. The sound recordings were deposited with the Harris Museum, after they had been loaned to the editor of the NSPCC book of Guild anecdotes and memories.

During the eighteen months before the Guild there were numerous lectures and lecture programmes focusing on the forthcoming celebrations and on the history and character of Preston. The Guild Office staff made available a list of eight lecturers who were prepared to speak about the Guild and the town, and they gave between them an estimated 260 talks, to over 8,000 people. The groups addressed ranged from the Preston and District Winemakers' Circle and the Institute of Bankers to the Southport branch of the Parkinson's Disease Society and the Longton Ladies Lifeboat Guild. These, and 'private' lecturers, carried the message of the Guild far and wide in Lancashire and beyond, and played an important part in publicising and promoting the forthcoming event.

Local libraries, museums and colleges were widely used for public lectures with a Guild theme. The County and Regimental Museum in Stanley Street held a lecture series on Preston and Lancashire topics during April–August 1992, while the Harris Museum and Art Gallery held several series of lunchtime lectures in the period before the Guild. The lectures at the Harris proved to be an outstanding success—the gallery in which they were held was usually packed to capacity. The lectures were free, and with the attractive time and very central location this ensured that the attendances were excellent. Four series of lectures were held between February 1991 and March 1992, and a fifth followed the Guild between October and December 1992, providing in total some twenty-two lectures. Subjects chosen included buildings, the borough regalia, the battle of Preston, maritime history, guild costumes, Winckley Square, the Civil War, education and, of course, the Guild itself.

The University of Central Lancashire and British Aerospace collaborated to hold a prestigious series of lectures by expert speakers of national and international repute. BAe offered hospitality before the lectures to guests from their own company, the University and the Borough Council, and attendance by the public was very satisfactory, with an average of eighty people at each lecture. The programme included talks by Melvyn Bragg on the role of the writer; Brian Durrans of the Museum of Mankind, on the origins of time capsules; Keith Eastwood of the North West Gas Historical Society, on the Preston Gas Light Company (Preston being the first provincial town in Britain to be lit by gas) and Dave Russell of the University's history department, on the origins of the football league—which was founded in Preston. To commemorate Guild Year the Institution of Electrical Engineers chose Preston as the venue for its 1992 North West of England Faraday Lecture. It was held on 21 October in the Guild Hall, and was presented by speakers from British Gas who spoke of the role of electrical sensing equipment in their industry and in our daily lives.

The success of the series of lunchtime lectures at the Harris Museum inspired the holding of a programme of concerts by members of local schools. They were put on in Gallery 6 at the Harris, also at lunchtime, and were sponsored by British Gas. Again, the numbers of people who attended were very pleasing, and the performers found the experience exhilarating and rewarding. The handicapped children from Moorfields School performed action songs and played percussion instruments, and their concert attracted particular attention.

Tree planting programme

Throughout Guild Year Lancashire County Council was anxious to make a major contribution to the Guild and to promote projects which would be of permanent benefit to the town. Among the suggestions put forward was a tree-planting programme. The County was already undertaking a major programme of planting as part of its continuing range of environmental improvement works, but the 1992 Guild offered an opportunity to focus attention on Preston, and eventually six major tree-planting schemes were adopted for the Borough. These were located at the following places:

§ The Birches/St Luke's Nursery, Ribbleton Lane (birch and pine);

§ Oakleigh, Home for the Elderly, Lawson Street (London plane and Swedish birch);

A tree-planting programme was one of the contributions made to the Guild by Lancashire County Council. This scene was at St Luke's Nursery, Ribbleton Lane. (Lancashire County Council)

§ Deepdale Centre, Deepdale Road (tulip trees and rowans);

§ William Temple High School [now Archbishop Temple School] (oak, bird cherry, rowan, silver birch, hawthorn, guelder rose, blackthorn, dog rose, goat willow);

§ Corpus Christi High School, St Vincent's Road (rowan, ivy, hawthorn, guelder rose, dog rose);

§ English Martyrs RC School, Sizer Street (beech, silver birch);

In addition to these larger projects, single commemorative trees were planted at thirteen other sites within the Borough of Preston, including Sharoe Green and Fulwood libraries, Brieryfield and James Street nursery schools, and six different homes for the elderly. The plantings took place in late March and early April 1992, and at St Luke's Nursery in Ribbleton Lane a special ceremony was held on 8 April. The Chairman of the County Council, David Nelson, planted a silver birch with the help of Sophia Sidhu, one of the pupils at the nursery who was celebrating her fourth birthday; the Mayor of Preston, Miss Mary Rawcliffe; and ninety-year-old Miss Ethel Welch, a 1902 'Guild Baby' who was living at The Birches Old People's Home nearby.

Another tree-planting ceremony, held in early March, marked a double commemoration. Not only was 1992 Guild Year, but it was also the 150th anniversary of the founding of Preston's second-oldest surviving business, James Starkie and Sons Ltd. For 130 years the family firm, well known to generations of Prestonians, made wire products in its converted mill premises in Cotton Court, off Church Street. In 1975 it ceased to do wire-working, but began to concentrate on the wholesaling of wire products and hardware from new premises in Raglan Street. To commemorate the anniversary, in the year of the firm's eighth Preston Guild, the chairman, Jim Starkie, and his wife Edwina, donated 150 trees to the Borough, and at a ceremony helped with the planting of these in Ashton Park.

Age Concern events and activities

The elderly citizens of Preston, and visitors to the town, have long occupied a very important place in the celebration of Preston Guild. As the 1992 Guild literature and stationery proclaimed, the Guild was a celebration of Preston past, present and future, and many elderly people have vivid memories of past Guilds which they watched or in which they participated. Proud claims are made about attendance at previous Guilds, and there is much fond and happy nostalgia about those glorious events. Each Guild is 'history in the making', and the sense of having been a witness to, or a contributor to, a historic event is strong.

This is a feeling which has always been present, and the strenuous efforts which elderly people have made to attend the Guild have been considered newsworthy for over 150 years. In 1842, for example, a man in his nineties walked to Preston from Poulton-le-Fylde in order to see the Guild! For some people in Preston today the 1992 Guild was the fifth which they had attended, and for many more it was the fourth. Because of the thirty-year break between the 1922 and 1952 Guilds nobody now can have been present at six Guilds, although in the past that was, for somebody over a hundred years old, a theoretical possibility.

Special attention was paid in the 1972 Guild to the needs of the elderly, and in 1992 the same example was followed. Preston and South Ribble District Age Concern participated fully in the Guild celebrations, and arranged a varied and interesting programme of events to try to ensure that none of the elderly residents of the area was forgotten. In April 1992 an Olde Tyme Music Hall revue was held at the Charter Theatre, and over 500 people enjoyed the entertainment of times past, performed by amateur talent. This was followed, in May, by an Olde Tyme Champagne Ball at the St Thomas' Centre, where there were more than ninety guests, all of whom fully entered into the spirit of the occasion. In June came one of the highlights of Guild Year—a mammoth street party for elderly Prestonians, held in the Covered Market. More than 800 people enjoyed refreshments, music and dancing in a party atmosphere, assisted (and filmed by!) the Granada TV 'A' team.

Age Concern held an Arts and Crafts Competition for the elderly, during which some 300 entries were received and a special prize was awarded to the oldest entrant, and the organisation also entered a float in the Community Procession on 3 September. The float was supported by 150 regular users of the Age Concern Centre at Arkwright House in Stoneygate. None of the Age Concern events could have taken place without the very generous sponsorship which was received, with much heartfelt gratitude, from over thirty individuals and organisations.

Drama and music activities before the Guild

*dge Hill College presented a dram-
ised version of Charles Dickens'
'Hard Times' at the Harris Mu-
um in March.
Preston B. C.)*

The Guild Players, a local amateur group established for Guild Year, held a series of performances in local nursing homes, day centres and hospitals during April and May. They aimed particularly to entertain the elderly, and their specially written short play, entitled 'A Seat at the Guild', looked at Guild episodes in the

life of an excited and noisy local household, in 1922, 1952 and 1972, as the Guild changed and the lifestyles changed too. The project was organised and directed by the Framework Community Theatre, with help from the Borough and County Councils, North West Arts and North West Shape, and the performances, which brought back many memories and struck familiar chords in the minds of the audiences, were much enjoyed and appreciated.

While the early preparation for the Guild was under way, students at Edge Hill College, Ormskirk, devised, produced and presented a dramatised version of Charles Dickens' *Hard Times*. Dickens came to Preston when he was writing the book, and it is generally considered that the fictional 'Coketown' was modelled on the town. For this reason the College was asked by the Guild Office whether it would be prepared to present the play in Preston during Guild Year. The Director of the College agreed, as it was thought that this would help to strengthen its links with the wider community. With this in mind, the project was also financed by the College. Performances were given between 25 and 28 March in the Rotunda of the Harris Library and Museum, using costumes which had been acquired from a TV dramatisation of a Dickens novel.

The concept was that of a promenade production, with the audience closely involved and mixed in with the action: hassocks, borrowed from the parish church, were used so that people could sit around a particular scene if they wished to do so. Attendance was excellent, and the capacity audiences included parties from a number of local schools. Sponsorship was received from thirteen organisations and companies, and there was much satisfaction with the results of the project—not least, it was found for the first time that the Rotunda lends itself very well to small-scale and intimate dramatic productions, and could be used for this purpose in the future.

Preston College has an open air theatre, built in 1986 but seriously under-used since then. It was decided that Guild Year would be an excellent opportunity to have a formal opening of the theatre, and to promote its potential, so that organisers of drama, musical events and other arts media would be aware that the theatre was available—one of the other Guild Year events to take place here was the Multi-Cultural Arts Festival. For the official opening BNFL agreed to sponsor a production of 'Hamlet' and this was performed on 30 June, in the presence of the Guild Mayor. The actors were a professional company, the Compass Theatre Company of Sheffield. There was a very good attendance— over 800 people were present at the beginning of the evening, and an excellent rapport developed between actors and audience.

Unfortunately the major disadvantage of open air theatres in England—the weather—afflicted this production, just as it did the Arts Festival. Very heavy rain began just before the interval, and the performance was moved inside to continue in the refectory. Tina Burchill of the *Evening Post* reported that 'they all died happily ever after, even if the college canteen didn't bear much resemblance to the ramparts of Elsinore Castle'. Nevertheless, 'Hamlet' in the open air was a great success: the writers of a letter to the *Lancashire Evening Post* said that the event 'would be their abiding memory of the 1992 Guild', and the College authorities hope that the theatre will now be much more fully used.

'A Georgian Evening at Lark Hill' was a very imaginative production staged by local amateur actors and actresses at Lark Hill House, now part of Cardinal

Newman College, during late August. The idea arose from the researches undertaken by local historian Margaret Burscough, who has written the history of the house (which was the home of Samuel Horrocks and his family). The production involved a dramatic reconstruction of life in the house in the early nineteenth century, using letters and other contemporary documentary sources. The audience, described as 'guests', were entertained with punch and canapes before being shown to their places by a 'member of the family'. Music and song were included, and afterwards the 'guests' joined the 'family' for a Georgian supper. In total about 450 people watched this memorable and unusual show.

Musical events for Guild Year included a unique production of Verdi's 'Nabucco', performed by Preston Opera at the Guild Hall on 22 August. This was a massive undertaking, with a set design—75 feet by 54 feet, and 25 feet high—based on the concept of the Hanging Gardens of Babylon. It took four weeks to make, and after the performance some criticism was voiced by some members of the audience that the design was in fact too large: it was said that the view of parts of the audience was blocked by the chorus standing on the raised arms of the set. There were over 200 performers, and the Guild Hall was filled to capacity for the event. 'Nabucco' was a very ambitious project which—these criticisms apart—was a resounding success. That a performance on such a large-scale and with such complex staging could be put on so effectively was a real tribute to the skill and enthusiasm of all concerned.

On the following day, after the scenery from Nabucco had been swiftly dismantled, the Guild Hall was the setting for 'One More Song', an evening of mainly barbershop harmony held by the Red Rose Chorus of Preston. There was a very high standard of performance by each of the groups present, all of which were immaculately dressed and disciplined, and the very large audience thoroughly enjoyed the evening. The Red Rosettes of Preston, a ladies' barbershop group, were there, and the Saddleworth Male Voice Choir sang works from the 'conventional' repertoire. Special guests were the Red Rose Chapter of Lancaster, Pennsylvania, and two award-winning quartets, Mainstream and Quattro, provided contrasting contributions.

The organisers of the Guild had included street theatre in their plans, as a less formal and more impromptu aspect of the celebrations which could be carried on during the summer in different parts of the town and would not require elaborate and complicated organisation. About twenty-five different acts performed in the district on Saturdays during the months from May to September. In the town centre there were usually large and appreciative audiences, even in bad weather—on such occasions the facilities of the Harris Museum and Library were used. Street theatre performers also went to several of the fetes, galas and fairs held by villages in the rural parts of the Borough, including Grimsargh, Woodplumpton and Barton. These were a great success, especially as some of the organisers made the performances a highlight of their day's programme.

The major disappointment was the attempt to hold performances of street theatre in housing estates. There the performers attracted very small audiences, either because of lack of effective publicity or lack of interest. This was in itself a major disappointment, since bringing drama to everyday situations had been an aim of the programme, but more serious in many ways was the physical abuse and verbal hostility which the entertainers suffered—equipment was stolen or damaged, and performers were assaulted. These episodes reflect very great discredit upon those concerned, and were one of the few black marks gained by Preston and its people during the whole of the great and varied programme of Guild Year events. Bad weather was also a problem in some instances, and it was felt that the most successful events—other than the town-centre performances—were those which had a ready-made audience gathered for another purpose, such as a fair or gala.

During Guild Week itself all the street theatre acts were concentrated on the Flag Market or nearby streets. Audiences were generally good, despite the wet weather, but when processions were due spectators chose in preference—though not unexpectedly—to secure good places for viewing those. One enterprising and cheeky group of entertainers, lacking an audience in consequence, simply joined in the procession! The acts were many and varied, and included community artists who did face-painting, kite-making and puppet-making. The programme was funded jointly by the North West Arts Board, Lancashire County Council and Preston Borough Council.

The owners of the Miller Arcade, P & O Properties, and the traders operating in the arcade, ran a programme of activities with a Victorian theme from 24–29 August. These included street theatre, magic, music and circus acts. Among the performers were Martini's Magic; the Grinnigogs, performing in costume and

Throughout the summer a great diversity of street theatre and entertainments could be seen in different parts of the town.
(Preston B. C.)

playing lutes; and the Preston Wates, who played music in a Victorian country style.

A very different type of entertainment should have been provided by the Walk The Plank company, billed as 'the world's first company of performers, musicians and visual artists to take to the high seas'. They performed in and from a converted Norwegian ferry, and their programme was scheduled to include two shows. One was 'The Blue', an extraordinary 'play' which featured 'swash-buckling fights on the poop deck, strange sounds in the cargo holds, and Blue creatures hauled aboard in nets ... Giant cranes and didgeridoos, the entire Royal Biological Oddity Corps, and a high speed chase through the Engine Room make this family show unmissable'. The second was 'Blue on Fire', a medley of light and fire, music and image, in which 'bizarre machines are launched from the vessel; a strange waterborne procession bursts into flame; and the ship erupts with smoke and pyrotechnics'.

The ship was moored in the middle of the dock, and spectators around the dock edge thus had an excellent potential vantage point as well as those who boarded the ship for performances. Unfortunately the shows were due to take place during the weekend before the Guild, and the weather was appalling. There were extremely high winds which, tearing across the dock, whipped the water up into huge waves and battered the gallant ship. Torrential rain lashed at the hardy souls who ventured forth to watch the show. Consequently much of the 'Walk the Plank' show had to be curtailed, and the Monday evening sound and light spectacular was also very considerably reduced.

Garden Competitions

The *Lancashire Evening Post* and Barton Grange Garden Centre took the lead in promoting the 'Design a Guild Garden' competition. This invited amateur gardeners to 'let their imagination take over to create an average sized suburban semi-detached garden of their dreams' on a plot 30 feet by 50 feet. They were to take into consideration the ease of maintenance, moderation in costs of construction, and suitability for use and enjoyment by all members of a household. The competition closed on 1 June, and was judged by John Busbridge of Barton Grange, Peter Topping of Barton Grange Landscapes, Nigel Conway (Preston Borough Parks Manager) and Phil Welsh of the *Lancashire Evening Post*.

The two semi-finalists were Andrew Kirkham and Sheila Heyes, both of Fulwood. Their designs were constructed on Moor Park as part of the Proud Preston Exhibition, and members of the public were asked to vote to select the outright winner. As a result of this Mrs Heyes was given first place, and won £1,000-worth of Barton Grange vouchers, and Mr Kirkham won £500-worth. Five other runners-up received prizes of garden furniture, shrubs and bulbs. There were over eighty entries, and the task of the judges was very difficult because of the high quality of the designs submitted.

A more traditional feature of Preston Guild is the Best-Kept Garden Competition, which was held during 1992 as in previous Guild Years. Entries were divided between two areas: the North of Preston section was sponsored by Barton Grange Garden Centre and Preston Borough Council, while the sponsors of the South of Preston section were Turbary House Garden Centre and South Ribble Borough Council. The competition was promoted by the *Lancashire Evening Post* and was launched at the end of June. Judging took place over a four-week period, with a representative of each garden centre and each council being on the panel: here, too, the judges had an extremely difficult task in deciding between the entries. The eventual winners of the Best-Kept Garden Competition were:

Best Back Garden	Mr and Mrs J. Malcolm Gill House Avenue, Lea
Best Hanging Basket	Mr W. Fordham Wellbrow Drive, Longridge
Best Business Premises	Mrs A. Hunter Hunter Fold House, Beech Grove
Best Back Yard	Mr C. J. Turner Powis Road, Ashton

Events and exhibitions at the Harris Museum and Art Gallery

The Harris Museum and Art Gallery has been closely associated with the Guild and Guild events ever since 1882, when the foundation stone of the building was laid during Guild Week. The Museum was opened in 1893, and since then has been a focal point of activities in successive Guilds, just as its building is one of the dominating architectural features of the town centre. Not least, in recent Guilds it has been used for several formal ceremonies as well as many receptions and presentations. During Guilds up to 1922 the Town Hall, on the site of what is now Crystal House, provided the civic setting for ceremonial events, such as the proclamations, Mayoral addresses to the crowds, and the great banquets, as well as the Guild Court itself. The partial destruction of the Town Hall by fire in 1947, and its subsequent total demolition, meant that in 1952 and 1972 events were shared between several other buildings, and the Harris Museum steps were used for the public proclamations.

After the completion of the Guild Hall, just after the 1972 Guild, the problem of where to hold the great events was solved, but the Museum steps are still the only suitable location for the major proclamations and the public appearances of the Guild Mayor. The building itself, being of such outstanding architectural significance, is a worthy setting for such grand civic occasions, although the Flag Market below is not without its problems—not least, at the 1992 Guild the trees, which were much larger than in 1972, obscured the view for a good many people!

The Harris Museum itself played a crucial role in the Guild, with its very successful year of exhibitions and special events, and as the setting for a range of other activities, including receptions and lunchtime Guild lectures. The list below shows the major exhibitions which the Museum and Art Gallery staged during

Guild Year 1992, and the visitor figures—which, as can be seen, were extremely rewarding:

Once Every Preston Guild	(1 Jan–31 Dec)	approx 140,000
Leonora Carrington	(1 Feb–21 Mar)	13,568
Guild to Guild	(22 Feb–10 Oct)	34,129
The People's Show	(23 May–1 Jul)	approx 15,000
Fine Material for a Dream	(3 Apr–13 May)	5,132
The Landscape Art of L. S. Lowry Landscape Contemporaries	(11 Jul–19 Aug)	13,232
Life Lines	(31 Aug–17 Oct)	16,427
The Ride of Life	(7 Nov–6 Jan)	approx 28,000
Preston in 1992		36,756

The total of visitors to these ten exhibitions was more than 300,000, which was an exceptionally high figure fully justifying the major effort which had been made to provide a wide range of stimulating events. The emphasis throughout Guild Year was on Preston, Lancashire, and the Guild itself, and much of the work was devoted to highlighting the Guild and its place in the history, culture and society of the town. For the Museum and its staff 1992 was a hectic, busy and exciting time, and a splendid prelude to 1993, its own centenary year.

The 'Leonora Carrington 1940–1990' exhibition, showing the work of this Lancashire-born artist, had earlier opened in London and attracted much media interest. The Harris held a reception for members of the Carrington family who live in the Preston area, and some of them were able to provide fascinating memories of her. The visitor figures were excellent, and people came from as far afield as Nottingham, Peterborough and Edinburgh.

Midsummer saw a dual exhibition. 'The Landscape Art of L. S. Lowry' highlighted a little-known aspect of the work of this perennially popular Lancashire artist, and was a marvellous opportunity to see material that is rarely, if ever, exhibited. 'Lancashire Contemporaries', which was sponsored by Building Design Partnership, looked at the work of seventeen painters, sculptors, photographers and animators who have Lancashire connections. Workshops were held in conjunction with this, and the exhibition included work by the Preston-born Oscar-winning animator, Nick Park. The exhibition also included a very large and somewhat rusty metal sculpture which was placed in—or, according to some, almost filled—the ground-floor Rotunda area within the Harris Building: it attracted instant notoriety and massive press coverage and seemed, at least to a few of the correspondents of the *Lancashire Evening Post*, to signal the end of civilisation—once it had gone, of course, everyone forgot about it.

'The People's Show' was immensely popular, and attracted one of the best attendance figures of any exhibition in recent years. This extraordinary exhibition displayed the things which people collect in their own homes—not the priceless, inside-a-glass-showcase material of museums and galleries, but moustache cups, frogs (in any form except live!), cricket memorabilia, flour graders, badges, and almost one hundred other collections—endearing, fascinating, bizarre, funny, delightful or just plain daft! There was enormous press interest, and some of the collectors were besieged by interviewers: media coverage included features on Radio 4's 'Kaleidoscope', Granada TV's 'What's New', and many newspapers and magazines. So popular was the exhibition that it is hoped to make it a regular event, and a National People's Show Festival is planned for 1994.

'Guild to Guild' was organised by the Commission for New Towns, and illustrated the changes that had taken place in the Preston area since 1972, which was not only the previous Guild Year but also the point at which the development of the Central Lancashire New Town began to make serious progress.

'Life-Lines' opened on the first day of Guild Week, and proved to be especially popular with families who were in the town centre for Guild events. They particularly enjoyed the participatory elements and the combination of work by amateur artists and school children with pictures on loan from the Arts Council. Local people were extensively involved in the Family Art and Community Groups sections, costumes were loaned by the Caribbean Carnival, and the Asian Ladies Embroidery Project was on show. 'Preston in 1992' was an end of year photographic exhibition which portrayed the town during Guild Year, and especially during Guild Week itself, as revealed by the cameras of the Preston Photographic Society. Their record will form an important resource for future local historians.

During Guild Year the staff of the Museum and Art Gallery worked on and promoted a wide range of other Guild projects. These included, among others, the Schools Guild Oral History Project, in which children at several local schools interviewed relatives about their memories and recollections of past Guilds;

'Once Every Preston Guild', which ran throughout Guild Year, was among the most successful exhibitions ever staged by the Harris Museum.
(Author's collection)

Town Walks; Dressing Up For Fun—a Guild fancy dress event; Create a Memory—a workshop to decorate mugs and plates with Guild designs; and 'The Butcher, The Baker, The Candlestick Maker', a schools' drama performance based on an early medieval Guild.

Dominating Guild Year at the Harris, though, was the outstandingly successful exhibition 'Once Every Preston Guild', officially opened by the Earl of Derby on 22 January. It attracted an astonishing number of visitors and maintained its attendance figures throughout the year. There were two aspects to the exhibition—the physical presence of the Guild in the form of objects and artifacts, and an audio-visual display. The Harris' extensive collection of Guild artifacts and memorabilia—badges and insignia, costumes, souvenirs, posters and photographs, crockery and portraits of Preston and its Guild Mayors—together with borrowed items such as historic documents, and the borough regalia and Guild Mayoral robes (which were borrowed back for Guild Week!), made a fascinating and informative display, accompanied by specially written information panels which presented a potted history of the Guild. Also included in this part of the exhibition was an audio-visual presentation which Christopher Ratcliffe, of Building Design Partnership, had produced in 1972: it anticipated what Preston would be like in 1992, and the comparison between the predicted and the actual was most interesting!

The audio-visual presentation was a very professional and effective 'sound and light' performance, produced by 'Spoken Image' of Manchester in conjunction with the Museum staff. Dramatic and humorous reconstructions of the history of the Guild, performed by an actor, were interspersed with slide sequences, all with a background of appropriate music and sound effects, and a commentary spoken by Preston-born TV newsreader, Fiona Armstrong. The exhibition was highly praised from all sides, and has since gained a number of national awards and commendations.

The University and Colleges and the 1992 Guild

In 1992 Preston became a university town, with the creation of the University of Central Lancashire from what had been Lancashire Polytechnic—and before then Preston Polytechnic, and before that the Harris Institute. The granting of university status was accompanied by a heated controversy over the name of the new institution, for many people and local organisations felt that the word 'Preston' should have been included in the title, but there is no doubt that Preston is proud to have a university and that many benefits have been and will be gained from its existence—it is already a large institution, and expanding fast, and this must be to Preston's advantage.

The University was able to play a significant role in the Guild of 1992, with a wide range of projects. The Rector, Mr Brian Booth, was present at many of the official events, while the innovative work of the University's Art and Fashion Department was dramatically highlighted by the remarkable sea-green ceremonial robes and caps which its students had designed for the Gentlemen of the Select

The unveiling of the new nameboard of the University of Central Lancashire, with the Rector, Brian Booth (left) and the Guild Mayor (right). (Photo, University of Central Lancashire)

Vestry. Their eye-catching costumes, at once modern and medieval, looked superb in the ceremonial events and processions at the opening and adjournment of the Guild Court.

The Lancashire Polytechnic Students Union, as it was then, held a very successful concert in Avenham Park on 23 May, and the 'celebrity' lecture series organised by the University for Guild Year attracted much attention. Second-year art students produced ten works of art for display in the town centre during late May, including a four-foot concrete arch and a fist of bricks. The project was given outside sponsorship by Marks and Spencer. A Guild Reunion of the 'Class of 42' was held by the Alumni Association, to commemorate the Guild which did not happen! Sixty-four former pupils of the Junior Technical School were present, and the event was so well received that it is hoped to make it a regular occasion.

The University Arts Centre, which was converted some years ago from the former St Peter's Church, Fylde Road, was the setting for a series of Guild Year events which formed part of the wider Guild programme. These included a presentation by the Limelights Theatre Company, which is made up of students from Cardinal Newman College, of Peter Hartley's 'Jacobite—the Preston Fight'. The play, performed on several evenings in February, is about the 'battle' which was fought at Preston during the 1715 rising. As well as its usual range of concerts and musical performances, the Arts Centre also housed the British Gas exhibition 'Gas in Preston from 1816' and several other exhibitions during the summer.

The most unusual and challenging University-based project was Radio Guild FM, conceived in the autumn of 1991 by members of the School of Journalism at the Lancashire Polytechnic. Their aim was to provide a community radio station which would broadcast throughout the Preston district during the two weeks at the heart of the Guild celebrations. It was felt that the other local radio stations could not, because of technical, programming and journalistic constraints, cover the events in this concentrated way, and it was hoped that Radio Guild FM would bring Guild coverage of a very immediate and direct kind to those in the district who were unable to witness what was going on at first hand. A Special Events Licence was granted by the Radio Authority to allow the public broadcasting to take place.

The project made excellent use of the School's professional standard studio and broadcasting facilities, but as much of the content as possible was broadcast from sites around the town, as it was happening. The University underwrote the technical and establishment costs, but almost all of the operating was done on a voluntary basis. The station broadcast on an FM frequency of 100.7 Mhz between 7 a.m. and 10 p.m. each day, with an overnight sustaining service provided by Red Rose Gold. Local and professional broadcasters offered their services as sequence presenters, a local studio prepared custom-made jingles, and technical, research and reporting services were provided by students of the University of Central Lancashire and some from other universities who were in Preston for the long vacation. Much help was also received from local people who offered their services spontaneously and without charge.

Radio Guild FM programmed a 50:50 balance between speech and music, structured around five sequences and beginning with a breakfast show, which included conversations with special guests and details of the events for the day ahead. This was followed by a mid-morning show, based in the AA shop in Cheapside, involving live broadcast of interviews with Preston people as well as detailed commentary on the events and processions during Guild Week itself. In the afternoon the show came from the Proud Preston Exhibition on Moor Park, and covered all aspects of this—unfortunately very unsuccessful—event. A tea-time show was broadcast from the studio at the University, and covered events to come and retrospect on the activities of the day. Finally, the late show, also from the University, looked forward to the following day and had interviews and conversations with special guests.

The results were beyond the wildest expectations of the organisers. Over the fortnight the number of people listening to the station grew very rapidly, and by the end of Guild Week it seemed that almost everybody in the town was listening at some stage. There were very many interviews with almost all people involved in the Guild, as well as outside broadcasts from all over the town (including a street party in heavy rain!). Mini-broadcasts even came from the tower of St Walburge's church and from the passenger seat of the world's oldest Rolls Royce.

It was evident from letters and telephone calls that the people at whom the service was particularly aimed—the elderly, the housebound, and others who could not reach the Guild—were especially enthusiastic about the station. During the coverage of the first procession telephone callers pleaded with the broadcasters to 'play no more music—stay with the Commentary on the Procession, it's wonderful'. Their wishes were granted, and no more music was played during any of the procession commentaries: it was instant listener power!

Because of the immediacy of the service, well-illustrated by the response to those listeners, it was possible to broadcast immediate updates on travel and traffic problems, and to keep the public accurately informed of what was happening in different parts of the town. The University was delighted that its public profile had been raised to such good effect at a key time, and regarded its investment as very profitable. And this venture, with its modern technology and innovative concept, is sure to provide an example for the organisers of the 2012 Guild.

Local colleges also made a very significant contribution to the Guild. Preston College students assisted with the production of scenery and props for the Schools' Pageant, and the College hosted the Lancashire Education stand at the Proud Preston Exhibition. The College had floats in the Community and Torchlight Processions, and a student from the College delivered, with great skill, one of the Latin orations at the opening Guild Court. Preston College also promoted the professional production of 'Hamlet' which is described in the section on drama.

'Gertie and Her Guild Machine', seen here in 1990, was the pre-Guild play produced by Cardinal Newman College for local schools. (Preston B. C.)

Cardinal Newman College produced the pre-Guild play 'Gertie and her Guild Machine', which toured local primary schools during 1990 and 1991. 'Gertie', a play intended to heighten the awareness of the forthcoming Guild among the children of the town, was commissioned by the Guild Committee and was written and produced by Peter Hartley, a laboratory technician at the College. It told of a time machine which went back through the centuries to previous Guilds. The production, which involved thirteen students, required some complex and challenging changes of costume and effects. The College also produced and performed 'Jacobite—The Preston Fight' at the University Arts Centre. The College Principal and a pupil were orators at the opening of the Guild Court, and the College made a major contribution to the Schools Pageant and other dramatic and artistic performances during Guild Year. Its Lark Hill building, which had been the family residence of Samuel Horrocks, was loaned for the presentation of the much-acclaimed 'A Georgian Evening with the Horrockses'. In another dramatic reconstruction, the Sealed Knot stormed the College playing fields on 15–16 August!

Guild school and education projects

Because the Guild takes place so rarely, it is a completely new event for all schoolchildren—no child at school can possibly have experienced the Guild before, or understand its particular qualities and meaning, and so there is always much scope for the development of special events and activities. These are generally aimed at explaining the Guild, its origins and its symbolic importance; at building on the idea of the Guild to demonstrate ideas such as 'community', or investigating aspects of local history and oral history; using the Guild as an opportunity for imaginative and creative work in a wide range of artistic media; and celebrating the Guild by entertainments, parties and festivals for the school. As well as all these individual activities and projects, there are many other roles for schools—participation in processions, visits to Guild events, and—above all, perhaps—the great Schools Pageant on Avenham Park.

All these many dimensions make the Guild Year a time of great enjoyment and excitement for individual schools, and the different projects can be very beneficial to children and teachers alike—although, it must be said, often very exhausting and wearying to the latter. Writing in their school logbooks, headteachers from the Preston area in 1882, 1902, and 1922 frequently express variations on the sentiment that 'the sooner it's all over and we can get back to normal, the better'!

In 1992 there was a huge range and variety of school activities, and many new and exciting projects were undertaken. The work of the Preston area schools, including those in South Ribble district and parts of Ribble Valley and Fylde, was assisted and developed by the Education Officers at the Guild Office, whose task was to provide all manner of practical help and information, as well as affording access to literature, giving talks and making arrangements for school events. They also had the major work of planning and organising the great Schools Pageant.

One task which had to be undertaken at the beginning was the arranging of school holidays for 1992. This was the first Guild at which Lancashire County Council had been the education authority for the Preston schools, and so it was closely involved in the preparations, but there was also a considerable element of individual decision by the schools concerned. The problem, as in previous Guilds, centred on the Schools Pageant and its timing; on whether or not schools should close for Guild Week; and on the question of whether there should be an extra holiday or simply a re-arrangement of the standard holiday length. Much debate ensued—the local branch of the National Association of Head Teachers even had the temerity to pass a resolution that the Pageant should take place in the summer term and not during Guild Week—and by the middle of 1991 little agreement had been reached.

The basic position by this time was that the County agreed that many local schools would have to close during Guild Week, like it or not, because of problems of access; that the sponsors who were interested in supporting the Schools Pageant saw it—quite correctly—as a Guild event, and so were strongly opposed to the idea of shifting it to the early summer; and that all agreed it would be very unfortunate if the Guild was to lose its schools content, after 150 years. Eventually, further discussion with the Chief Education Officer, Andrew Collier, resulted in a very amicable agreement and a great deal of invaluable practical, technical and strategic support for the schools' participation in the Guild and its events. It is significant that some South Ribble schools, as well as those in Preston, chose to adopt the arrangement and were able to participate.

As planning for the Guild began in earnest it was realised that there was a pressing need to make educational material available to schools. Paul Cross, the headteacher of St Andrew's Church of England School, Ashton, was commissioned to produce a local history pack dealing with the history of the town and the significance of the Guild, and to relate these to the history curriculum. Unfortunately, circumstances meant that there were serious delays in preparation of the material and it did not appear until January 1993, after the close of Guild Year. However, since it contains general material on the teaching of local history in Lancashire it continues to have relevance and to sell well.

A feature of every Guild in the last century and a half has been the distribution of medals to schoolchildren. When the idea was first introduced, in 1842, it was expected that these would only be given to those who had actually participated in Guild events, but there was such a demand for medals from everybody else that the Corporation began to produce them for all children of the Borough—just as they did for national events such as coronations and jubilees. Ever since the mid-nineteenth century, therefore, all schoolchildren in the Borough have received a special Guild medal.

In 1990 it was decided that a design competition would be held, so that the 1992 Guild medals would have a particular distinction. The competition, which covered not only the medal for schools but also the general Guild medals, was arranged by BWP Consultants, and generous prizes were offered in several categories. It was open to all secondary schools and sixth-form colleges in the Preston education district, and was judged by Dick Atkinson (the Chairman of the

Guild Committee), Professor Sir George Grenfell-Baines of Building Design Partnership, and Ron Dutton, a professional medal designer from Wolverhampton. Over 150 entries were received, from nine schools in the area, and the overall winner was thirteen-year-old Sanjay Nayee of Tulketh High School. Ramish Limbachia, aged fourteen, of Fulwood was chosen designer of the medal for schoolchildren. They received their prizes and awards at a Mayoral reception on 23 January 1992. Eventually 23,000 medals were produced for distribution to schoolchildren in Preston and district.

The local Rotary Club, in conjunction with the Preston Philatelic Society, organised the printing of a special Guild envelope, to be used by local businesses during the Guild period. Schools were given the opportunity of buying the envelopes and selling them for school funds, and a design competition was arranged. The specification was that the design should have no more than three colours, should include the words 'Preston Guild 1992', and be suitable for use on an envelope. There was much interest in the competition, and over one hundred entries were received from twelve schools. The winner was ten-year-old Hiten Patel of St Augustine's RC primary school, and the prizes were presented by the Mayor, Miss Mary Rawcliffe, on 24 March. The best entries were later exhibited in the Community Gallery at the Harris Museum. Eventually 160,000 envelopes were sold, of the 200,000 printed—delays in printing reduced sales opportunities. The unsold balance has been distributed free to charities.

Technology and its place in education were supported and emphasised by three Guild projects. The organisation known as STEEL—Science, Technology and Engineering Education in Lancashire—was founded in 1976 and holds an annual fair. Its aim is to promote science and technology in schools at all levels, and it receives funding from, among others, the business community, the County Council, universities and colleges. In 1992 it decided to hold its annual fair in Preston, to mark Guild Year. The Fair was staged at the University of Central Lancashire between 6 and 13 July, with financial assistance from British Aerospace, Building Design Partnership, Leyland/DAF, Thomas Banks & Co (coal merchants), Dutton Forshaw and the University itself. Thirty-five schools took part, and many members of the public and schoolchildren visited the exhibition and fair.

In October 1991 British Nuclear Fuels Ltd agreed to sponsor a special Guild competition, with a technology theme, for primary and secondary schools within its travel-to-work area. After discussion it was decided that the schools should produce curricular-related projects concerned with the subject of 'energy'. The project could be delivered in any medium which was thought appropriate— 'newspaper' formats, playlets, videos, exhibits, models and poetry were all suggested. Prizes of £2,000- and £1,000-worth of computer equipment were offered for primary and secondary schools, together with smaller awards for runners-up.

After a disappointing initial response the competition was very successful, and a high standard of entries resulted. The joint winners in the secondary schools group, Ashton High School, Preston (energy sources) and Our Lady and St John, Blackburn (a conservation project) each received £1,500. In the primary group Fleetwood Charity School, Newton Bluecoat School, Preesall, Catforth and Eldon (Preston) primary schools each received £750. Awards were presented on Saturday 27 June by Lord Shuttleworth at the Living Countryside event in Moor Park.

The Preston Area Industry Education Liaison Group and Preston Area Compact, led by the Chief Executive Miss L. Duckworth, arranged a Guild project in conjunction with the Guild Office. It was associated with the Preston Area Enterprising Technology Project, a major initiative which is spearheaded by the Education Business Partnership in the Preston area. The aim was to encourage the development of curricular-based 'enterprising technology' projects in the academic year 1991–2, and to involve small teams of high school pupils in research, design, production and costing. The students would gain wide-ranging skills in problem-solving, experimental design, team work and technological innovation and assessment, while employers would be able to initiate or strengthen links with schools.

Entrants were asked to submit their best projects for exhibition and inclusion in the competition, and BP gave help with its Technology Bus, which was used for student workshops, training sessions for teachers, and receptions for employers. Twelve of the best entries were exhibited at Moor Park High School on 23 June 1992. The Enterprising Technology Project was also represented at the Proud Preston Exhibition in Moor Park during Guild Week.

School events and activities before the Guild

There were so many schools' activities in the eight months before the Guild that it is impossible to describe, or even to mention, all of them. What follows is therefore a review of the main areas of the work and activities of local schools, and a selection of specific projects undertaken and events held.

Many schools held special fairs, fetes or festivals in the early summer, to commemorate Guild Year. Some were new for 1992, while others were a regular annual event which was given a special Guild flavour. Lea Endowed Church of England School had a Guild Summer Fair, which was opened by the Guild Mayor and Mayoress. Our Lady's High School developed an impressive Guild Project, but it also had a Guild Awareness Week and a Guild Summer Fair. Pupils of Fishwick County Primary School had a very exciting time on 9 July, when they were entertained by a 'Blue and White Guild Disco'—an afternoon session for infants and an early evening event for the juniors. An outside disc jockey was brought in, and parents subscribed to the cost. Longridge County Primary School organised a Guild street party, while Tulketh High held its own 500-strong Guild Procession around the neighbourhood, thus strengthening its links with the community—several other Preston schools held similar events.

St Pius X Preparatory School in Garstang Road held a Guild Day, in which everybody was transported back to Victorian times, with special costumes and mouthwatering cream teas at Victorian prices—3p each! At the William Temple High School the Guild Summer Fair had several impressive events, including a display by the Black Knights Parachutists, the High Fly Team, and Thwaites Dray Horses. The Guild Mayor was among the 2,500 visitors. Ashton High School Guild Summer Fair was given a seventeenth-century feel, and there were treasure hunts, punch and judy, a miniature railway and marching and pipe

he Lea Endowed C. of E. Primary
:hool held a Guild Summer Fair,
·ith plenty of period costume.
'reston B. C.)

bands. Broughton High School had a Guild Fayre which included a procession through the village, and at Cliff House Day Nursery a children's party was held, with the Guild Mayor and Mayoress as guests, together with local senior citizens: the children were too young to understand the idea of the Guild, and were told that the party was for Preston's birthday!

There was plenty of opportunity to carry out valuable art and drama projects, and the Guild enabled some schools to give public performances and exhibitions of their work. For instance, Christ the King High School was the initiator of the very imaginative Hallé project which, according to the Head of Music, Joan Parkhouse, was intended 'to heighten the profile of music within the school and to stimulate interest in the school in the local community'. Pupils from Christ the King and four of its feeder primary schools—Ss Ignatius, Augustine, Teresa and Joseph—joined in a master class for the Guild in conjunction with the Hallé Orchestra itself. Six groups performed, and each had a player from the orchestra as its leader: a public performance with the Hallé Orchestra was given on 12 July.

Ashton High School and the Framework Community Theatre joined forces to produce 'The Living Newspaper', in which news items and advertisements from the Guilds of 1952 and 1972 were brought to life in short sketches, using specially designed costumes. Performances were given at the Harris Museum on 25–26 June. The School also contributed a Guild song, 'We are proud', which told of Preston's 1,000-year history: it was written by two of the teachers from the school, and the proceeds from the sale of cassettes went to local charities. As far away as distant Kirkham, the Carr Hill High School organised a Guild Year Arts Week starting on 9 March. John Cotterall from the Guild Office provided an introductory talk explaining the significance of the Guild, and there was a wide range of activities: art, drama, literature, pottery workshops, theatre visits, an artist-in-residence and writers talking about their work.

Penwortham Girls' High School presented 'A Pageant of Music in England', which showed developments in and influences on English music from the medieval period to the present. Costume tableaux were shown, and a dozen primary schools joined in the project. It was staged at the Charter Theatre for two nights, and attracted capacity audiences. Broughton High School Art Department organised a photographic competition on the theme 'Images of Preston', for pupils, parents and friends of the school. It encouraged participants to look at their familiar surroundings with a new and artistic eye, and the results were excellent. A musical evening was held at which the winners were presented with prizes donated by local firms. Children from Lea Endowed Primary School made a 'Guild Pond', decorated with bunting and flags, and kept Guild scrapbooks, while some of them also designed a Guild tea towel.

In several local schools there was a strong feeling that a more permanent record of the Guild was needed, and they sought to mark the occasion by doing something which would have lasting value and appeal. Many schools therefore undertook ambitious projects to design and build Guild gardens, or commemorative windows and wall panels, or to write and illustrate Guild publications. Our Lady's High School chose to produce a 'Guild Year Book', recording the activities of the school between January and September 1992. The work was carried out by ten fourth-year girls, who photographed and recorded school events, visits and visitors, and daily life. They took the pictures, wrote captions and text, and undertook layout and design work. Three hundred copies of the book were then printed by a specialist firm, and were sold to children and parents—with obvious entrepreneurial talent the designers ensured that every child in the school appeared somewhere in the book! The project provided excellent experience in photography, writing and design, and in business methods.

St Leonard's Church of England School, Walton-le-Dale, decided that its project to commemorate the Guild was to be the planting of thirty native species trees in the school grounds and the nearby churchyard, while at Fishwick Primary School the Guild Mayor planted a whitebeam tree donated by Spout Farm nurseries of Longridge. At Higher Walton Church of England School, which was opened in 1864, the school carried out a historical investigation into the seven Guilds during its lifetime, 1862–1992. The people of the village, and their daily lives and lifestyles, were researched, and art work was produced. Some of today's residents—and old photographs of former residents—were used as models for a thirty-foot square mural which was painted on the gable end of the village butcher's shop by Peter Owen, a professional artist who transferred the work of the pupils to this new site. The mural was unveiled in a ceremony on 11 January 1992, after the project had attracted much local support and enthusiasm. The designers hope that it will last until the Guild of 2012, as a reminder of that of 1992.

At Our Lady's High School the Guild was commemorated by a much larger building project, in which the school redeveloped a former bungalow within the grounds to provide a conference centre with information and resource unit, small library, rooms for private study, and word-processing and computer facilities. A Guild Committee, which included pupil representatives, was established to plan the school's Guild involvement, and one of the ideas put forward was for a commemorative window in the new building. This was constructed by Preston College after a county-wide design competition. The winner, Gerry Richards, had been artist in residence at the school during 1991: his design incorporated many of the significant buildings of Preston, in a range of rich red, purple and golden glass. It was unveiled by the Bishop of Lancaster on 3 February 1992, and the school's annual report notes that the building 'affords a tranquil and elegant environment ... elegant generally in its ambience and particularly because of the commemorative window'.

Middleforth Church of England School has developed a particular interest in pottery and working with clay, and in the past has made special tiles and tile pictures. It was felt that this would be a very appropriate way of commemorating the 1992 Guild, and so the pupils and staff designed and made a six-foot square wall panel with a design of Preston buildings and the Preston crest. This was installed in the entrance hall of the school, and was unveiled by the Guild Mayor and Mayoress on 24 November 1992. Lostock Hall County Primary School children produced a mural, eighteen feet by seven, depicting the Harris Museum and the Flag Market and other symbols and emblems of Preston.

Priory High School, Penwortham, made a 'disposable' record of a very remarkable sort—pupils were asked to create a Guild sausage. The winning recipe has since been produced by a butcher in Longton and is still selling well. The school also constructed a Guild Garden, with a pond, shrubbery and flower beds, in one of its courtyards, and produced and sold a 1992 Guild Year Calendar. It is striking that so many of the schools which carried out these projects are in South Ribble district.

A permanent reminder of the Guild which will be of special benefit to many was the project to renovate and bring back into use a hydrotherapy tank at the Elms Special School. The school caters for children with profound and multiple handicaps, and was in great need of such a tank for therapy sessions—warm water is used to relax and free limbs, a treatment which is simple but very beneficial. The disused tank was situated at the former Preston Royal Infirmary building, and with the help of Conlon Construction Ltd., the Preston Health Authority and the Preston & District Spastics Group it was possible to remove and renovate it and to make the necessary alterations to the school building to provide suitable accommodation. The tank was officially opened by the Deputy Mayor, Miss Mary Rawcliffe, on 24 September 1992.

Some schools held sporting events. Several participated in the major sports and activities day at the West View Leisure Centre, described in the previous chapter, while Lostock Hall High School attracted special attention by promoting a very ambitious Table Games Tournament, in joint celebration of the Guild and the Silver Jubilee of the school. Secondary schools from all over Lancashire were invited to take part in the competition, which was held in the Rotunda of the St George's Shopping Centre on Saturday 4 April. They were asked to hold their own heats during 1991 to find winners who could go forward to the Guild Tournament—the games chosen were chess, darts, table tennis, draughts and dominoes, and over seventy pupils from fifteen schools were represented. The winners and runners-up came from Tarleton, Blackburn, Tulketh, Walton-le-

Dale, Ashton, Chorley and Lostock Hall itself, and there was a good deal of public interest from shoppers and passers-by.

The accountancy firm of Alliott, Rawkins & Holden asked to be able to contribute to the Guild celebrations, and wanted to do something which would benefit children. It was decided to work in conjunction with the Preston School-children's Fund (the former Clog Fund) and to offer a working and educational day out in the country for a group of twenty children. The field study centre at Hothersall Lodge was chosen as the venue, and Shearings Coaches provided free transport. The Harris Charity, which has for many years done much work with and for children, was also involved. The children enjoyed a day spent pond-dipping, exploring woodland, and undertaking field studies and environ-mental appreciation exercises on Longridge Fell. It was an excellent day, and very valuable for the children. Alliott, Rankins & Holden have expressed a wish to repeat this type of venture in future Guilds.

Our Lady's High School held a highly successful and well-publicised history exhibition during Guild Week. It looked at the development of local amateur football, and was opened by Tom Finney. The exhibition was very popular, and attracted extensive media attention, and as a result it is planned to repeat it in the future and to show it at the Harris Museum. A very different kind of sport—the making and flying of kites—was the subject of an event in May. Two workshops for schools were held, at Moor Park High and Ashton High, and although attendance at the latter was disappointing a good participation was reported from Moor Park. The kites were flown at the Aerial Weekend held on Ashton Park in mid-May, and the *Lancashire Evening Post* reported that they 'almost stole the show' and that scores of local children who had brought their own kites were admitted free.

Oral history and the recording and writing of memories of Guilds were chosen by some schools for Guild Year work, and there were several more general projects. Other schools did local history research and investigation making use of the Guild as a theme. The mural project at Higher Walton, for example, involved looking at life in the village during the 130 years since the building of the school. Children at St Peter's Church of England Primary School undertook 'Guild Memories' studies, and the Guild Mayor presented twenty-five prizes for the best work.

The 'Return of the Vikings', held on Avenham Park on 13–14 June and the 'Storming of Preston' by the Sealed Knot on 15–16 August gave opportunities for schoolchildren to do historical investigation of a very unusual kind. 'The Vikings' is a major topic within the national curriculum, so the presence of some real-life (well, almost!) Vikings was very exciting, especially as Kim Siddorn, their chief (and, in another incarnation, Director of Regia Anglorum which holds Viking events) travelled everywhere in costume, with spears and shields and helmet. He gave a seminar to teachers, with videos and information packs, and at least nineteen schools then invited him to visit during early March. When the Vikings invaded, in mid-June, they built a village encampment, and this was visited by many school parties.

The 'Storming of Preston' introduced another period of history. Schools were invited to contribute to a major exhibition of Civil War project work, held in the Community Gallery at the Harris Museum, and artwork, maps, written work, photographs and drawings were sent and exhibited. There was good media coverage and sponsorship was made available by Royal Mail. Prizes were awarded for the best entries. The playing fields of Cardinal Newman College were the scene of the Civil War encampment in mid-August, but for three months ahead of this members of the Sealed Knot in full costume had been visiting local schools, carrying arms and equipment: over forty-five such visits were made. The children, of all ages, were captivated and found the whole experience fascinating and very instructive—'living history', as one teacher described it.

Contemporary history was revealed and recorded for posterity in the 'Children's Lives in '91' project, carried out under the direction of Harris Museum staff with sponsorship from Marks and Spencer, as part of a longer-term programme. The children at five local schools—Savick CP, St Mary Magdalene RC Penwortham, Brockholes Wood CP, Tulketh High and Ashton High—recorded their impressions on a range of topics, including home and family life; leisure activities and part-time work; television; the world; the Guild; superstitions; and story-telling. Four of the schools then moved on to a Guild project, in which parents, grandparents and friends were interviewed about their memories and attitudes to the Guild past and present. The tapes have been deposited in the Museum as part of its stock of oral history material.

Youth organisations and the Guild

Preston Girl Guides were involved in three events for the Guild. A religious service, attended by over 1,500 local Rainbows, Brownies, Guides and Rangers, was held on 17 May at the Guild Hall. On 20 June there was a camp fire in Avenham Park from 7.00 p.m. to 9.00 p.m., attended not only by girls from the Preston area but also others from Manchester, Blackburn, Chorley and Ormskirk. Money was raised for the Derian House Children's Hospice Appeal, and it was reported that about 2,000 guides had been present. A total of 1,025 members of the various groups joined in the processions during Guild Week, and the Saturday Torchlight Procession included a Guides float with an international theme.

The 120-strong National Band of the Church Lads' and Church Girls' Brigade gives an annual concert in areas where the Brigade is strong. There are about one hundred companies in the North West, including eighteen in the Diocese of Blackburn, and it was thought appropriate to hold the 1992 concert in Preston. The Guild Hall was chosen and on 3 May an audience of almost 1,500, including the Deputy Mayor, heard an excellent concert performed by young people from all over the country. The Band was very pleased with the response, and thought that the Guild Hall was one of the best places in which they had ever played. Local groups active in the movement include St Matthews, Emmanuel, St Anne Moor Nook and St Lawrence and St Paul, Longridge. The concert was sponsored by, among others, the Royal Bank of Scotland and branches of the British Legion.

The Guild in the Villages

In 1974 the old County Borough of Preston was abolished, and the new Borough created. Its boundaries were much more widely drawn, and places such as Fulwood, Grimsargh, Woodplumpton and Broughton were, for the first time, brought within the Borough of Preston. In 1992 these areas shared fully in the Guild celebrations, as did the areas of South Ribble which are close to the town but not part of it administratively.

At Cottam, which in 1992 was still physically separate from the built-up area of Preston but which in 1993 was being linked to it by sprawling acres of new housing estates, the whole village turned out for a giant party. The church field was packed with families, and a marquee was erected. A former Guild Queen, aged seventy, was the guest of honour, and a Country & Western group provided the musical entertainment at an evening Guild Hoe-down. At Longton, on 25 July, two hundred children joined in a celebration Guild party at the Memorial Ground in School Lane, with food, a bouncy castle, games and a disco. The event was financed by the village, with the help of the local business community.

Grimsargh Festival was held for a full week in June, and had a special Guild theme, while in Woodplumpton the weekend of 12 June saw the Parish Guild Event, with a village procession, field events, dancing, craft stalls and sideshows, and a local history and archive exhibition at St Anne's church. The event was organised by the Parish Council, in conjunction with the Anglican, Catholic, Methodist and Free Methodist churches in Woodplumpton, Catforth and Cottam.

'GIFT '92'

Peter Metcalfe, secretary of the Harris Charity, suggested to the Borough Council that the 1992 Guild would be an ideal opportunity to launch a joint scheme for a furniture supply service for needy people in the Preston district. The charities involved are the Preston Council for Voluntary Service, St Vincent de Paul, Church Representatives and Age Concern. The aim is that unwanted furniture will be collected, repaired, stored and distributed as required. GIFT stands for Guild Initiative for Furniture Trust: there are fifteen trustees, and the patron of the venture is the Mayor of Preston. The scheme was launched on 9 October 1992, under the slogan 'Don't just tip it—GIFT it'. The Deputy Mayor, Miss Mary Rawcliffe, said that 'GIFT '92 is a wonderful way to ensure that the community spirit of the Guild lives on'.

Chapter 5

The civic and ceremonial events of Guild Week

A S THE PROGRAMME OF ACTIVITIES and entertainments unfolded during
Guild Year, and as the preparations became more intensive, so the
excitement about the forthcoming Guild mounted. Attention began to
focus upon the end of August, when a sequence of concerts and other spectacular
events would culminate in Guild Week itself, for at least six hundred years the
traditional climax of the celebrations. Throughout its long and illustrious history
the Preston Guild has always been focused upon Guild Week, even though
festivities and popular carnivals may have been carried on in the days before and
after. The period of six days which begins on the Monday after the feast of the
decollation of St John the Baptist is, together with the Sunday immediately
before, the time when almost all the official and civic events are held, and—most
important of all—during which the Guild Court sits and Guild Burgesses may
renew their membership of the Preston Guild Merchant.

Over the centuries the arrangements for Guild Week have altered considerably, particularly with the addition of new processions, but the essential character, and many of the specific events, have been unchanged for hundreds of years.
The civic ceremonies begin three weeks in advance of Guild Week, with the
official public proclamations which announce that a Guild is to be held, and
summon those who wish to attend. The first civic event of the week is a mayoral
procession and a church service on the first Sunday, and then on the Monday
morning the Guild and Guild Court are formally opened. The rest of the week
is filled with processions and other events, some of which are additional to the
original pattern but over the past century and a half have become integral to the
tradition. On the Saturday morning the closing ceremonies, and adjournment of
the Guild Court, take place. A new feature which has quickly become an essential
ingredient of the official recipe is the midnight speech by the Guild Mayor,
preceded by fireworks, at the closing of the Guild.

The proclamations

Preston Guild was an event of the utmost importance in the commercial and
social life of the medieval town and, as was the case on other momentous
occasions such as elections, the deaths and accessions of monarchs, and

The crowds packed the Flag Market to witness the historic occasion. (Lancashire Constabulary)

announcements of glorious victories in battle, a public proclamation of its imminence would be made. This had the practical purpose of reminding all those who would want to participate, or to renew their membership of the Guild, that they had to make application to do so. Proclamations of this sort would have been made by the town crier, who until the eighteenth century would have stood at the town's medieval market cross, in the Flag Market.

The Guild was always proclaimed three times, on the Saturdays before its opening. Saturday was the chief market day in medieval Preston, and on those days the largest number of people would be gathered in the town, conducting their trades and businesses and using the market to buy and sell. It was thus the most public occasion at which proclamations could be made. Advance notice of the Guild was essential if burgesses were to renew their membership, although by the seventeenth century the fact that many burgesses lived far away from Preston meant that other ways of announcing the forthcoming Guild might also be required—for this reason formal invitations were sent to leading Guild Burgesses.

The proclamation of the Guild has continued, although for well over two centuries it has also been announced in newspaper advertisements. Because of the rarity of the celebrations it is likely that most people were well aware of the forthcoming Guild, but the public announcement remained and has done so to the present day. In 1992 the customary pattern was followed, and on three successive Saturdays the moving and dramatic ancient ceremony was held with great pomp and dignity. To be able to listen to the proclamation of the Guild in the Flag Market afforded the audience a direct link with medieval Preston, as they joined in a tradition which represented eight hundred years of history. As always, large crowds gathered to witness and appreciate the unique ceremony.

The first proclamation was made on 15 August 1992. The waiting crowds were entertained by street theatre and by members of the Sealed Knot Society who paraded up Friargate in seventeenth-century costume. At 11.30 a.m., in the Harris Museum building, the Guild Mayor and Mayoress, Councillor and Mrs Harold Parker, received invited guests, who included members and officers of the Council, representatives of the various parish councils in the district, ex-Mayors of the Borough, and pupils from some of the high schools in Preston. At 11.50 a.m. the assembled guests proceeded to the steps of the Harris Building, overlooking the Market Square, while members of the Sealed Knot Society formed a guard of honour.

At 11.57 a.m. the regalia party, carrying the superb civic regalia of the ancient borough of Preston, preceded the Guild Mayor, the Mayoress and the Stewards and other officers of the Guild to the steps, and the Guild Mayor was greeted by a fanfare played by the trumpeters of the 14th/20th King's Hussars and the King's Own Scottish Borderers. The mayoral party took its place on the balcony, and at 12 noon precisely the Sergeant at Mace, using the time-honoured formula, called for silence:

OYEZ!   OYEZ!   OYEZ!

All manner of persons here present, whether inhabitants within this Borough or Foreigners, draw near and give your attendance to the reading of the proclamation of the holding of a Guild Merchant in this year one thousand nine hundred and ninety-two.

The Clerk of the Guild then read out the first proclamation of the Guild, advertising that it was to be held on 31 August next, and that all burgesses should on that day attend the Mayor and Stewards of the Guild, while any of those who wished to renew their privileges and liberties of membership of the Guild must make appropriate claim to do so. A full text of the proclamation is given in Appendix 8 of this book. As always, the proclamation ended with the magnificent statement that all was to be done 'according to the tenor of the letters patent of our late Sovereign Lord King Charles the Second and others his Royal Progenitors, Kings and Queens of this Realm, and according to the laudable practice and customs of many Guilds Merchant heretofore held within this Borough. GOD SAVE THE QUEEN'.

Thus could centuries of history be encompassed, and Charles II be referred to as though he had only recently departed. After the close of the formal proclamation the Guild Mayor addressed the crowds, and spoke of the sense of history, over hundreds of years, which the proclamation evoked: 'This ceremony has changed little during that period and it is right that we should continue to re-enact the history of our town in the traditional way. Enthusiasm and excitement is growing in anticipation of the celebrations in Guild Week, and I hope everyone will share in the festivities and events which will take place throughout the town during that week'. The Guild Mayor then offered the warmest of welcomes to all who had come to the town for the 1992 Preston Guild from elsewhere, and particularly from overseas. The first proclamation ceremony concluded with the singing of the National Anthem.

The second proclamation, made on 22 August, followed the same pattern. Among the guests this time were members and officers of the Borough Council, representatives of local high schools, the magistracy and parish councils within the Borough, and the mayors of the boroughs of South Ribble and Chorley. A parade through the town centre by historic commercial vehicles was the prelude to the civic ceremonial. The traditional Pot Fair was, as is customary in late August, being held on the Flag Market. Although consideration was given to relocating the stalls, it was eventually decided that this was not necessary, and in the event no problems were encountered: indeed, as the Pot Fair is an almost equally historic feature of the Preston calendar it was perhaps appropriate that the two should have coincided.

Two officers of the Duke of Lancaster's Own Yeomanry provided a colourful guard of honour for the Guild Mayor, while trumpeters from the Queen's Lancashire Regiment augmented the fanfare: the band of the regiment also played the National Anthem at the conclusion of the ceremony. The proclamation was read by the Clerk of the Guild, and then the Guild Mayor addressed the crowd, which was considerably larger than on the previous Saturday. He used the example of the Pot Fair to emphasise the history and tradition which lies behind, and gives so much strength to, the Guild and the town of Preston, and then paid tribute to the great effort which the town was making to ensure the success of the Guild: 'We hope this will attract businesses of all descriptions to look to Preston as a place where the people are hard-working, skillful, warm and friendly, and as a town where investment will generate a significant return'.

The third, final, and most important proclamation was held on 29 August, at 12 noon, two days before the official opening of the Guild and Guild Court. A much larger guest list included the Bishop of Blackburn, the Chairman of Lancashire County Council, the members and officers of the Borough Council, ex-Mayors and ex-Mayoresses of the Borough, senior Guild Burgesses, Members of Parliament and County Councillors representing the Preston area; representatives of the magistracy and local parish councillors; high school students; guests from Preston's four twin towns—Almelo, Recklinghausen, Nimes and Kalisz; and representatives of Preston Lions and Preston Rotary, the two organisations which had overseen the tour of the Guild emblems and scrolls through North America and Australasia. The waiting crowds were entertained by street theatre performances and by the superb Russian Police Band, which was in Preston for the International Tattoo organised by the Lancashire Constabulary.

Immediately after the reading of the proclamation the Guild Mayor received a special scroll of friendship from each of the four twin towns, presented by the Mayor of Almelo, Mr H.G.J. van Roekel; the Deputy Mayor of Nimes, Madame V. Bombal; the Mayor of Recklinghausen, Herr J. Welt; and the President of Kalisz, Mr W. Bachor. After these presentations Dr Norman Leigh and Mr Geoffrey Lockley, of Preston Lions, handed to the Guild Mayor the scrolls which had travelled with the Preston Guild emblems around Australasia, and which had been signed by expatriate Prestonians throughout Australia and New Zealand. The Guild Mayor thanked them, and the Lions, for organising the tour. He then announced that they were awaiting the arrival of the similar scrolls which had been sent around North America, and which had only arrived at Manchester Airport on the previous day.

With perfect timing, and exactly on cue, as he finished this statement the police motorcycle outriders which had been escorting the emblems and scrolls from Manchester Town Hall emerged from Church Street, and runners from Preston Harriers climbed the steps to the Harris Museum balcony to make their presentation to the Guild Mayor. Councillor Parker then spoke with feeling to the very large crowd which was assembled in the Market Square. He drew attention to the international links which Preston had developed, through its own citizens and their families who had gone overseas, but who still remembered their Prestonian heritage, and by means of the twin town network, which had provided Preston with very strong links with European towns. He singled out Kalisz in Poland, which had only recently been twinned with Preston, and which had a thousand years of its own history, and he gave a special welcome to the representatives of Kalisz, attending their first Guild celebrations.

The Guild Mayor also gave prominence to the role of the children of Preston in this Guild, reminding his audience that the School Children's Pageant on Avenham Park would be the highlight of Guild Week, and that those who watched processions and events should take along their children to see, 'for they are the links to the next Preston Guild 2012'. He concluded with a proud statement about Proud Preston, and a message of hope: 'we should all be proud of our town, for no where else in the world can they celebrate such a unique event as Preston Guild. What better way could we illustrate that pride and community spirit than if that minority amongst us who commit acts of vandalism or behave badly towards their neighbours, joined with all of us and for one week at least, shared our pride and pleasure and enjoyment ... God Bless Preston Guild 1992'.

The band of the Queen's Lancashire Regiment played the National Anthem, and then the regalia party preceded the Guild Mayor, the Clerk of the Guild, and the police chiefs of the Russian and Italian police bands to the saluting base which was situated immediately below the Harris Museum balcony. The Guild Mayor took the salute during a march past of the three international police bands which were present, from Russia, Germany and Italy. Afterwards a buffet reception for invited guests was held in the Art Gallery of the Harris Museum.

The Guild Mayor's church procession (Guild Sunday, 30 August)

In accordance with ancient custom the Guild Mayor attended divine service at the parish church of St John on the morning of the Sunday before the start of the Guild. As is usual, a formal notice was published in the local newspapers in advance, inviting those who wished to attend upon the Mayor to be present at the Guild Hall at 10.30 a.m. Before the procession to the church a reception was held for those who had honoured the Guild Mayor with their presence. These included the members and chief officers of the Borough Council, the Honorary

From top left:
The great standard of Preston, tightly furled, leads the borough regalia at the head of the Guild Mayor's Church Procession. (Author's collection)
Ex-servicemen and borough councillors walk past the Miller Arcade during the Church Procession on Guild Sunday. (Author's collection)
The band and drums of the Lancastrian Brigade during the Guild Mayor's Church Procession. (Author's collection)
Left:
Leaving the parish church of St John after the civil service on Guild Sunday. (Preston B. C.)

Recorder of the Guild (Judge Anthony Jolly), ex-Mayors and Mayoresses, Mayors of several of the adjacent districts, the Chairman of Lancashire County Council, senior officers of the armed forces and police, magistrates, many Guild Burgesses and 'a large number of ladies and gentlemen of the Borough'.

The procession, which is of great symbolic significance as it is the first formal public procession of the Preston Guild, and brings together many facets of the town and its society, included representatives of the Special Constabulary; the St John Ambulance Brigade and the British Red Cross Society; the Sea Cadets, Army Cadets, Air Training Corps and Boy Scouts; high school and college students; local clergy and ministers; council officials; Guild officers; representatives of other local authorities; ex-Mayors of the Borough and ex-Chairmen of Fulwood Urban District Council and Preston Rural District Council; members of the armed forces and police officers; magistrates; and ordinary citizens of Preston,

They were accompanied by the Lancastrian Brigade Band of Corps and Drums, and the short processional route was lined by detachments drawn from the Sea Cadets, Army Cadets and Air Training Corps. Near the head of the procession were carried the standards of the Borough of Preston, including the great blue banner pennant depicting the lamb of Preston which had been given to the Corporation by the Countess of Derby in 1902. The gleaming borough regalia were borne ceremonially ahead of the Guild Mayor who, with the heavy and ornate gold chain of office around his neck, wore his magnificent purple robes of office, lined and bordered with fur, and the characteristic three-cornered Guild Mayoral hat. The morning was cool and blustery, with the occasional light shower, but for the procession itself the weather stayed dry.

The service was conducted by the Revd Robert Ladds, Rector of Preston and Guild Mayor's Chaplain, assisted by the Revd John Francis and the Revd Denis Blackledge. The sermon was preached by the Lord Bishop of Blackburn, the Right Revd Alan Chesters, and the Intrada Brass Ensemble provided musical arrangements during the proceedings.

The Guild Court (Monday 31 August)

The official celebrations for the Preston Guild Merchant have always started with the opening of the Guild Court, which since the late sixteenth century has traditionally been on the first Monday after the feast of the decollation (or beheading) of St John the Baptist. Until the Reformation the patron saint of Preston was St Wilfrid, but he seems to have been dropped in favour of St John sometime in the middle of the sixteenth century. Although for centuries the people have gathered well in advance of that day, and there have usually been events and festivities before the opening, this remains the formal and official start to the Guild Merchant. It is an occasion of great splendour, pageantry and solemnity, and it represents directly, and almost unaltered in its content, the medieval heart of the Preston Guild.

The Honorary Recorder of Preston, Judge Anthony Jolly, whose untimely death in September 1992 marred the post-Guild euphoria. (Lancashire Evening Post)

The Guild Mayor's chaplain, Revd Robert Ladds, Rector of Preston (Preston Citizen)

The feast of St John the Baptist is on 29 August, and in 1992 the opening day therefore fell on Monday 31 August. In terms of the weather, at least, the omens for the official start of Guild Week seemed very discouraging. The *Lancashire Evening Post*'s headline that day was simple and straightforward: WET! WET! WET!.

The paper reported the prediction of local meteorologists that the town was heading for one of the wettest Augusts on record, while seasoned Guild-watchers reckoned that—if the weekend's torrential rains and high winds were anything to go by—the 1992 Guild was going to take place in some of the worst weather they could remember. Nevertheless, the weather did not deter thousands of spectators who came to watch the civic procession—and, fortunately, the rain and wind died away by the afternoon, when the first of the two Church Ecumenical Processions was held.

Following the traditional order of proceedings on these occasions, laid down and carefully followed in Guild after Guild, His Honour Judge Anthony Jolly, the Honorary Recorder of the Borough, and the Guild Mayor's Chaplain, the Revd Robert Ladds, were received by the Clerk of the Guild, Antony Owens, at the Town Hall. The Recorder and the Clerk were wearing their full legal robes and lawyers' wigs. The three men drove to the residence of the Right Worshipful the Guild Mayor, Councillor Harold Parker, and there tendered their respects and offered congratulations to him and to the Guild Mayoress, Mrs Enid Parker. The Guild Mayor, in his magnificent robes and chain of office, and the Guild Mayoress wearing her chain of office, then travelled by car into the town centre, preceded by the Recorder, the Chaplain and the Clerk of the Guild. At the Lancaster Road entrance to the Town Hall the Guild Mayor and Mayoress were greeted with a ceremonial fanfare from the trumpets and drums of the Queen's Lancashire Regiment and the 14th/20th King's Hussars. The regalia party were in position at the entrance to the Town Hall.

On entering the Town Hall the Guild Mayor and Mayoress were greeted with due ceremony by the stewards of the Guild, and then at 9.00 a.m. they received their distinguished guests, who included the Lord Lieutenant of Lancashire, Simon Towneley; the Right Honourable the Earl of Derby; the Right Honourable the Lord Clitheroe; the Archbishop of Westminster, His Eminence Cardinal

a abundance of gowns and robes, ademic, legal and clerical, as the ic procession arrives at the Guild all for the opening of the Guild urt. (Lancashire Constabulary)

Basil Hume; the Lord Bishop of Blackburn, the Right Revd Alan Chesters; the Roman Catholic Bishop of Lancaster, the Right Revd John Brewer; the Moderator of the Preston and District Free Church Federal Council, the Revd Fred Wilson; the Chairman of the North Lancashire District of Methodist Churches, the Reverend Michael Wearing; the High Sheriff of Lancashire, Mr Keith Gledhill; two of the MPs for the Borough of Preston, Mrs Audrey Wise and Mr Nigel Evans; the local MEP, Mr Michael Welsh; the Chairman of Lancashire County Council, Mrs Josephine Farrington; the Mayor of Almelo, the deputy Mayor of Nimes, the Mayor of Recklinghausen and the President of Kalisz, representing Preston's four twin towns; the Mayors or Chairmen of the thirteen other district councils in Lancashire; members of Preston Borough Council; and other people prominent in the life and business of the town and Borough of Preston.

At previous Guilds it had been customary for the opening of the Guild Court, and the accompanying ceremonies, to be followed by the Mayoral Procession through the town centre to the parish church, where a civic service would be held. In 1992 the adoption of such a plan would have given rise to major problems, because the parish church was being used for a major Guild Flower Festival, and so could only conveniently accommodate some 380 people. Approximately 2,000 guests and participants were expected to attend the opening Court in the Guild Hall, and the officers of the Borough Council considered that it would have been well nigh impossible to make arrangements to 'extract' 380 of these in order to form the procession to attend the church service.

The Clerk of the Guild and the Guild Mayor's Chaplain therefore decided that a more effective solution would be to hold the service in the Guild Hall itself, so that the entire audience could participate. This was agreed by the Guild Committee on 15 July 1992, and it was also determined that, because there would no longer be any need to process to the church, the Civic Procession should instead be held before the opening of the Court. Therefore, from about 9.45 a.m. the procession began to assemble in Lancaster Road, and at 10 a.m. it departed for the Guild Hall, in the following order:

Mounted policemen
Masters and Wardens of Trades
Guild Burgesses
Freemen of England and Wales
Police
Firemen
Ambulancemen
Trade Unions
Representatives of Professions
Magistrates
Clergy and Ministers
Gentlemen of the Select Vestry of Preston
Band
Councillors
The Preston Borough Regalia
Chief Superintendent

Deputy Town Clerk   Clerk of the Guild   Treasurer of the Guild
Guild Stewards
Honorary Recorder   GUILD MAYOR   Guild Mayor's Chaplain
Lord Lieutenant
Under Sheriff   High Sheriff   High Sheriff's Chaplain
Hon. Freeman T. Finney   Guild Mayoress   Hon. Alderman
Deputy Mayor   Deputy Mayoress
Lord Derby   Lord Clitheroe
Other senior Guild Burgesses
Church of England Bishops
Roman Catholic Cardinal and Bishop
Free Church and Methodist representatives
Members of Parliament and European Parliament
Officers of Her Majesty's Forces
Judiciary
Chairman of Lancashire County Council
Chief Constable   Chief Executive & Clerk of County Council
Mayors and Chairmen of other district councils
Ex-mayors of the Borough
Ex-Mayoresses and Mayors Consort of the Borough
Ex-Chairmen of Fulwood U.D.C.
Chairman and Deputy Clerk of Magistrates Bench
Rector of University of Central Lancashire and Principals of Preston
College and Cardinal Newman College
Students from Preston College and Cardinal Newman College
Twin Town Representatives
Chief Officers of the Council
Other ladies and gentlemen

For the first time representatives present at the ceremony included those from the nursing profession, who were seated with other professions. Representatives of the different organisations which had sponsored the Guild Merchant, and the various ethnic minority groups within the town were also present.

As the Civic Procession was walking through the streets of the town centre, the other people who had been invited to attend the ceremony were taking their seats in the Guild Hall. For the first time, the guests of Guild Burgesses were seated together with the Burgesses in the main body of the Guild Hall. The procession arrived at the Guild Hall at 10.15 a.m., and members of the platform party were at once escorted to their places. At 10.30 a.m. a magnificent ceremonial procession entered the great hall of the Guild Hall and, to the sound of medieval music, made its way to the platform. It comprised the following:

The standard bearer, with the great standard of the borough
Silver mace bearer   Gold mace bearer   Sergeant-at-Mace
Silver oar bearer   Beadle
Halberdiers
Deputy Town Clerk   Clerk of the Guild   Treasurer of the Guild
Honorary Recorder   GUILD MAYOR   Guild Mayor's Chaplain

Lord Lieutenant, High Sheriff Under Sheriff, Guild Mayoress
and Deputy Mayor

A dramatic and brilliant ceremonial fanfare was given by the trumpeters and drums of the Queen's Lancashire Regiment and the 14th/20th King's Hussars, and the Guild Mayor then took his seat in the State Chair, with the Chaplain on his right and the Guild Mayoress and the Honorary Recorder on his left. The Clerk of the Guild and his Deputy took their places at a table below the platform, immediately in front of the Guild Mayor, with the bearers carrying the regalia to their left and right. On the table were placed the Guild Roll of the 1972 Guild Merchant, the proclamation which was to be made, and the account or declaration of the Guilds Merchant which had hitherto been held in the Borough, and which would shortly be read out by the Clerk of the Guild.

A further trumpet fanfare was given after the platform party and the Guild Mayor were seated, and then the Sergeant-at-Mace made proclamation:

OYEZ! OYEZ! OYEZ!

All manner of persons that are Free Burgesses of this Borough of Preston in the County Palatine of Lancaster, whether Inhabitants within this Borough or Foreigners, who have had Public Summons or Notice to appear at this time and place for the more solemn holding and keeping of a Guild Merchant within and for this Borough of Preston, according to Ancient usage and Custom thereof, draw near and give your attendance.

He then further proclaimed:

OYEZ! OYEZ! OYEZ!

The Mayor of this Town strictly chargeth and comandeth all persons here present to keep silent whilst an Account or Proclamation of several Guilds Merchant which have heretofore been holden within this Borough, together with the Authority by which the same are and have been held and continued, is in reading. GOD SAVE THE QUEEN!

The Clerk of the Guild then read the recitation of the charters of the Borough and the account of the previous Guilds, back to the charter of King Henry II granted in 1179. The full text of the recitation is given in Appendix 9 of this book. The Clerk of the Guild's recital, which followed precisely the traditional wording used on such occasions for over three hundred years, brought the record up to date by declaring that Guilds Merchant had been held 'in the first and twenty-first years of the Reign of her present Majesty Queen Elizabeth the Second', and that

Now another Guild Merchant according to the Rights, Precedents, Practices and Ancient Customs of this Borough, commences this present Monday, the thirty-first day of August, in the forty-first year of the Reign of Her present Majesty Queen Elizabeth the Second, and in the year of our Lord One thousand nine hundred and ninety-two, before the Right Worshipful Harold Parker, Mayor, and Richard Atkinson, Ian Whyte Hall, Joseph Hood, Dennis Kehoe and Ronald Philip Marshall, Stewards,

Anthony Charles Jolly, Honorary Recorder, and Antony Owens, Clerk of this Guild.

As was customary, it was proclaimed that the mayor, stewards and clerk would sit at the Town Hall each day during the Guild Week, to receive the claims of burgesses on behalf of themselves, or their sons, or—and this was a break with the traditions of eight centuries—on behalf of their daughters. The Sergeant-at-Mace then declared that all the rights and privileges of the Guild were now devolved into the hands of the Guild Mayor and Stewards. This continued the time-honoured procedure whereby at each Guild celebration the membership of the Guild Burgesses lapsed, and all of them who wished to renew had to claim it afresh by submission to the power and authority of the Guild Mayor.

The clerk opened the Guild Books, the membership rolls of the Preston Guild Merchant, and called over the names of the Guild Burgesses. The reading out of the names, which is the central part of the ceremonial at all Guilds, signifies an invitation to renew privileges and membership. The person who is thus called acknowledges his—or now and in future Guilds 'her'—renewal and shows submission by rising and bowing to the Guild Mayor and the Clerk of the Guild. The first name to be called was that of 'Edward John Stanley, 18th Earl of Derby, son of Edward Montague Cavendish, Lord Stanley, deceased': the admission of the Earl of Derby as the most senior of all the Guild Burgesses is a tradition which dates back to 1542, when members of the Stanley family first appear in the Guild Rolls. Lord Derby's name was followed by that of 'Ralph John Assheton, the Right Honourable the Lord Clitheroe, Peer of the Realm, Son of Ralph Cockayne, Baronet, deceased' and 'Reginald Stanley Gray of Askam-in-Furness, Inn Keeper, brother of Joseph Frederick, former alderman of the Borough and Mayor of the Guild of 1972 deceased'. It is another tradition that the Guild Mayor of the preceding Guild, or his closest relative, is numbered among the senior Guild Burgesses. The other senior burgesses who were members of the platform party were then called.

At this point the Clerk of the Guild turned to the body of the hall, and called the renewals or admission of some 400 Guild Burgesses who had previously indicated that they would be present or would be represented by a proxy. Each of those present in person rose and bowed to the Clerk and the Guild Mayor, but proxies were not required to do so. For the first time in over eight centuries women were included among the participants in this ancient ceremony on an equal footing: the list began with 'Alker, Rachel Louise, daughter of Neil' and continued with many more. Some of those who were admitted were tiny babies and small children, and there was much spontaneous applause and enthusiasm as these were held above their fathers' or mothers' heads to signify their assent to the admission. The youngest admission, which was by proxy, was of Claudia Charel Vickers, daughter of Gary Vickers of Wooloware, New South Wales, Australia, who was born on 28 August 1992 and was thus only three days old when enrolled as a Guild Burgess.

A full list of the names of all the 1992 Guild Burgesses is given in Appendix 5. The numbers enrolled at the Guild of 1992 were as follows:

Burgesses renewing Freedom
> (In)   325
> (Out)   25

New burgesses admitted
> (In)   427 [of which daughters 253]
> (Out)   31 [of which daughters 21]

> TOTAL   808 [of which daughters 274]

When all the names had been read the Sergeant-at-Mace called for silence, and the Clerk of the Guild then read out the names of the officers of the 1992 Guild: the Guild Mayor, the five Stewards, the Honorary Recorder, and his own name as Clerk. Following a trumpet fanfare, he continued with a further proclamation, declaring that the Guild Merchant was now open and would remain so for all its traditional purposes, and to allow all other burgesses who wished to claim liberties to attend the Clerk at his office in the Town Hall, where the Guild Books would be kept open for the enrolling of names. At 11 a.m. on the following Saturday, the proclamation continued, the Court would be held once more in the Guild Hall and there the orders would be made, the books sealed, and the Court adjourned for another twenty years or until a new Guild shall be held. The complete text of this proclamation is included in this book as Appendix 10.

The Principal of Cardinal Newman College, Peter Newsome, then introduced Cathy Hume of Preston College and Alex MacLaren of Cardinal Newman College, the students who would, following the centuries-old pattern of the Guild celebration, deliver Latin orations containing topical and witty allusions. There was a major break with tradition in the inclusion of two orators, for in all Guilds before 1952 one pupil of the Grammar School had spoken, and in 1972 a boy from the Sixth Form College. The new arrangement worked very well, and the students were outstanding. Their delivery was faultless, their voices clear, and their pronunciation and inflection excellent—the listeners might reasonably have suspected that they regularly spoke Latin as a matter of course! The complete text in English and Latin of the four orations (including those given by the Principal of Cardinal Newman College and the Honorary Recorder) is given as Appendix 11 of this book.

Cathy Newman's oration noted one of the most remarkable features of the 1992 Guild. Referring to the tradition of the orations, she said that in times past a boy from the Preston Grammar School had spoken, 'iam mihi denique, puellae tantum, dimidia pars honoris huius traditur. O Tempora, O Mores!' ('but now, in these modern times, a half of this honour has been given to me, a girl! So changed are things today!). Her oration also referred to a matter which had been the subject of great and heated debate during Guild Year—the title of the town's newly created university: 'Academiam ... habet municipium nostrum, non nomine Prestoniensi guadentum sed certe situ, quae fundamentis clarissimis conlegii Harris erigitur' ('Our town now has a University; it is not blessed with the name of Preston, but at least with a Preston site! It is founded on the well-known Harris college').

The oration given by Alex MacLaren referred to the immense changes which had been taking place in Preston, and to great events in the history of the town—the visit of the Queen during the celebrations of the 800th anniversary of the first charter in 1979; the closure of the port and the redevelopment of the dockland area; the loss and contraction of famous and familiar industries; and—another topical reference—the building of new roads, and the considerable confusion which reigned in Preston's traffic system in the first half of 1992: 'ponte novissimo se supra flumen tollente, vehicula plurima itinere novo et miro commeant. Nec pauci sunt qui conqueruntur se non iam posse itinere recto domum redire!' ('A new bridge soars across the river and many vehicles use this wonderful new route—although not a few complain that they can no longer go home by a direct road').

The Honorary Recorder, Judge Anthony Jolly, replied to the two orations, beginning his Latin speech with characteristic wit: 'Annos prope octingentos quidem Gilda Mercatoria huius municipii habita est; minus viginti annos oratores nostri hi nati sunt; inter quos terminos ego denique gradum incertum consecutus sum' ('Preston Guild is nearly eight hundred years old. The last two speakers are each under twenty years old. I am somewhere in between'). Again referring to the name of the University, that bone of fierce contention, he claimed that 'Cum sim rogatus ut brevi loquar, necesse est ut nomen amplissimum Academia nostrae novae praetermittam'! ('I have been asked to keep my oration reasonably short, and that necessarily deters me from referring to Preston's new University by its full name'). He went on to praise the merits of Preston, its varied community, its educational achievements, its role as a regional and county capital, its place as a centre of communications, and its strong links with Europe through the four twin towns.

The Guild Mayor replied, thanking especially the two students and their excellent Latin—a tradition which he hoped could be maintained in future Guilds—and emphasising the historical continuity which these ceremonies represented. He drew attention to the way this was reflected in the presence at the Guild Court of some 300 Burgesses from the 1972 Guild Roll, and how the admission of women showed that the Guild could change with the times and acknowledge changes in society.

He pointed to an uncertain future, as local government reorganisation seemed likely to change once more the status and boundaries of Preston, and he urged that this should not be allowed to affect the traditions of the Guild. There were other uncertainties—the severe unemployment in the town, and the loss of major industries, were serious problems. Preston, however, was a town of resilient people with considerable skills and a work ethic which had overcome such setbacks in the past, and he urged that we should be resolute and use our qualities to seek other employment. The Guild Mayor, like the Recorder, warmly welcomed the involvement of the twin towns and the ties of friendship and co-operation which had been forged with them. He concluded by expressing his pleasure at being able to preside over the Guild Court, and thanked his colleagues who had allowed him this privilege.

One of the new Burgesses of the Preston Guild Merchant, Elizabeth Beatrice Molyneux, granddaughter of Cyril Molyneux, a former Mayor of the Borough, was on that day celebrating her eighteenth birthday, and to rousing applause the Guild Mayor asked her to come to the platform and receive a bouquet of flowers from the Guild Mayoress. The Clerk then announced a short interval for refreshments.

Following the interval the religious service was held. Among those present on the platform were the Lord Bishop of Blackburn, the Cardinal Archbishop of Westminster, the Roman Catholic Bishop of Lancaster, the Gentlemen of the Select Vestry (who were wearing the superb new sea-green ceremonial robes which had been designed for them by the Art and Fashion Department of the University of Central Lancashire), the churchwardens and choir of Preston Parish Church, and Dom Edgar Miller OSB, monk of Ampleforth and a Guild Burgess. The Guild Mayor and Mayoress, the Honorary Recorder, and the Clerk to the Guild were also seated on the platform.

The service was conducted by the Revd Robert Ladds, Rector of Preston and Guild Mayor's Chaplain, assisted by the Revd John Francis. Lessons were read by Councillors David Borrow (Leader of the Council), Joseph Hood (Leader of the Conservative Group) and Ronald Marshall (Leader of the Liberal Democratic Group). Intercessions were led by the Revd Canon Eric Chard (Diocesan Ecumenical Officer), the Revd John Furmage (Fishergate Baptist Church), the Revd Dennis Blackledge (St. Wilfrid's Roman Catholic Church) and Captain Rosemary Rogerson (Salvation Army Citadel). The Homily was given by the Rector of Preston, and the Lord Bishop of Blackburn gave the Blessing.

The Guild Hall provided a fine setting for the Guild Court and the religious service which followed. It can accommodate a very large audience, and because it is purpose-built for great musical events and entertainments the layout and acoustics are of a high standard. The Guild Court was a theatrical event of the highest order, and the pageantry, splendour and colour of the occasion were deeply impressive. From the sight of the massed orange-red, purple and gold robes of the many clergy present, to the colourful and historic costumes of the regalia bearers, and the sumptuous purple and fur robes of the Guild Mayor himself, the effect was one of drama and magnificence.

This was more than matched by the ceremony itself, for here was that tangible link with Guild over eight centuries, back to the original purpose and role of the Guild Merchant when it was established just over a century after the Norman Conquest. The proclamations and orations, the calling of names and the acknowledgements by the burgesses, the robes and the titles, and the symbolic place of the Guild and its ceremonies in the life and civic consciousness of Preston—all were continuing history. Every participant and every spectator must have been deeply aware of being present at a remarkable event and aware, too, of the rare privilege which this afforded them.

Balls and dances

A very important part of the traditional Guild celebrations was the range of balls, dances and banquets provided by the Corporation or by private organisations. Some were public events, and tickets were sold to anybody who wished to come and could afford to do so, while others were by invitation only and were very exclusive affairs. Richard Kuerden's account of the 1682 Guild gives particular attention to this aspect of the celebrations, and includes a very detailed description of the Mayoral banquet, its organisation and the food which was eaten. It would seem that for him, at least, the banquet was the high point of the week! Lavish and costly banquets, and equally prestigious dances and balls, continued to be a major feature of the Guild until the early years of this century.

In 1952, however, these events were very much reduced in scale, because the combination of austerity, rationing, and lack of money meant that the sumptuous meals and glittering decorations of previous generations were no longer feasible. Furthermore, there was a growing opinion that very expensive elitist events were out of keeping with the spirit of the modern Guild, in which there was a much greater emphasis upon the participation of the townspeople of Preston as a whole. The 1972 Guild saw only a modest banquet, a very tame affair in comparison with the ostentatious spreads of earlier generations, but the dances and balls which were held then were as successful and popular as ever. When the 1992 Guild was being organised it was decided that the vexed question of banquets could be resolved by the obvious expedient of not holding them at all; they had simply become an anachronism.

Therefore the Guild of 1992 was the first since detailed records began at which no official civic banquet was held. Nevertheless, two Civic Balls and a Carnival Ball were held, and the organisers drew on the experience of the Guilds of 1952 and 1972 in arranging these. Buffet meals were provided for all the guests; the Celebrity Restaurant was used for the Guild Mayor and his guests, while the majority of those attending were accommodated in a large and splendid marquee erected on the terrace of the Guild Hall.

The Guild Inaugural Ball was held on Monday 31 August, and was attended by 672 people—rather fewer than had been anticipated. It was sponsored by NORWEB, and music was provided by Andy Ross and his Orchestra and the City Lights Show Band. Before the dancing began the Guild Mayor spoke of the pomp and ceremonial of that morning, as a tradition going back over eight hundred years was re-enacted, and he anticipated a memorable and majestic evening. The second ball, the Guild Mayoral Ball, was on Wednesday 2 September and was sponsored by InterCity. The 527 people present were entertained by the band of Her Majesty's Royal Marines, Commandos, and by Ray McVay and the Ray McVay Orchestra and Singers. The Carnival Ball, on Friday 4 September, had 724 guests. It included music by the Mike Jones Band and the Terry Lightfoot Jazz Band.

Mayoral Reception for Overseas Visitors (Thursday 3 September)

As travel became easier with the development first of fast steamships and, more recently, of air transport, it became possible for significant numbers of people to come to Preston Guild from overseas—particularly North America and Australasia. In 1952 the influx was such that a special mayoral reception was held in their honour, and it proved to be an outstanding success. The 1972 Guild saw

the event repeated, and in 1992 it was decided that the reception would be made larger and more varied, since it was expected that more overseas visitors than ever before would be present.

The Mayoral Reception for Overseas Visitors was held on the evening of Thursday 3 September in the Guild Hall, and not only the visitors but also their Preston friends and relatives were invited to attend. The event was sponsored by *Lancashire Life* magazine, and was given extensive publicity in the local press, local radio and the magazine itself. The Stewards of the Guild, the Deputy Mayor and Deputy Mayoress, members of the Guild Committee, the Assistant Parish Priest and the Band of the Queen's Own Lancashire Regiment assembled to meet the guests, who were admitted to the hall at 7 p.m. Displayed on the elevated stage area were the Guild Scrolls of Friendship. There were sixty-three of these, from sixteen countries, and they bore the names of over 1,200 ex-Prestonians, together with their messages of greeting and friendship.

The Guild Mayor's party, who included the Clerk of the Guild and the regalia bearers, entered the hall at 7.40 p.m. In theatrical and dramatic fashion the lights had been dimmed, and a single spotlight illuminated their arrival as they descended a staircase to the sound of a fanfare from the military band. The regalia party lined up in front of the stage, and the spotlight then shone on a

The Mayoral Reception for Overseas Visitors (3 September). (Preston B. C.)

large Union Flag high up in the Grand Hall while the band played the National Anthem. It was estimated that about 1,700 people were assembled in the hall.

In his address, the Guild Mayor welcomed all those present, and paid tribute to those who had come so far to be in Preston for the Guild. He read the text of a message sent from the Queen at Balmoral, conveying her thanks to the people of Preston for their loyal greetings and wishing the Guild success. Refreshments were then served, and the Guild Mayor and Mayoress mingled with the crowds.

From 8.15 p.m. Uzorockye, the visiting folk ensemble from Tver in Russia, provided a very colourful and entertaining song and dance routine, which delighted the visitors and emphasised not only Preston's links with Europe as well as with the Commonwealth, but also the remarkable political changes which had recently swept across Eastern Europe. The band of the Queen's Lancashire Regiment then gave an impressive marching display, with nostalgic and patriotic arrangements including tunes such as 'She's a Lassie from Lancashire' and Elgar's 'Pomp and Circumstance'. This was followed by a spectacular and highly unusual performance in which fluorescent drumsticks, illuminated only by ultra-violet light, 'danced in the darkened hall in animated percussion'.

The Guild Mayor signed countless autographs, and reminisced and chatted with many visitors. The scrolls of friendship received much attention, attracting large and interested crowds, and the public address system was used with good effect to assist guests to contact long-lost friends. The names of all visitors present at the reception were later written in the Overseas Visitors' Book. At 9.30 p.m. the Guild Mayor made a short speech of thanks and farewell and, to the strains of 'Auld Lang Syne', he and his party walked slowly back up the long staircase. As he made his final wave and departed, red, white and blue balloons descended onto the crowds beneath, in a particularly moving finale.

The involvement of the twin towns

In July 1991 an invitation to attend the Preston Guild was sent to the mayors of Preston's four twin towns—Almelo in the Netherlands, the Polish city of Kalisz, Nimes in southern France, and Recklinghausen in the Ruhr district of Germany. Each town was invited to send a delegation of up to six representatives for the six days of the Guild Week, and each accepted. A total of nineteen delegates from the twin towns came to Preston for the celebrations, and they were entertained in splendid style, with a packed programme of exciting and colourful events. The delegation from Recklinghausen was accompanied by an unofficial party of twenty-four visitors, who included members of housing associations, the city council, and local press and radio officers. Almelo was also represented by a stand at the ill-fated Proud Preston Exhibition.

Special arrangements were made to accommodate the twin town visitors at the Forte Crest Hotel on Ringway, and they participated in the various civic receptions and other ceremonial events during Guild Week. Their programme was designed to allow them to witness and experience the full pageantry of the Guild, and to see as many of the associated processions, shows and special events as possible. During the course of the week they exchanged civic gifts and official greetings with the Guild Mayor, something which had been a feature of the 1972 Guild, and at midnight during the Guild Inaugural Ball the Guild Mayor made a special presentation to Alderman William Pingen of Almelo, who was celebrating his 50th birthday.

The guests from the twin towns provided a welcome and topical European dimension to the Guild celebrations, for 1992 was a year in which Europe was, for good or bad, very much in the news. The speeches made by the Guild Mayor and other officials at several Guild events emphasised the role of Preston within Europe, and the twin town arrangements are a tangible proof of connections which already exist. The guests and the members and officers of Preston Borough Council were able to use the opportunity of Guild Week to discuss ways of strengthening and reinforcing the existing ties between the towns, and all agreed that it was a valuable and successful visit, which they had greatly appreciated and enjoyed.

The Guild Mayoress's Church Visit (Friday 4 September)

In the late eighteenth century the ladies who were present at the Guild, accompanying their menfolk, seem to have rebelled against their own lack of involvement. They were allowed to watch some of the events, to attend some of the dinners, to be dancing partners at the balls, but nothing else. In 1762, therefore, we have the first record of a separate Ladies' Procession, in which the wives, daughters and sisters of the gentlemen attending the Guild walked over a short route through the town centre, led by the Guild Mayoress accompanied by the Countess of Derby. The ladies wore their most decorative costumes and their finest jewels and trimmings, and were protected from the over-familiar attentions of the masses who lined the streets by a cordon of gentlemen carrying white staffs.

The Guild Mayoress (Mrs Enid Parker) and the Guild Mayor walk in the Guild Mayoress' Church Procession. (Lancashire Evening Post)

The Ladies' Procession became a favourite feature of the Guild thereafter, and the newspaper reporters became almost incoherent with enthusiasm in describing the splendour of the costumes, the magnificence of the spectacle and, of course, the exquisite charms and beauties of the ladies themselves. However, the procession never developed into a fully fledged grand event, on the scale of the opening procession of the Guild, and it remained a comparatively modest affair—only a limited number of ladies joined in, and the processional route was very short. After 1842, when large numbers of women (as distinct, in the Victorian view, from ladies) participated in the ordinary processions, as representatives of churches, schools and trades, the need for a distinct 'ladies' procession' diminished. It began to change, and was subtly altered to become the Guild Mayoress's Church Procession, and in that guise it has continued to be a part of the civic programme to this day.

In 1992 the Guild Mayoress's Church Procession was held on Friday 4 September. The official description of the event conveys its traditional origins and character very well: 'at 11.00 a.m. the Guild Mayoress and the ladies of the Borough attended Service at the Parish Church'. The Guild Mayoress, Mrs Enid

The Women's Red Cross assemble in blustery weather before the start of the Guild Mayoress' Church Procession. (Preston Citizen)

Parker, was accompanied by the wives of the Clerk of the Guild, the Honorary Recorder, the Guild Stewards, the Assistant Town Clerk, lady magistrates and Borough Councillors, Mayoresses of adjacent boroughs, the Chairman of Lancashire County Council (Mrs Josephine Farrington), Mrs Audrey Wise M.P., ex-Mayoresses of the Borough, policewomen, representatives of fifty-eight women's organisations from throughout the Borough, and girls from local schools and colleges. In keeping with custom, there were just four men present in the procession—the Guild Mayor, the Clerk of the Guild, the Honorary Recorder and the Guild Mayor's Chaplain, and to signify that this was a civic and ceremonial occasion the Borough regalia were carried in state before the Guild Mayoress and her husband.

The approach to the church was lined with ladies from local voluntary organisations and girls from Preston's youth groups. There were over seven hundred ladies in the procession, and it was noted that 'remarkably if not entirely comfortably, most of these were accommodated within the Church!'. Because of the space occupied by the Guild Flower Festival fewer than four hundred people could be seated in the body of the church, and it proved to be necessary to relay the proceedings by a public address system to an overflow congregation of almost five hundred. This was the best attended of all the church services during Guild Week. The service was conducted by the Revd Robert Ladds, Rector of Preston, assisted by the Revd John Francis and Father Denis Blackledge, and the sermon was preached by the Right Revd Jack Nicholls, the Anglican Bishop of Lancaster. The County Hall Singers, conducted by Joan Brandwood, provided the musical accompaniment.

The Adjourned Guild Court (Saturday 5 September)

Balancing the splendid official opening ceremonies for the Guild Court, held on the Monday morning, was the adjournment ceremony on the Saturday morning of Guild Week. Ever since the first detailed account of a Guild Court, provided in 1682 by Dr Richard Kuerden, and probably for a great deal longer than that, this ceremony has been the occasion for rejoicing at what has happened during the week, tinged with a certain sadness and wistfulness—for retrospection about the Guild which has gone, and anticipation of what the twenty years until the next Guild might bring.

It is the grand conclusion of an outstanding week, the winding up of an event which has been long planned and over which many people have spent very many hours in discussion, preparation and hard physical labour, the ending of a brief but spectacular period which has been eagerly anticipated by the town and its people for months, even years. Thus it cannot fail to include an element of regret: it will be another twenty years before the like is seen again in Preston, and a proportion of those who have participated or been spectators will not see another Guild. Yet, as the Guild Mayor emphasised in several occasions during the 1992 Guild, there is an unbroken link from Guild to Guild, and a chain of continuity—the children of Preston represent the Guilds and Guild burgesses of the future. They are what connects, generation after generation, the past, present and future of the ancient Guild Merchant of Preston.

The Adjournment of the Guild Court is, like the opening session, an event of great solemnity and magnificence, but there is no formal procession through the streets of the town. Instead, while the invited spectators took their seats in the great hall of the Guild Hall, the guests and members of the Borough Council assembled from 10 a.m. onwards on Saturday 5 September, and at 10.50 a.m. the platform party took its place. The platform party included several of the most senior and most prominent Guild burgesses and the Guild stewards; the leader of Preston Borough Council; the Honorary Alderman; Mrs Audrey Wise M.P. and Mr Michael Welsh, M.E.P; the Lord Bishop of Blackburn, members of the judiciary and the Chairman of Lancashire County Council; magistrates, the Chief Superintendent of Police, the Rector of the University, and the Clerk of the County Council; chief and deputy chief officers of the borough, and Mayors and Mayoresses of several other district councils in Lancashire. A large number of Guild Burgesses, and members of the public, sat in the body of the hall.

Meanwhile, a procession was formed in the following order, and at 11 a.m., to the sound of accompaniment of medieval music, the Guild Mayor and his civic party took their places:

The standard bearer, with the great standard of the borough
Silver mace bearer   Gold mace bearer   Sergeant-at-Mace
Silver oar bearer   Beadle
Halberdiers

Deputy Town Clerk   Clerk of the Guild   Treasurer of the Guild
Honorary Recorder   GUILD MAYOR   Guild Mayor's Chaplain
Guild Mayoress   High Sheriff   Deputy Mayor

The Sergeant-at-Mace ordered all those present to attend, and the Guild Mayor then rose and, in exercise of the privilege of his office, admitted several new in-burgesses. These were people who were not existing Guild Burgesses by previous hereditary right, but henceforth were admitted as such and would be able to exercise all burgess rights and to transmit their burgess-ship hereditarily. It has always been the case that the Guild Mayor had the right to admit a small number of individuals free and gratis to the Guild. Usually, as in 1992, some of those so admitted were people who had been of service to the Guild and the Borough Council, while the remainder were the personal choices of the Guild Mayor himself.

Those admitted by the Guild Mayor in this way in 1992 were Richard Atkinson, Ian Hall, Joseph Hood, Dennis Kehoe, and Ronald Marshall, Stewards of the 1992 Guild and (with the exception of Councillor Marshall) former Mayors of the Borough; Joan Ainscough, Ronald Ball, Robert Butcher, Dorothy Chaloner, Joseph Pownall, Mary Rawcliffe, Albert Richardson, Arthur Taylor, Nancy Taylor, Gerard Walmsley and Joseph Ward, all of whom were former Mayors of the Borough of Preston; Anthony Jolly, the Honorary Recorder of the Borough; Raymond Jones, the Honorary Alderman of the Borough; Antony Owens, the Town Clerk and Chief Executive of the Borough, and the Clerk of the Guild of 1992; Florence Cooke and Thomas Finney, for their services to the town and Borough of Preston; and two members of the Guild Mayor's own family—his brother, George Parker of Irlam, and his baby grandson, Henry Thomas Parker-Robinson. The Clerk of the Guild then announced that the Right Worshipful the Guild Mayor, Councillor Harold Parker, was admitted 'generally and gratuitously' as an in-burgess of the Guild.

He then held up the Guild Book of New Orders to the Guild Burgesses assembled in the Hall, and declared that a Guild Merchant had been held in Preston 'on Monday, the Thirty-first day of August, being Monday next after the Feast of the Decollation of Saint John the Baptist in the forty-first year of the Reign of Her Majesty Queen Elizabeth the Second, by the Grace of God, of the United Kingdom of Great Britain and Northern Ireland and of Her other Realms and Territories Queen, Head of the Commonwealth, Defender of the Faith, in the year of our Lord One thousand nine hundred and ninety-two'.

After this he proclaimed, as his predecessors had done at every Preston Guild for at six least hundred years, that the Mayor and Stewards 'by and with the full assent and consent of the said Burgesses of the Borough now here present, have ordained and hereby ordain, That all and singular Bye-laws and Ordinances of this Borough and of the Guild thereof, now lawfully in force, be performed, observed, obeyed and kept in all things according to the tenor and effect of the said respective Bye-laws and Ordinances'. The Guild Mayor then enquired of those present: 'Brethren, do you approve of these Ordinances so done by us, and which are consonant to Regal Authority and the laudable customs of preceding Guilds?'. The Burgesses replied, as with one voice, 'So be it' and the Guild Mayor responded, 'GOD SAVE THE QUEEN'.

The Guild Burgesses having in this way voiced their approval of the bye-laws of the Borough, the Guild Mayor signed the Book of Orders, and the Clerk of the Guild held it up for public view, declaring in ringing tones, 'Here is your Law, GOD SAVE THE QUEEN', to which the burgesses replied, 'AMEN'.

The Sergeant-at-Mace then proclaimed the end of the official part of the ceremonies:

OYEZ!   OYEZ!   OYEZ!

This Grand Guild Merchant's Court is adjourned for twenty years or until a new Guild Merchant's Court be held and duly proclaimed

which was received with a final acclamation of 'GOD SAVE THE QUEEN'.

In the account given by Dr Richard Kuerden of the Guild of 1682 there is a detailed description of the procedures for the adjournment of the Guild Court, and the pattern followed in 1992 was faithful in every important respect to that of three centuries before. Unquestionably, though, this was already a ceremony of immense antiquity when it was first recorded in the reign of Charles II: Richard Kuerden was a learned antiquarian, and he recognised that what he saw and described then was a survival from a very distant past, half a millenium before his own time.

The holding up of a book of laws, and its approval by popular acclaim, is a vestige of a very early form of government and administration, the folk-moot or people's gathering, which was superseded in the twelfth and thirteenth centuries by the beginnings of borough councils and 'local government' in a more modern sense. Here, in this ceremony, we have a direct and extremely powerful link with the time before Preston was a borough, indeed, almost before it was a town. Preston is remarkably fortunate to have retained such a remarkable link with the past, in a ceremony which has been cherished over the centuries and which lives today at every Preston Guild.

Although the official ceremony was now over, there were speeches of thanks and of acknowledgement. Councillor Ian Hall, Guild Steward, proposed a vote of thanks to the Guild Mayor and Mayoress, and paid tribute 'on behalf of the citizens of this ancient and historic Borough ... for a job done extremely well. To be available for such an extensive programme of celebrations and to do it with dignity and obvious pleasure and pride, is no mean achievement, and a simple "thank you" seems inadequate. It is said, however, with sincerity and genuine appreciation'. Councillor Hall noted how the 'new' areas of the Borough—Fulwood and the rural districts which had, since the last Guild, been brought within Preston's boundaries—had responded to the Guild in a magnificent fashion, and had joined in as true Prestonians. He had also been impressed by the enthusiasm of neighbouring communities in South Ribble and Ribble Valley districts.

He drew attention to the Guild spirit, which had shown itself in so many ways, and urged the use of that spirit and feeling of community to help to overcome Preston's present commercial and economic difficulties. The Guild itself had been supported by council members, officials, advisers, voluntary organisations and individuals, and Prestonians, both born and adopted, were free and forthcoming in their response. Guild Week, he said, 'is a time where we all ... reflect and recognise our duty towards each other. Friendship, respect for person and property, a helping hand in times of need and a genuine love for each other should be at the forefront of our thoughts ... without reservation we are proud of our town and proud to be a part of its history and dedicate ourselves to its future prosperity and continued prominence'.

Councillor Joseph Hood, Guild Steward, seconded the vote of thanks. He fully endorsed what Councillor Hall had said, and declared that when he had seconded Councillor Parker's nomination as Guild Mayor 'I pointed to the fact that he would serve the town well as a communicator and ambassador for Preston past, present and future. I think everyone would agree that he has acquitted himself splendidly in this important role'. Councillor Hood pointed to another of the changes in the town since the last Guild—as well as having wider boundaries, it now embraced citizens from different ethnic groups. One thing had remained constant, though: 'the support which has manifested itself so strongly for this ancient and traditional celebration. Preston is unique and long may it remain so'.

He spoke of the re-enactment of old customs and traditions, the happy memories which they evoked for the more senior citizens, and the way in which the next Guild, when many present would no longer be here, will be carried on by the children who had participated so magnificently in the Guild of 1992. The Guild would continue into the next millenium, and 'in centuries to come people will still be able to use the old adage, "Once Every Preston Guild". In a vivid summing-up of the Guild Week of 1992, Councillor Hood said that it had been 'hectic, enjoyable, momentous, exhilarating, and without doubt has laid a heavy burden, not only on the Town Hall staff who have been the main organisers, but also on the Guild Mayor and Mayoress ... it will have been the most exciting and exhausting week of their lives, but they have stayed the course well and stuck to the task manfully and with dignity. They can reflect on a job well done on behalf of the citizens of this proud and ancient borough of Preston'.

The Guild Mayor thanked Councillors Hall and Hood, and admitted that it had been 'a very demanding few weeks', but that he and the Mayoress had been carried along by the spirit of the Guild and that had given them the stamina necessary to carry out their duties. He expressed the view that, when the history of this Guild was written, it would be seen as one of the finest Guild Merchant celebrations ever held. He had, of course, very many personal memories of the events of the past week. One which was special was the sight of tiny children being held up by their parents at the opening Court of the Guild, to be admitted as burgesses. If anything summed up the continuity of the Guild, he believed, it was that.

His other memory, the Guild Mayor said, was of the cleansing vehicles which followed the processions. In this he struck a chord with many of his listeners, who had also been deeply impressed by the exceptional efficiency and good humour with which the men from the Cleansing Department had carried out their task—in vehicles carrying the proud but tongue-in-cheek legend 'Purveyors of Clean Environment Services'! Councillor Parker had noticed how the cleansing vehicles seemed to get a louder cheer than almost any other part of the processions, and he told the Court that 'By the Wednesday it had so touched one of the drivers that he stopped his vehicle, got out of the cab, and took a big bow!'.

The Guild Mayor went on to declare that many would remember, for the rest of their lives, what had happened and what they had seen during this Guild Week, and he said that the Guild had demonstrated to the rest of the world the skills and business abilities of the people of Preston. 'The lights will soon be lowered on the 1992 Guild but ... Preston Guild will live on and we must all pledge ourselves to ensure that we go on to even greater things in the Guild of 2012. Tell your children and your grandchildren that they are the custodians of future Guilds. The Guild Book is closed. Nothing must prevent it being re-opened in 2012'.

In conclusion, the Guild Mayor announced that a telegram of loyalty and allegiance had been sent to the Queen, 'on the celebration of our Guild Merchant granted to us by Your Majesty's predecessors long ago'. He then read out a message which had been received in reply, in which Her Majesty conveyed 'her warm thanks to you and the people of Preston for your kind message of loyal greetings, sent on the occasion of the Preston Guild. Her Majesty received this message with much pleasure and sends her best wishes to all concerned for a very enjoyable and successful occasion'.

A vote of thanks to members of the Council and the Guild Committee and Stewards, and the various officials, was moved by Andrew Wilson, the Under Sheriff for the County of Lancashire and a senior Guild Burgess. The vote was seconded by another senior Guild Burgess, John Brandwood of Penwortham, and the Honorary Recorder responded on behalf of the Guild officials. The ceremony then ended, and the Guild Mayor and Mayoress and their distinguished guests left the platform. A reception and buffet luncheon for the Guild Mayor's party was held at the Town Hall, while members of the Council and other invited guests enjoyed luncheon at the Celebrity Restaurant.

Service of Thanksgiving (Sunday 6 September)

At the conclusion of a week of magnificent ceremonial and exciting celebrations, the Guild Mayor attended a Service of Thanksgiving at the Parish Church. As on the previous Sunday, a reception was held beforehand at the Guild Hall, and then the Guild Mayor, with a large number of distinguished guests and ordinary citizens of the Borough, processed through the town centre to St John's church. Here the service was conducted by the Revd Robert Ladds, the Revd John Francis and Father Denis Blackledge, and the sermon was preached by the Right Revd Ian Harland, Lord Bishop of Carlisle. Lessons were read by the Guild Mayor, the Clerk of the Guild, and Sir Bernard de Houghton, a senior Guild Burgess and Lay-Rector of Preston. After the service the Guild Mayor dispensed his customary generous hospitality to the guests in the Grand Hall of the Guild Hall.

The Guild Farewell Ceremony (Saturday 5 September)

Since the Guild of 1922 it has been traditional for the Guild Mayor to address the crowds who gathered in the Market Square on the last night, and this tradition has grown in scale and importance since that time. The Guild of 1992 was to be no exception. Planning went ahead, and a detailed scheduled was arranged: it was intended that the Guild Mayor and his guests would watch the Torchlight Procession, then go on to Avenham Park to watch the Firework Display before returning to a reception at the Harris Museum. There, at midnight, the Guild Mayor would make his address. Unfortunately these detailed plans did not allow for the immense number of people—over a quarter of a million by some estimates—who were packed into Avenham Park and adjacent streets, and who prevented the Guild Mayoral party from reaching the Park despite heroic police efforts. The Guild Mayor and his guests therefore had to return to the Harris Building much earlier than expected, and thus—although they missed the fireworks—they had rather longer to enjoy the reception, which was generously sponsored by Matthew Brown plc.

At two minutes to midnight the regalia bearers led the Guild Mayor and Mayoress onto the steps of the Harris Building, to be greeted by the cheers of the thousands of people assembled in the Market Square below. On the stroke of midnight the Guild Mayor addressed the crowd, referring to the wonderful spirit of goodwill which had permeated the entire Guild celebrations, and to the way in which this had contributed to the huge success of the Guild of 1992. He expressed his appreciation of the support which he and the Mayoress had received from all sections of the community during this very busy period. The crowd gave three cheers for the Guild Mayor and Mayoress, who then linked arms with other dignitaries and joined with many thousands of others in singing 'Auld Lang Syne'. A great cheer was raised as the Guild Mayor gave a final farewell, and returned to the Harris Building. Guild Week 1992 was over.

As so often in the past, the *Lancashire Evening Post* summed up the memorable and fascinating events of Guild Week: 'community spirit is alive and well and living in Preston. If anyone had doubts about the true value of the Guild, then they were surely dispelled amid the astonishing scenes on Saturday evening. It was the night when the whole town stood shoulder to shoulder to celebrate the town's history; that they did so with so much good humour, so much respect and so much pride is a remarkable testament to every single one of them'.

*A well-deserved rest for the Guild
Mayor at the end of a hectic but
rewarding week.
(Lancashire Evening Post)*

Chapter 6

The churches and the schools
during Guild Week

THE CHURCHES OF PRESTON and district now play such an integral and warmly received part in the celebration of the Guild Merchant that it is hard to appreciate how recently—in historical terms—they began to participate. Only in 1842, a mere 150 years ago, was there the first official contribution from any of the churches of Preston. There is no evidence to suggest that, even before the Reformation, it had any significant religious connections. This sets the Preston Guild apart from many of its medieval contemporaries, for guilds in the Middle Ages frequently had very strong ties with particular churches or particular saints, and religious worship played an important part in their ceremonial activities. Indeed, guilds were very often named after saints, and had their own chapels in parish churches.

In the case of Preston none of this seems to have been the case—at least as far as the available documentary and other evidence is concerned. This suggests that the Guild Merchant of Preston was always a secular body and that, although it participated in services and made use of the parish church during its celebrations, that was the limit of its religious activities. After the Reformation, from the Guild of 1542 onwards, any religious element would in any case have been far more limited, because Guild religious observances often had strong overtones of Roman Catholicism, and that was unacceptable to the authorities. Therefore from at least the Guild of 1542, for three hundred years, the church played no formal part except in connection with the holding of a civic service during Guild Week.

By the time of the first eye-witness account of the Guild, that of Richard Kuerden in 1682, the civic service was held in the parish church of St John at the conclusion of the mayoral procession on the Monday, the opening day of Guild Week. This seems to have been the case as long ago as 1500, when a formal procession gathered at Maudlands and then went along Friargate to the town centre, and finished at the parish church for a service. Also by 1682 the Mayor's Chaplain, invariably the rector of Preston, was present at most important official events—and was an enthusiastic participant in the great banquet which Kuerden describes in such detail!

Until the early eighteenth century there was only one Anglican church in the town—the parish church of St John—and until the 1690s it had been the only official place of worship. That is, there were several unofficial and semi-clandestine Catholic chapels from at least the reign of James I, and from the early 1690s several nonconformist chapels and meeting houses were licensed. During the eighteenth century, however, the numbers of churches and chapels multiplied. Two more Anglican churches were founded—St George's in 1725 and Holy Trinity in 1813, while several Roman Catholic chapels, and numerous nonconformist places of worship were established by the 1820s. One common factor between all of these disparate churches and chapels was that none of them played any part in the Guild celebrations. Neither did the congregation of the parish church: all were excluded from participation. The Corporation, which administered and organised the Guild celebrations, was exclusively Anglican and Tory, but not even the Anglicans played any formal role in the proceedings—their only official contribution came as part of the civic service.

In 1835, however, the Corporation was reformed, under the terms of the Municipal Corporations Act of that year, and its Anglican–Tory monopoly was broken. The reformed Borough Council, which took office at the beginning of January 1836, had a strong Whig and Nonconformist contingent, and no longer was it possible for those running the town and planning the Guild to be blithely unaware of—loftily to ignore—the non-Anglicans. Even without this religious/political change, the Guild of 1842 was destined to be very different from its many predecessors. For the first time it was designed as a celebration of the people and for the people, and for the first time many new aspects of Preston were represented.

Most notably, the churches and the schools of the Borough and of adjacent townships such as Ashton and Fulwood were allowed to join in, and to become participants in Guild Week events. They had their own processions and events, and the Guild of 1842 was therefore the first time that Roman Catholics and nonconformists played their part. In a town where both these denominations were very numerous and influential this was, to many people, a long overdue development—though others disagreed. The church and schools events of 1842 proved to be extremely popular with those who participated and with the thousands of spectators and bystanders, and in the planning of the 1862 Guild there was no question but that these new features would be a central aspect of the entire celebration.

Unfortunately, the organisers of the Guild of 1862 had to contend with a potentially disastrous diplomatic question. There was strong dislike and friction between the three main denominations in the town. The Catholics and the Protestants were at loggerheads, while within the Protestant community there was very considerable mutual suspicion between Anglicans and nonconformists—and even between different nonconformist groups. This wrecked any hope which the organisers had entertained of planning a single church contribution.

The original intention was that there should be a single procession, the longest yet seen at any Preston Guild, to include Anglicans, Roman Catholics and Nonconformists, in that order—an order based on the nominal numerical strength of each denomination (although the Anglicans would never have ceded first place even if numerically inferior). Within each section the individual parish churches or chapels were to have been separately represented, but the arrangements for these would be left to the different denominations. The Nonconformists—and especially the Wesleyans—steadfastly refused to cede second place to the Roman Catholics, saying that the Protestant churches should march together, and eventually the idea of a single procession was abandoned. Instead, three separate ones were held, divided on religious grounds and not following identical routes. At the end of the day the children from all the different church schools congregated in the recently opened Avenham and Miller Parks and sang patriotic songs. This was an immensely popular event, and it set a precedent for the participation of schoolchildren which led directly to the famous 1922 pageant, the forebear of the modern Guild pageant.

Separate processions for each of the three main Christian denominations remained the rule for the next century. During that period the religious processions became a central feature of the Guild, and attracted many thousands of participants and spectators. Their significance was demonstrated by the presence of numerous leading churchmen of national importance—a total of thirty-six bishops were in Preston at different times during Guild Week in 1972. But still there was no unity, and still the division into three processions continued. Although an ecumenical procession was considered in 1972 the idea was dropped, but on the Sunday before the Guild a Walk of Witness was held. This went through the town centre to Avenham Park, where an open-air service was held. The Walk was attended by official representatives of all denominations, as well as by many ordinary people, and it was a significant pointer to the future. Anglicans, Catholics and Nonconformists also joined together in the civic service at the parish church. Thus, although the three groups each had a separate official procession, a sharing of worship did take place.

In 1992 it was intended, from the outset, that all would be different. The concept and reality of ecumenicalism had grown apace during the intervening twenty years, and the idea no longer produced such hostility and antagonism: the Pope had visited England, and joint worship was now a common feature of public and private events. Furthermore, all the churches realised the immense value of gathering together for a great celebration such as this: it was an opportunity not to be missed. In 1992, therefore, there was for the first time in the history of the Guild a full-scale ecumenical service and a two-part ecumenical procession.

Church activities before and after Guild Week

Although the greater part of the effort of the Preston churches was devoted to the celebrations and processions of Guild Week itself, there was of course a wide range of other activities during the year. Some of the individual churches made special contributions, and a number of them combined to participate in the Church Heritage Walks which are described below. Others, however, had particular problems during Guild Year, and were prevented from doing as much as they would have liked.

St Walburge's Roman Catholic church, with its extraordinary spire which is Preston's most prominent and best-known landmark, has traditionally been a very active church community which has played an important role in the Guild. Unfortunately, in 1991 it was discovered that the church fabric was threatened by a massive outbreak of dry rot. Although remedial work carried out in 1992–3 should make the fabric safe, this problem, and the fact that work was in progress in the church, prevented the parish from making the large contribution to Guild activities which it had hoped to do. On 30 August, however, the Archbishop of Westminster, Cardinal Basil Hume, attended to preside over a special Guild mass—the church had been specially cleaned up and tidied for the occasion, but although the original intention had been to hold an ecumenical service it was realised that in the limited space available this would not be possible. During his visit the Cardinal agreed to support the appeal which would raise funds for the restoration work, and he consented to become the president of the appeal committee. Later in the year, although not part of the official Guild celebrations, St Walburge's opened its tower to visitors, and many people queued for the rare chance to see the finest possible view of Preston, and many miles of the surrounding countryside.

Fishergate Baptist Church also suffered from problems during Guild Year, but these were the result not of nature but of the inhumanity of man. In June 1991 the controlled explosion of an IRA bomb at the next-door Army Recruiting Office had resulted in severe structural damage, which was being repaired during 1992. A Church Heritage Tour visit on 13 June allowed visitors to review the progress of the restoration, and on this occasion a ceremonial trowel, used in the laying of the original foundation stone, was stolen from an exhibition in the school room. The service to commemorate the 209th Anniversary of the church was held on Guild Sunday, 30 August, and the opportunity was taken to offer special thanks for the work of restoration and refurbishment.

A programme of organ recitals at the parish church was arranged after a request from the Guild team. At the 1952 and 1972 Guilds this was a popular feature, and in 1992 the Borough Council had a particular interest because it had recently invested £40,000 in the restoration of the 1802 organ, originally installed by the self-taught organ-builder James Davies of Lea Town, just outside Preston. The recitals were given by Roy Massey of Hereford Cathedral on 22 May, Ian Tracey of Liverpool Cathedral on 6 June, Philip Crozier and Sylvie Porier from Canada, on 13 July, and the locally born prize-winning recitalist Julie Ann Carr on 30 September. Audiences were satisfactory, averaging about a hundred, and the series was considered to be an outstanding opportunity to appreciate the different styles and approaches of five recitalists. The recitals were generously sponsored by British Gas and the Friends of Preston Parish Church Organ, and the profit made was given to the parish church funds.

Two Church Heritage Tours were organised, for 13 June and 26 September, to allow visitors and local people to see some of the little-known and under-appreciated architectural and historical treasures of Preston. The first tour visited St Wilfrid's RC, the parish church of St John, Central (Lune Street) Methodist, Fishergate Baptist and St George's churches, and the second English Martyrs, St Walburge's, All Saints, St Ignatius and, again, St George's. At the last-named a display of silver and vestments was put on, and there and at the parish church the visitors were able to hear the organ.

English Martyrs and St Walburge's had souvenir stalls, and St Walburge's allowed access to the tower, while at Central Methodist church the guide had the visitors singing a Wesley hymn! Some thirty to forty people came on the two trips, although many more came specially for the St Walburge's section of the second visit. Each church provided a spokesman or guide, who explained the history and architectural features of the building, and any points of special interest. The idea was well received, and it is particularly unfortunate that a request via the Racial Equality Council for a similar tour of places of worship of the various eastern religions met with no response.

As one of its special events to commemorate Guild Year the Carey Baptist church arranged a visit by a sixty-strong Czechoslovakian choir, which played and sang English, Czech and Slovak religious music. The service, which attracted a congregation of more than forty people, was held on 11 July. During Guild Week itself the Carey Baptists participated in a partnership mission, in which five couples visited Preston to represent American Baptist churches. Lea Methodist church also brought overseas visitors, with representatives of an evangelical church at Solingen, Germany, attending for Guild Week and joining the Lea contingent in the ecumenical procession on the Tuesday.

The New York Salvation Army Staff Band came to the town on 1 June, for a Guild concert at the Guild Hall as part of its 1992 national tour. There was a civic reception, and the concert had an audience of well over 1,000 people. The international Salvation Army leader, Commissioner David Baxendale, visited Preston during Guild Week, and led services at the Citadel and at an open air meeting in Friargate on 29 August: he also participated in the Guild Court and the ecumenical service in Avenham Park. On 4 December the Salvation Army's Festival of Christmas Carols was its final contribution to the Guild Year celebrations.

On the social side of church activities, the Roman Catholic Catenian Association held a grand Banquet and Ball in the Guild Hall on the Saturday before Guild Week, 29 August. The event, which was organised by Preston Catenian Circles 14, 144 and 235, was advertised as 'The premier Catholic event of the Guild celebrations', and was honoured by the presence of the Archbishop of Westminster, Cardinal Basil Hume, and four other bishops.

St John's Parish Church and the 1992 Guild

The parish church of St John has always played a major part in the celebration of Preston Guild. The earliest surviving record of any Guild event is that which is noted on the reverse of the Guild Roll of 1542 and which refers to the holding of a procession during the Guild of 1500, along Friargate from Maudlands (the site of the present St Walburge's church) to the parish church, where 'after the Forsaid procession a Mase with solempnytie of the holy goyste solempny to be herd with the Maior & Aldermen'. This, half a millennium ago, was the distant ancestor of the religious service on the opening day of the Guild. Events which were held at the church in subsequent Guilds included not only religious worship, but also concerts and musical recitals, and since the nineteenth century it has also been used for exhibitions.

The former Rector of Preston, the Revd Michael Higgins, left Preston in June 1991 to become Dean of Ely, but he had already set in motion the planning of the church contribution to the 1992 Guild. On his departure arrangements were made to ensure that the planning of Guild events and activities continued during the 'interregnum' before the appointment of the new rector, and committees were established to deal with the proposed Flower and Quilt Festival, the organ recitals, and the work of the church itself during the Guild. The new Rector, the Revd Robert Ladds, arrived in November 1991, and shortly afterwards was invited to become the Guild Mayor's Chaplain, an office which is far from merely honorary: it involves attendance and participation in a wide range of services, processions and ceremonies throughout the year.

The ecumenical theme of the 1992 Guild, an exciting development which was strongly supported by all denominations and churches in the town, meant that the parish church had a special role. The new Rector was very conscious of the way in which centuries of Guild tradition would be intertwined with new approaches to Christian worship, and to participation in the community celebra-

A hitherto unknown watercolour by Beattie was used for the cover of several official Guild programmes: this detail shows St John's parish church (1851). (Society of Jesus, Winckley Square)

*The 1992 Guild Mayor,
Councillor Harold Parker.
(Preston B. C.)*

*The town centre was
brilliantly illuminated at
night: the Flag Market is
seen here on New Year's
Eve, at the start of Guild
Year.
(Preston B. C.)*

The Preston Guild Town Criers' Competition, 23 May. (Preston B. C.)

A raggle-taggle Scottish army crosses Avenham Park during the Storming of Preston by the Sealed Knot in mid-August. (Lancashire Evening Post)

The Guild Mayor addresses the crowd after the third proclamation of the Guild, on 22 August.
(Preston B. C.)

The scene inside the Guild Hall during the Guild Court: the Clerk of the Guild (right of lower table) is reading out the names of the Guild Burgesses.
(Lancashire Constabulary)

The street-cleaners, who followed every procession, were favourites of the crowds, and were singled out for special mention by the Guild Mayor. (Lancashire Evening Post)

Enthusiastic worship despite the rain at the Ecumenical Service. (Lancashire Evening Post)

The vestrymen of Preston, in their remarkable new robes, were seen in several church and civic events during the Guild.
(Preston B. C.)

Great care was taken to en-sure that the costumes made for the Schools' Pageant were historically authentic.
(Lancashire Evening Post)

The Uzorochye Folk Group from Russia attracted much enthusiastic attention throughout Guild Week. (Preston B. C.)

Mersey Street, which won a prize for its decorations, really enjoyed its street party. (Lancashire Evening Post)

*The internationally known
opera singer, Sarah Walker,
in full voice during 'Opera
in the Park'.
(Preston B. C.)*

*Bass North West, with their
superb Shire horses, provided
a traditional element in the
great Trades Procession.
(Lancashire Evening Post)*

Which one is wearing fancy dress? Community spirit during the first-ever Community Procession.
(Lancashire Evening Post)

Members of Preston's Sikh community in the highly successful Community Procession.
(Preston B. C.)

tions and events. One of the first demonstrations of this was the opportunity offered by the Milk Race, which took place on 31 May. The Preston leg of the race finished outside the church, and it was decided to use this occasion as a 'demonstration of active intent', on the part of the church, to be as close as possible to all aspects of the Guild. The church building was open, food was served, the bells were rung, the choir sang on the church steps, and the Rector had a place on the official stand. On 13 May, in another demonstration of openness and ecumenicalism, a concert was held at the church by the Brigham Young University Orchestra, from Salt Lake City, as part of its world-wide tour. The event was organised by the Church of Jesus Christ and the Latter Day Saints, and raised £1,000 for the Church Urban Fund. St John's was packed with visitors from as far afield as Cumbria, Liverpool and Manchester.

There were numerous special services during the year in addition to those held in Guild Week. Regular services were given a special 'Guild year' emphasis, and it was decided that the traditional services of Guild Week itself should be upgraded, each with a distinct flavour. A hitherto unpublished Beattie watercolour, showing Church Street, was used as the cover of all the orders of service: it had been discovered in St Wilfrid's Presbytery, and was reproduced by permission. Special services included the Judges Service on 2 June; the State Visit of the Guild Mayor to the Church on 7 June, with the Revd Dr John Andrew, a former Rector of Preston, as preacher; and, on the same day, the service of reunion for the Loyal Regiment, with dedication of a memorial to a former colonel by the Archdeacon of Lancaster.

The Flower and Quilt Festival, held at the parish church between 29 August and 6 September, was a particularly impressive contribution to the Guild celebrations, and attracted wide acclaim and great admiration. A festival on this theme had been held at the 1972 Guild, but that was considerably smaller than the ambitious conception of the 1992 display. The choice of the subject of the Festival was itself symbolic of a Christian theme. The Rector, the Revd Robert Ladds, wrote in the introduction to the programme that 'part of the beauty of flowers is their transitory quality. By contrast the Quilts will last for scores of years into the future. In this there is perhaps a message; a truth. It is the message echoed by this Church and its long history. The message is that the Christian faith is lasting and eternal; yet is ever new and fresh. It is the very fabric of our lives against which we experience all the events of today and of the future'.

The festival brought together the Quilterer's Guild and the National Association of Flower Arrangement Societies: seven Lancashire clubs and societies affiliated to the N.A.F.A.S. participated, and the organisers, led by the churchwarden Mrs Jo Ratcliff, had the valuable services of Gold Medal winners Ann Coulton and Margaret Whittaker. The festival was a triumphant success, and the interior of the church was a breathtaking display of colour and beauty. Visitors were enchanted and delighted by what they saw, and the quality of the work, both of the quilters and the flower arrangers, was quite exceptional.

Purchase of the souvenir programme allowed the holder to make as many visits as he or she wanted, and so no precise figures of attendance are available, but the best estimates suggest that about 15,000 people visited during the week. Sponsorship was received from British Aerospace, and £20,600 was raised for church funds, while the raffle for a quilt produced £6,885. Money was given to

Derian House and the Blackpool Victoria Hospital as well as to the parish church.

After the Guild was finished it was said that the relationship between the church and the Guild organisers within the Borough Council had been the best in living memory: indeed, one observer closely involved in the organisation of the church events said that it was 'not a case of Church and Borough, but Church and Borough acting together'. The close co-operation between 'church and state' and the prominent and essential part which the parish church played in the Guild were recognised in April 1993, when Preston Borough Council resolved to grant the freedom of the Borough to the parish church. This generous and imaginative gesture was warmly welcomed by all.

The Ecumenical Service in Avenham Park (30 August)

The Walk of Witness and open air service held in Avenham Park during the 1972 Guild, had been very well received by the congregation and by the 'administration' of the different churches involved. It had inspired many people with the idea of large scale ecumenical worship, and in the intervening twenty years the old divisions had begun to break down. There was therefore an excellent example to follow for the 1992 Guild, which would inevitably have a much greater emphasis on the sharing of worship and Christian faith. As before, the Sunday at the beginning of Guild Week—the so-called 'Guild Sunday'—was the chosen date, and Avenham Park was the natural venue. There was already seating for 10,000 people and the arena also had a large stage, which had been used for a pre-Guild show and would be used during Guild Week for concerts and for the Schools' Pageant later in the week.

In April 1990 delegates from the Anglican, Roman Catholic and Free Churches met, to begin planning the open air service, and it was soon agreed that the event should if possible be livelier and more impact-making than that which had been held in 1972. Since a very large congregation was anticipated, and there would therefore be a comparatively long period during which crowds would be gathering and waiting for the service to start, a 'warm-up' personality would be needed to maintain enthusiasm and create the right mood.

At various times the organising committee included Monsignor O'Dea and Canon Michael Taylor, representing the Roman Catholic churches; Canon Stanley Finch, the Revd Robert Ladds and the Revd John Francis (Church of England); the Revds John Beardsley, David Mann and Michael Wearing (Free Churches); Frank Hartley and John Cotterall (Guild Office) and Canon Chard (Secretary, Lancashire Church Leaders); Superintendent Gary Price (County Constabulary), Martin Haworth (Preston Borough Council) and Peter Hartley (Cardinal Newman College drama section).

The Committee sent invitations to several leading church figures, asking them to come to the Guild to take part in the Ecumenical Service, and it was enormously encouraged and inspired when acceptances were received from the Archbishop of Canterbury, Dr George Carey; Cardinal Basil Hume, Archbishop of Westminster, Dr John Newton, Chairman of the Liverpool Methodist District; and Dr John Biggs, Moderator of the Free Church Federal Council. The plans for a major ecumenical event received a further boost when Graham Kendrick, the widely known and very popular Christian musician, agreed to provide a musical introduction to worship, and to accompany the singing. Some Roman Catholics from the Preston area had been hoping that the Pope would visit the Guild celebrations, and a petition asking him to do so was delivered in November 1991, but this was never a realistic possibility—nonetheless, the presence of the leading churchmen left nobody in any doubt as to the symbolic significance of the Guild and the real importance attached to the ecumenical service.

Many local church organisations helped with the detailed arrangements for the ecumenical service, providing volunteers to undertake a wide range of essential tasks and duties. For example, assistance with taking the collection, which ultimately amounted to £1,998.44, was provided by the Knights of St Columba. Special arrangements were made to seat those visitors with wheelchairs, and the Mary Cross Trust supplied two interpreters for people for hearing difficulties. Because many churches were sending coachloads of visitors the organising committee and the police co-operated to provide parking areas in West Cliff, while Preston Bus ran a shuttle service to and from the bus station.

The programme for the service was as follows:

> Thanksgiving
>> Reading
>> Reflection on the theme (Dr Newton)
>> Hymn
>
> Celebration
>> Reading
>> Drama
>> Reflection on the theme (Archbishop Carey)
>> Songs of Celebration
>
> Commitment
>> Reading
>> Reflection on the theme (Cardinal Hume)
>> Prayers (led by Dr Biggs)

Other prayers were led by Monsignor O'Dea, the Roman Catholic Vicar General, and by Canon Stanley Finch, the Anglican Rural Dean. The attendance at the service was very encouraging, and it was thought by the organisers that Graham Kendrick and his band, together with the presence of the three leading international churchmen, helped to make the event such a success … despite nature's attempts to cause maximum disruption by hurling all the worst possible weather at Avenham Park that afternoon. The congregation was estimated at about 7,000, which was considered a remarkably high figure in the circumstances—although it is clear that, in good weather, a turn-out several times larger might have been seen. The special Guild poly-ponchos proved their worth many times over, and a remarkable number of the audience stayed until the end.

Undoubtedly the conditions in which the service took place did detract from its impact, for the weather was appalling—the worst in the whole of Guild Week, which was itself one of the wettest and windiest of any Guild in recorded history.

The Archbishop of Westminster, Cardinal Basil Hume, and the Archbishop of Canterbury, Dr George Carey, with other leaders during the Ecumenical Service. (Lancashire Evening Post).

The worshippers showed remarkable staying power and fortitude, and members of the congregation revealed that they were made of sterner stuff than the Royal Marines, whose planned concert at the dock on Riversway that evening was cancelled because of the atrocious weather. Ignoring or braving the lashing wind and torrential rain, the worshippers enjoyed the event and many people found it a deeply rewarding experience: one lady of 94 was heard to say that 'I might not live long after this, but it's a wonderful way to go!'

The report of the service in the *Evening Post* noted that 'Worshippers sang from beneath a sea of umbrellas as a spiritual light filled the park despite the driving rain'. Cardinal Hume, in his address, pointed to a metaphor—the adversities posed by the weather, he said, 'were a reminder of the adversities to be faced in life', while Dr Carey, the Archbishop of Canterbury spoke of the realisation that the churches needed each other and could learn from each other. He reflected on how, just over a century ago, the Guild of 1882 had been marred by communal violence and strife between the churches, but that now it was possible for unity and togetherness to be real. Cardinal Hume picked up that theme, reminding his listeners that 'we no longer walk as strangers but as pilgrims together'.

The Ecumenical Processions

Ever since the churches first began to participate in the Guild, their processions have required a great deal of careful organisation. In the mid-nineteenth century this produced many headaches for the Guild's planners, as the different denominations squabbled over precedence and routes: holding three separate processions may have solved the disputes over the order of the different denominations, but it produced three times as many differences of opinion over routes and other organisational matters. The religious strife which was an ugly and endemic feature of Preston in the second half of the nineteenth century boiled over into violence at the 1882 Guild, when the Orange Order attacked the Roman Catholic procession.

Detailed planning was particularly complex because, even in the second half of the twentieth century, these processions involved very large numbers of walkers drawn from many different individual churches. All of the participants, and the themes and messages which they conveyed, had to be co-ordinated and orchestrated by those planning the individual processions.

In the knowledge that, for the first time, the 1992 Guild would possibly see a combined procession involving all the denominations, the contribution of the local churches to the 1992 Guild was the subject of serious discussion at a very early stage in Guild planning. Already by the spring of 1990 the shape of their participation was becoming clear. On 1 May 1990 a strategy meeting was held between the Town Clerk, the Senior Guild Co-ordinator (Neville Bridge), the Guild Processions Co-ordinator (Martin Haworth), the Bishop of Blackburn, the Roman Catholic Bishop of Lancaster, and the Chairman of the North Lancashire district of the Methodist Church.

This high-level meeting considered the radical proposal that, for the first time in Guild history, there should be a joint and unified approach to church participation. The idea of a single monster procession—which would probably have been one of the longest on record—was soon abandoned for practical reasons, and instead it was decided that two Ecumenical Church Processions should be held, one on the Monday and one on the Tuesday. In previous Guilds the three separate processions were each of considerable length, and it was clear that these could not be combined within a single one without it becoming far too long and unmanageable; the holding of what were, in effect, first and second instalments, was therefore suggested. The plan, like the decision to make the churches' contribution entirely ecumenical, was very widely welcomed.

An organising committee was established on 4 December 1990, composed of six representatives from each of the three Christian communities in Preston. It chose a single vigorous and decisive theme for the processions, one which emphasised the ecumenical spirit and the co-operation between the groups, as well as highlighting a message for everybody in the world at large: GOD SPEAKS TO ALL. The organising committee also agreed that the two processions, which had already been accepted, should be arranged on a geographical basis using the A6 London Road–North Road–Garstang Road line as the approximate division. On the first day, the Monday of Guild Week, the churches east of the A6 would process, and on the following day those to the west.

This arrangement worked extremely well, and the skill and effectiveness of the organisers was apparent in the smooth operation of the processions on both days. The organising committee was chaired by the Right Revd Monsignor Canon P. G. O'Dea (St Anthony RC) or the Very Revd Canon S. J. Finch (St John, Broughton, C of E), and the Secretary was Mrs M. Vaughn of St. Gregory the Great RC church. The Revd Martin Cripps (St Cuthbert C of E) undertook much of the inter-church liaison, while a great deal of the detail of the project was finalised by a sub-committee comprising the Revd Cripps, the Revd J Robinson (St Jude with St Paul C of E), the Very Revd Canon M. Taylor (English Martyrs RC), Mr Leo Warren (St Wilfrid RC), and Mr J Hodgson (Free Churches Federal Council).

The Monday (east of town) procession involved fifty-eight floats, eleven bands and 3,800 walking participants, while on the Tuesday the west of town procession included fifty-six floats, nineteen bands and 4,200 walkers. The total participation was therefore no fewer than 114 floats, thirty bands and more than 8,000 walkers, together with several hundred other people who rode on the floats and took part in the tableaux. The organising committee ordered medals, for sale to participants, bearing the processional motto, 'God Speaks To All'. The Borough Council gave financial support of £5,650 to assist those smaller and less well-endowed churches which had found difficulty in raising the cost of their contribution to the processions.

One of the very heartening features of the processions was that in many parts of the town and surrounding areas all the local churches had joined forces in their own ecumenical movements. They worked together during the two years of planning, and pooled their enterprise and resources to put on combined floats and tableaux, marching together in an impressive display of genuine unity. One fine example from the parts of the borough which at the time of the last Guild in 1972 were not even within the boundaries of Preston was the 'Brock Valley Churches Together' section—twelve churches and chapels serving the small rural communities of the area around Goosnargh, Inglewhite, Claughton, Whitechapel and Bleasdale. There were four Anglican, three Roman Catholic, one Congregational and two Methodist churches involved, and the message they gave was of the importance of prayer. From the town, to quote but one example, the Deepdale Council of Churches, comprising St Gregory's RC, Guttridge Memorial Methodist, St Jude with St Paul C of E, and St Ignatius RC churches, had the theme of 'togetherness' and represented 'forgiveness, accepting, healing, peace and justice'.

The overall theme, GOD SPEAKS TO ALL, was followed on each processional day, but every church or group of churches was free to make its own interpretation, and to portray the message in whatever way it chose. There was a 'sequence of thought' which underlay the general message, and which was identified and explained in the programme:

1. Basic Christian Belief:
   We believe in one God, who is supremely revealed as Father, Son and Holy Spirit, who sustains and is involved in his creation.

2. God reveals Himself through the Bible:
   He made his covenant, his promise, with Noah, Abraham, Jacob, Moses and the prophets from Old Testament times. Christians see the fulfilment of God's promises in the New Testament, in the life and teaching of Jesus, and the salvation brought through his death and resurrection.

3. God continues to reveal himself in history:
   Through the centuries, saints and pilgrims in the faith have shown how

powerfully God has been able to act in history through those who have put their trust in Him.

4. Today's Church:

   Amidst the many troubles and needs of our world, Christians accept the responsibility for doing something in God's name to bring Christ's love into the hearts of individual lives and into the varied communities of today.

5. Our Future:

   As we go into the future in hope and faith, we do not know in detail where the way may lead, but we believe that the Holy Spirit will guide us into His truth and will give us the strength and courage we need. Jesus Christ is the same yesterday, today and for ever; all who call themselves Christians must go forward together, loving and supporting each other as we all seek to offer God's love to the world.

Heading the first Ecumenical Procession was a huge wooden cross: it was followed by an array of archbishops, bishops and leaders of the Free Churches.
(Lancashire Evening Post)

A splendid sequence of banners is in view as the first day's procession passes along Friargate.
(Lancashire Evening Post)

The first day's Ecumenical Procession was led by the most senior churchman present, the Archbishop of Westminster, Cardinal Basil Hume. He was accompanied by leaders of all the main Christian churches in Lancashire, including the Anglican Bishop of Blackburn and both Bishops of Lancaster. They followed an impressive wooden cross which was carried on an electric float, and signalled the start of the two-hour-long procession. During the morning it had been somewhat

Joy, enthusiasm and commitment during the Ecumenical Processions. Preston B. C.)

wet and windy, but the weather had improved by the afternoon, and the procession took place in sporadic sunshine. It was reported by the local press that many found this procession a particularly moving experience: 'for some of those watching it brought back fond memories of previous celebrations and tears flowed with the emotional recollections. But the event was just as popular with those who were witnessing history being made for the first time.' Ninety-two-year-old Gertrude Giddins of Ribbleton was watching her fifth Guild: she had seen that of 1902 in her father's arms. She told a reporter that 'I did not think I would see five Guilds, but I am really enjoying it. It's great'.

Describing the second Ecumenical Procession, which took place in fine weather with considerable amounts of sunshine, the *Evening Post* reported that 'the town centre streets were filled with the sounds of singing and music in a joyous celebration of God and the Guild … and God must have been looking down on his flock, as the stormy rain and winds of previous days held off throughout the three-hour procession'. On both days the many bands and musicians in the processions attracted particular attention, and generated a lively excitement. There were brass bands from all over Lancashire, jazz bands and groups, pipe and drum bands and Christian singers: all were entertaining in their own right, and an integral part of the success of the processions. Some floats had their own musicians, and these played religious music, while St Cuthbert's and the Calvary Christian Fellowship played music from the open tops of double-decker buses. All the emphasis was on harmony, togetherness, the joyous celebration of the Guild and happy celebration of ecumenical worship.

Many of the floats had excellent and imaginative tableaux and displays. On the second day the contribution of St Mary Magdalene, Lower Penwortham, was a float full of young ladies, in wimples and medieval costume, who were closely followed by a fierce dragon. The Longton Area Methodist Churches had a simple message: PEACE! But the message was translated into many languages, and held high on banners … SPOKOJ! HEDDWCH! VREDE! The traditional banners were proudly held aloft by church groups, mothers' unions and other organisations, while other walkers carried tall crosses, beautifully decorated statues of Our Lady, or large signs proclaiming the message of love and unity.

As is always the case in the churches procession, the costumes worn were often very attractive and unusual, having been specially made for the occasion. There was widespread use of flowers, foliage and ribbon to make splendid garlands and floral arches. Near the head of the procession walked the vestrymen of Preston, clad in their stunning new robes of sea-green, which had been designed for them by the fashion department at the University of Central Lancashire. The theme 'Ready to serve' was uniquely symbolised by Irene Barnes and Tony Strong, from the Lune Street Central Methodist Church, who were dressed as a tin of oxtail soup and a tin of lentil soup respectively! A particularly attractive form of dress was the beautiful and exquisitely embroidered traditional costume worn by members of Preston's sizeable Polish community: this has been a feature of the Guilds since 1952, when the Poles and Ukrainians who had come to

A glorious and colourful display of costumes, floats, regalia and banners, as many churches walked under the unifying theme 'God Speaks To All'.
(Lancashire Evening Post)

the town just after the Second World War first participated in the celebrations.

The Vice-Principal of Cardinal Newman College, Leo Warren, edited a booklet entitled 'Christians Together', detailing the eighty-eight churches which were participating in the two processions. The booklet sold the quite remarkable total of 20,000 copies, many of them to the 10,000 people who were involved in the processions but many others to people anxious to have a permanent souvenir of 'the biggest display of church unity ever seen in Preston'.

The churches, of all denominations, were delighted by the success of the ecumenical service and the processions, and by the marvellous display of unity. The Revd Martin Cripps, vicar of Fulwood St Cuthbert and one of the chief organisers of the events, said afterwards that they were 'thankful to God for the weather and that God, himself, had been glorified'. He thought that it was especially rewarding 'to see the hard work and effort come together in such a fine way'. The processions had been notable for their 'imagination, co-operation and execution', and the bishops who had participated in the Guild celebrations had been thrilled with what the churches had done.

The Schools' Pageant

During the Guild of 1862 Avenham Park, which was then only just being landscaped and planted with trees, was invaded by a crowd estimated at about 100,000 people. These were not participants in a Viking-period or Civil War re-enactment—they were the spectators at the first of the children's events which, at every Guild thereafter, were deservedly such an attraction. Those who watched in 1862, like those in 1992, braved heavy rain and high winds to enjoy their Guild—although, unlike those of the most recent Guild, they also had to put up with cinders, soot and sparks from the railway trains passing along the viaduct between Avenham and Miller Parks: many of the onlookers were actually watching from open goods wagons stabled along sidings, while trains steamed past.

At the 1862 event the children—some 25,000 of them according to eyewitnesses—gathered in the Park in orderly formation. All were wearing their best clothes, and many of them carried Union flags and red, white and blue banners. They sang a programme of favourite and stirring hymns and patriotic songs, finishing with a rousing rendering of 'Hurrah for England's Queen'. There was no attempt to stage dramatic scenes or to make a pageant in the modern sense, but the event itself was quite unprecedented in Guild history. Its success, and the admiration which it drew from all who watched it—not least the thousands of proud parents and relatives in the audience—produced a very favourable response, and the local newspapers reported in enthusiastic terms about this new Guild idea. The holding of such a gathering was therefore prominent in the plans for the next Guild, and at each celebration from 1882 onwards a children's event was included. These became increasingly complex and elaborate—though none has ever included as many children as the pioneering gathering of 1862—and gradually the events began to take on the format of a pageant, with the re-enactment of scenes and the wearing of special costumes, and with a historical theme.

In 1922 the Pageant was of a particularly high standard. It was conceived, written and directed by A. J. Berry, the Director of Education for the Borough of Preston. He had written *The Story of Preston*, a children's history of the town which was very favourably received, and followed this—after the 1922 Guild—with *Proud Preston's Story*, a popular account written for adults. Berry was of the firm opinion that 'no other place in England can in itself furnish more complete examples of an ecclesiastical and feudal past, with the expansion into an industrial present'. When he was asked, as Director of Education, to take responsibility for the 1922 Children's Pageant he decided that his production would reflect the 'ecclesiastical and feudal past', and trace the way it had changed into the industrial present. His idea was to stage a long series of varied and exciting scenes, illustrating events in the history of Preston. They were to be large in scale, in full costume, and with realistic props and scenery.

In 1922, therefore, children dressed as Danes—and ransacked the town; as monks, they prayed and chanted as they converted the heathens; as Queen Elizabeth and her courtiers, they looked proud and haughty as they granted a charter to the town; as Cavaliers and Roundheads, they fought fiercely for their opposing causes outside Preston; and as many other colourful characters they recreated exciting and momentous occasions from Preston's past. About ten thousand children took part, and it was estimated that some 30,000 people watched the Pageant on each of three days—a total of 90,000 spectators. The event was, perhaps, the most influential of any in the past two centuries of the Guild. It, more than any other, stirs the warmest memories among those who participated, and it made a deep impression upon all who were involved in it or who organised the Guilds which followed.

Thirty years later, in 1952, there was a different theme for the Guild Festival for Schools. During two days a total of 51,000 spectators saw 6,000 children perform a four-part presentation which had the theme of games and dancing—Children of Yesterday and Children of Today. This was in keeping with the spirit of the age—a post-war enthusiasm for cleanliness, health, freshness and joy, combined with forward-looking idealism. The cynicism, disappointment and doubt which assailed society forty years later were not yet apparent.

The Festival began with a pealing of bells, a fanfare of trumpets and the singing of the National Anthem, followed by the reading of a message sent by the Queen to the children of Preston. The second section, 'Children of Yesterday', included readings of selected excerpts from Preston's charters, to the accompaniment of songs from a large choir. Children dressed in appropriate costume represented the mayoral groups of the Guilds of previous centuries—they, as befitted mayoral parties, sat on a central dais and watched other children perform dances and pastimes characteristic of those times.

In the third part, 'Children of Today', the mayoral parties of the different centuries gathered together to watch colourful displays of the games and activities associated with physical education in the schools of Preston in 1952. The choir sang 'Nymphs and Shepherds' and, in a gesture which seems extraordinary in our world-weary and unconfident age, a section of the 1944 Education Act was read out. This part of the Pageant finished with a march-past of all those who had participated. Finally, as an 'Epilogue', the Children of Yesterday and the Children of Today joined forces to sing and dance round a great central maypole, gradually increasing in tempo and in numbers until the music and movement abruptly ceased. The mayoral parties of past centuries then left the arena, the dancing resumed, 'Land of Hope and Glory' rang out, and bells pealed.

The Guild of 1972 saw a more traditional pageant, in which history was once again the theme. About 3,000 children took part, and there were said to be 10,659 spectators—a very precise figure indeed! The children portrayed Preston past, present and future. The town in the past was illustrated by themes from the seventeenth century onwards, such as markets and fairs, the coming of the cotton industry, and the arrival of the railway. The schoolchildren were dressed in appropriate costumes, and acted out tableaux and dramatic presentations.

'Preston Present' depicted the cosmopolitan town of the early 1970s, with its business, commerce and family ties all over the world—new residents from the Commonwealth, Preston people who had migrated overseas, Preston's industries trading with countries north, south, east and west, and the town's flourishing international commercial life with its dock, its great manufacturing trades and its thriving economy. 'Preston Future' showed how the town might develop and prosper, with green field industrial sites, the Central Lancashire New Town, and its role as the capital of Lancashire. We are still waiting for the Preston citizen of tomorrow, the small boy in the fluorescent space suit, and the gleaming vision of new industries, bright new buildings and a bright economic future had lost much of its shine by the time the 1992 Guild came round.

For the Guild of 1992 the organisers reflected upon the experience of the previous years, and decided that the Pageant should look at the whole history of the town—it would, therefore, return to the idea which had underlain the Schools' Pageant of 1922. The Pageant of 1992, officially entitled *A Pageant of Preston: the Story of a Proud Town*, was organised by John Cotterall and Frank Hartley, from the Guild Office. They began work on the project in November 1989. Frank Hartley had been closely involved with the 1972 event, for which he was the producer, so he had a detailed working knowledge of the procedures involved in such an ambitious task. John Cotterall was an active local historian, and he was therefore particularly well suited to the role of scriptwriter.

Both, though, had a much wider role, in providing liaison and information for all schools in connection with the Guild, and in coordinating and forwarding educational activities during Guild Year. Because of the intense pressure on the time and resources of schools, teachers and pupils it was decided that the production must of necessity be more modest than in some of the previous Guilds. Notably, the secondary schools could not participate to any great extent in the pageant itself because they could not commit themselves sufficiently far ahead, but it was agreed that technical and backstage assistance, musicians and all solo speaking roles would be provided by them. The organisers made this decision personally, but were pleased to note that nobody from the schools ever questioned it or its wisdom.

There was no doubt about the choice of venue for the 1992 Pageant—it had to be held in Avenham Park, as had all its predecessors for 130 years. Nevertheless, the organisers had some misgivings about the problems which might be faced in bad weather, for there was disturbing evidence from the 1972 Pageant that rain and damp ground could cause serious problems for the performers. Their worries were fully justified, for the appalling weather of the first part of Guild Week 1992 almost forced the abandonment of the whole show, or its transfer to the much less suitable location of the P.N.E. football ground at Deepdale. A message for future Guild organisers, strongly emphasised by John Cotterall and Frank Hartley, was that a great deal of very careful attention should be given to the question of protecting the arena from the weather and sheltering the participants, and to preventing the damper ground in the less well-drained hollow of the arena from being churned up by vehicles and pedestrians.

There was, almost inevitably, a long period of planning and negotiation ahead of the rehearsal and production of the Pageant. The agreement of the Chief Education Officer and the District Administrative Officer was required, and many schools expressed some reluctance to join in because of problems with the timing of holidays. Eventually these difficulties were ironed out, by allowing schools to make flexible arrangements for holidays and days off, but it was a lengthy process. The production team was assembled in the spring of 1991: Frank Hartley and John Cotterall were joined by Fred Green, a retired headteacher with very extensive experience in sound work, and Joan Glynn, who organised and helped to produce the costumes—an extremely important and very time-consuming task. Brian Berry came in September 1991, and planned the back-stage work and the complex transport arrangements. This trio, like Frank Hartley, had helped in 1972.

A major concern of the organisers at an early stage was obtaining sponsorship. Eventually Lancashire County Council and British Aerospace agreed to become sponsors for the event. The County Council made a sizeable monetary contribution, and also agreed to cover the costs of transporting the children to and from Avenham Park. British Aerospace provided invaluable financial assistance, as well as a hospitality tent for distinguished visitors and other help. In total over £40,000 was granted by the two sponsors towards the cost of the Pageant.

Letters were sent to all schools in the Preston education district (area 6) in April 1991, inviting them to take part—only two schools in Preston, and, understandably, those in the Chipping area, decided against joining the Pageant. Thereafter the organisers maintained a regular flow of information, news, and requests for assistance and involvement to all participants. By the end of 1991 this was being supplemented with detailed work on the script, the music, the backstage activities and the logistical planning. An official letter, requesting participation and a firm commitment, was issued in January 1992 so that the schools could send copies to parents.

The script was so written that it was easily divisible between the different schools which would be contributing, according to the number of pupils and quantity of time and resources which each school could give. There was also the opportunity to make use of special features of each school—thus, those with a large proportion of children from Preston's ethnic communities were allocated scenes in which the modern town, or the coming of the Asian and Caribbean peoples, were portrayed. The division into sections also allowed each of the participating schools to rehearse and prepare on its own. The alternative would have been the need for many more large-scale rehearsals—a time-consuming and expensive option, and one which would have required complex organisation.

John Cotterall felt that 'the teachers in the various schools responded magnificently to this opportunity to prepare alone, and this saved the producer much heartache'. Preston schools collaborated for as long as can be remembered in a Preston Schools' Music Festival and it was their organisation, ideas and the enthusiasm of the teachers which were drawn on to help with the Pageant.

Choir rehearsals began in March 1992, but before then the Music Director, Mrs Mary Duckworth, had provided each school with music and a tape recording of the songs. She held a briefing meeting in January 1992 at Queen's Drive CP School, during which she went through the music and explained technical and teaching points. The choir members were drawn mainly from the primary schools, but to ease the burden on the smaller children some of the songs were performed by soloists from secondary and high schools. In contrast, the orchestra was made up solely of pupils from the secondary schools and sixth-form colleges. As in 1972, it was decided that the music and narration for the event should be pre-recorded, to reduce the risk of technical problems on the days of the actual performance, and to simplify the sound arrangements and to make it possible to sell recordings. After a long search for suitable premises, the recording sessions were held during April 1992 at All Hallows High School Sports Hall, Penwortham.

Making the costumes was a mammoth undertaking, involving hundreds of parents and school staff, as well as the children themselves. Joan Glynn visited all the schools, taking with her bags of material and samples, costume designs and patterns, and giving advice and instruction on what was required. Mothers and grandmothers assisted teachers. Almost all the costumes were made specially for the Pageant—only a few were bought—and there were some headaches with materials and designs which were, to say the least, unconventional. Some of the children had to dress up as terraced houses and mills, and thus had to wear brick-patterned material or paper. The original idea had been to use a plastic-coated fabric, but nothing suitable could be found, and the solution which was eventually adopted was to use heavy-duty polythene with brick-patterned wallpaper stapled on to it. There was extensive research to ensure historical authenticity.

In the words of Frank Hartley, 'these costumes looked most effective, but had their problems. The length … made walking difficult, [while] the lack of armholes made balancing on difficult muddy areas imperative, since a fall created not only dirty houses but also children who found it rather difficult to get up again, but the most serious problem was that the 'brick' wallpaper became very fragile in heavy rain and after the dress rehearsals two schools … had to make some careful repairs to some very soggy houses'. The costumes were also too wide to be worn in the bus bringing the children!

Properties and scenery were produced under the direction of a team of art teachers, headed by Ian McCormick of Preston College. They were constrained by the requirement that all the equipment and props which would be carried had to be small and light, as the actors were primary school children. The larger and more bulky stage props and scenery were handled by secondary school children, and so could be more substantial. Most of the lighter items were made of foam rubber and expanded polystyrene, and not only looked excellent but were also very easy to carry—just what the organisers and planners had in mind.

The ground conditions, already the subject of slight misgivings at the start of the preparations, became the object of ever more serious doubts as the day of the first performance approached. Avenham Park is an ideal venue for open-air events such as the Pageant, but long before the intensive use during the summer of 1992 there were signs of serious problems ahead. Drains in the basin of the arena had been replaced shortly before Guild Year, as a result of excessive flooding, and the ground was therefore soft and disturbed from the excavation work even before the events of the Guild began. From Easter 1992 onwards the Park had been used for many large-scale events as the Guild festivities progressed, and by late August there was considerable disquiet over its condition. Had the weather been clement the problems would probably have been minimised, but the prolonged and heavy rain over several days immediately before Guild Week was the worst possible outcome.

After all the many months of planning and hard work, the organisers and prospective participants were immensely dismayed by the disastrous weather which preceded Pageant Day—Thursday 2 September. The rain had been more or less continuous during the Saturday and Sunday, and was again heavy and prolonged on the Wednesday. After four days of downpours the ground in Avenham Park was in danger of becoming a treacherous quagmire—a problem exacerbated by the intensive use which had been made of the Park during the previous fortnight. The first official event in the Park, the great Ecumenical Service on the afternoon of Sunday 30 August, was attended by over 7,000 people, who worshipped in pouring rain. By the end of the service the main pathways, the grass and parts of the seating areas were heavily trodden and trampled, and very large patches of mud were appearing.

The next three days saw further deterioration: although the weather moderated somewhat, the ground was heavily waterlogged and the continued movement of people and vehicles had churned it up further. Large quantities of sand had been dumped in an attempt to improve the surface, but in the wettest parts this too had been submerged in mud and water. On Monday 31 August, the first day of Guild Week proper, the organisers were forced to give very serious consideration to the use of an alternative venue for the Pageant, and finally, on Wednesday 2 September a conference was called to decide whether the Pageant should go ahead, or be moved, or be cancelled outright.

Preston North End's Deepdale ground, with its then notorious plastic pitch, was suggested as the most likely option. But there was a great reluctance to abandon the Park, which was the most suitable venue, and is a magnificent natural setting for the Pageant. It was also—and this was a very important point—the traditional setting for this event, which is one of the high points of Guild Week. Equally important was the fact that all the rehearsals and technical preparation had been carried out using Avenham Park—there was simply not enough time to move elsewhere.

Frank Hartley told the *Lancashire Evening Post* that the Borough Council would 'move heaven and earth' to ensure that the event went ahead in its intended site: 'We have decided that we should go ahead on Avenham Park and we will do everything in our power to make the ground as good as possible. We hope people understand it won't be perfect but if we had moved it to Deepdale it would have been a question of the children going on to the pitch without any rehearsals or

A general view of Avenham Park during the great Schools' Pageant (Lancashire Evening Post)

a chance to get used to the new venue. That would almost certainly have ruined the Pageant'. Desperate efforts were made to ensure that the ground was dry enough to use, and to improve the setting. Huge quantities of matting, straw and sand were brought in to the arena to create a new drier surface, and the stands of seating in the performance area, used for previous events, were kept until the last minute to protect the ground from further rain.

The decision was taken: the 1992 Guild Schools' Pageant would not be defeated by foul weather and a quagmire underfoot, but would go ahead in the Park as planned. However, urgent remedial action would have to be taken to make the ground fit for use. At 8 a.m. on Thursday, the first day of the Pageant, a team moved in to lay a special type of aerated plastic sheeting across the whole area. This would allow any rain to seep through to the ground underneath, but would not allow the groundwater to well up to the surface. The sheeting was covered with a thin layer of sand, in which were marked out all the circles and segments needed for the guidance of the performers—in the event these became blurred and scuffed, but the performers coped valiantly with this difficulty. Workers from the Borough's Works Department laboured to clear up pathways and seating areas, prepare the arena and to provide dry routes around the stage. At 1.30 p.m., when the work was still in progress, the audience began to assemble.

The herculean efforts were worthwhile. The ground stayed usable throughout both days, and the Pageant was a great success. Most important of all, perhaps, was the weather, which at last was kind—or rather, less unkind! On the Thursday there were two short heavy showers during the afternoon (during which the performance was halted and the children attempted to find some shelter) but for most of the time the weather was dry. On the Friday the weather could actually be described as good—the sun shone and it was quite warm. Had it rained

*he Pageant was preceded by
ngthy and careful planning, and a
st amount of work went into pre-
aring the costumes and designing
e opisodes illustrating the history
`Preston.
ancashire Evening Post)*

heavily on either day the performance would have been seriously jeopardised, but for once the fates were smiling!

The Pageant itself was full of historical detail, with extensive verbatim quotations from writers, historical documents and other original sources, so the quality of the script was very high. The full length and breadth of the town's history was

Best of all were the children them-selves—part of the 650-strong choir and 150-piece orchestra at the Schools' Pageant.
(Preston B. C.)

shown by numerous short sharp scenes, accompanied by narration from a detailed text, and by the appropriate sound effects, background music and songs. It was an impressive canter through two thousand years, and—given the constraints of time, resources and the age of the actors—it is remarkable how much of Preston's past could be touched on. The script divided into several sections: Preston's Position; Early Times, Charters, Markets and Fairs; The King [James I] comes to Town; Plague and Pestilence; Civil War; Stuarts and Hanoverians; The Machine Age; Gaslight and Daddy Dunn; Trouble at 't' Mill; Benefactors; Fun and Games; World at War; Women Folk; Preston's Progress; Workaday World; British Aerospace; Leisure and the Arts; and The Quality of Life.

It began with Proud Preston's position, and described the location and accessibility of the town, including the terrible road conditions of the 1770s—'I know not the whole range of language terms sufficiently expressive to describe this infernal road [from Warrington]. Let me seriously caution all travellers to avoid it as they would the devil.' Other travellers' tales were told, and then the story of the town began. The children described the days of St Wilfrid and the origins of the lamb of Preston and the motto P.P. They portrayed the granting of royal charters and the holding of fairs and markets. The burning of the town by the Scots in 1322 was graphically depicted, with sounds of mayhem and pillage. Then followed a series of short scenes, in which the pageant of the town's history through the later medieval and Tudor periods was unrolled—the first-recorded Guild celebrations; the monasteries and their dissolution; the influence of the Puritans; and the visit of James I—including his celebrated banquet at Hoghton Tower.

War and plague were vividly brought to life—Preston was devastated by pestilence in 1630, and badly damaged in the Civil War which came only twelve years later. Roundheads and Cavaliers fought for the town, and the children demonstrated these uncivil conflicts with passion and realism. Restoration of the old order came, and then the renewed fighting between Jacobites and Hanoverians. The defiance of Preston's vicar in 1715 was shown, and 'Charlie is my darling' and the 'Skye Boat Song' were sung as the Jacobites' sojourn at Preston in 1745 was re-enacted. Now Preston became a great centre for society—children danced and sang as the elegance of the eighteenth century progressed, but their merry-making was rudely interrupted by strange noises coming from a house in Stoneygate. What was happening? Did the noises come from devils or witches, were they the work of demons and spirits? No! Richard Arkwright was at work, making his spinning jenny, and the Industrial Revolution was under way.

Cotton came to Preston. So did John Horrocks. The town was transformed. New mills, and ever larger mills, were built. Groups of children dressed as cotton operatives—first six, then twelve, then seventeen, then fifty, then eighty-five—demonstrating the expansion of the industrial might of Preston. Then they carried signs, to show the population of the town, and to demonstrate that the cotton industry had brought soaring growth—6,000 ... 12,000 ... 17,000 ... 50,000 ... 85,000 ... 96,000. The children formed into terraced streets of little houses. They showed, with great ingenuity and skill, the growth of the town from its small but not humble beginnings, to its industrial might and great size.

The great diversity and excitement, as well as the hardship and misery, of nineteenth-century Preston were revealed by the next phase of the Pageant. Daddy Dunn, the Roman Catholic priest, did much good work—helping to bring gas-lighting, founding the Savings Bank, and promoting the House of Recovery which eventually became the Royal Infirmary. Urchins from Fox Street School had their heads inspected for lice, and a lamplighter went on his rounds. Other children, working long hours in dangerous conditions in the factories and mills of Preston, joined in the 1842 riot in which five people were shot dead in Lune Street. The Cotton Famine and the Temperance Movement, the social distress and the attempts of the good and charitable to alleviate the misery—all were dramatically displayed.

Then there was light relief—the music hall. Dance routines, juggling, pierrots, and in a superb setting a scintillating scene splendidly spoken so smoothly and with such serene sublety by the master of ceremonies who talked of its 'mellifluous music, manipulative magic, magnificent maidens, multifarious movement and miscellaneous mirthfulness'. Sport was shown—Preston North End and all its rich history. There was a spontaneous round of applause on the second day when Frank Hartley interrupted the football sequence to announce that Tom Finney himself was in the audience. And then there was war—children in costume depicted marching bands of First World War soliders, and the haunting songs of that war rang out, while in the scenes showing the Second World War there were air raid sirens and the voice of Winston Churchill. Patriotic songs familiar to many—'We'll meet again' and 'The White Cliffs of Dover' were accompanied by dancing and queuing for rationed food.

The scene changed. The women of Preston's history came to the fore, among them Martha Thompson, Edith Rigby and Kathleen Ferrier. This led into the theme of Preston's Progress, and portrayals of the changes in the town since the Second World War. The coming of families from the Caribbean and Asia; the clearance of slums and building of new housing; roads and motorways and transport improvements; new shops and shopping centres; new industries and services. There was a special section devoted to the place of the sponsors, British Aerospace, in the history of the town, and to the arts and leisure facilities of Preston.

The Pageant ended with the theme 'The Quality of Life', looking at such diverse aspects as the twin towns and educational improvements, the dynamics of change in modern Preston, and the strength, numerous and sterling qualities, and enduring success of the town and its traditions. This was the final message: 'May these children inherit the same traditions, skills and courage as they face their future and may Guild 2012 ensure an even prouder Preston'. The choir sang 'We Are Proud', the song which had been specially written for the 1992 Guild by Ian Gray and Gary Cunliffe:

> We are proud
> Of the history which surrounds us
> Of the great events and names that
> Make the story of our town
> We are proud.
> To be children born of Preston
> Let us sing it clear and loud
> We are proud.
>
> This shouldn't be a thing we say
> Once in every twenty years
> When in our hearts
> We feel it ever day.

Despite the pressures on school and staff time, the Pageant of 1992 was at least comparable in scale with that held in 1972, and in some respects significantly larger. Almost four thousand children participated, from fifty-seven primary schools: of these 2,741 were involved in movement and dancing, 644 were in the choir, 125 were in the band and orchestra, and the remainder acted as stage-hands, marshals, soloists or narrators.

There had been a considerable amount of unfortunate adverse publicity before Guild Week, centred around the cost of the tickets, which was claimed to be too high—it was said that as a result parents and grandparents were being deprived of the chance to watch their children in the performance. Nevertheless, despite this and the appalling weather just before the start of the Guild, the Pageant was watched by a total of at least 13,000 people. This was almost a capacity audience—the Avenham Park arena could have accommodated about 8,000 people on each day—and the organisers felt, quite rightly, that the attendance was very gratifying.

The organisation, so careful and so meticulous over so many months, went very smoothly. The children arrived on time, and were efficiently directed and guided on entry to the arena. The arrangements for catering and costuming went very well, and all the technical organisation functioned without hitch. A particular tribute was paid to the council staff and others who had put in much extra time and effort to ensure that the arena was fit for use, and so guaranteed that the Pageant could go ahead as planned. The Guild Mayor, Councillor Harold Parker, wrote to all schools in the area thanking them warmly for their hard work and for making the Pageant such a success. He said that 'This time there were numerous problems to be overcome—not least with the weather—but the co-operation achieved by our local schools provided us with two memorable performances. The whole venture was in the best traditions of the Guild. I am conscious of the hard work and skill that went into the Pageant and you can all look back on a job very well done'.

The verdict after the performances was, like that of the Guild Mayor, unanimously favourable. Many letters were received from people who had attended the Pageant, full of praise for the way the children had coped with the difficult conditions on the Park itself, had presented and performed their parts, and had entertained their huge audience. A top television producer rang the Guild Office and left the following message: 'I just want to say what a marvellous production I saw this afternoon. I got wet but it didn't matter at all. I enjoyed it so thoroughly. I'm in awe, absolutely. I know what goes into this sort of thing and, believe me, it was marvellous. Many, many congratulations. I've seen the past two pageants and this one is better than both of them!'

An editorial leader in the *Evening Post* on Friday 4 September summed up what many people must have felt about the Pageant, and its triumphant success: 'It took just a few hours of glorious entertainment yesterday to prove beyond a shadow of a doubt that come the year 2012 the spirit of Preston Guild will be in safe hands. Those who witnessed the heart-warming schools' pageant on Avenham Park will remember all that is good about the young people of the town. From the superb music to the hundreds of colourful costumes to the infectious enthusiasm of the children—this was the tradition of the Guild encapsulated … They are the ones who in 20 years time will inherit some of the responsibility for the next Guild. Judging by what they have given to the town this week, they will not fail us.'

Honorary Freeman Tom Finney says a few words prior to switching on the Guild illuminations …

… but did not expect a slight technical hitch!
(Preston B. C.)

Chapter 7

The community events
during Guild Week

THE PROCESS whereby a celebration for the few became a festival for the many has already been described—the once-every-two-decades meeting of an exclusive organisation, with real participation only by the commercial and social elite, was changed in 1842 into a very different event. The emphasis thereafter was, increasingly, upon the participation of everybody in Preston. No longer would the pleasures of the Guild be 'tea, buns and gawping at the gentry for the people of Preston, and champagne, ices and the opera for the chosen few'. Instead, ever larger numbers of ordinary people joined in the processions and enjoyed the events and activities of the Guild. Although 'community' may be a fashionable word of the late twentieth century, the idea of 'community' involvement was already developing strongly in the Guilds of a century ago.

In 1992 the emphasis on the Guild as an event for everybody was stronger than ever before. The very theme—'A Celebration of Preston, Past, Present and Future'—points to the thinking which underlay the Guild: that it would be Preston as a whole which would be feted. The idea that the Guild glorified and praised the town is far from new—Richard Kuerden refers to it more than three hundred years ago—but in our day it has become a dominant element in the festival. The town means not only the bricks and mortar but also, of course, the townspeople, and they too were emphasised. Many speakers referred to the skills, the enterprise and the civic pride of Prestonians, and many drew particular attention to the 'Guild spirit', which had helped to make the 1992 Guild such a success and which was such a positive attribute for the future.

So the Guild of 1992 was about 'community'—the community joining in the events and activities, the community sharing the celebrations and helping its less fortunate members to play their part, the community using the Guild to build new ties and to develop existing strengths and qualities. The community events of Guild Week, with their bright, exciting and fresh appeal and their capacity crowds amply demonstrated these admirable features. Some community events are ancient—the Trades Procession is the best example—while some, such as the Community Procession which was held in 1992 for the first time, are very new. All are intrinsic to the success of the Guild, and all share the common characteristic—they are immensely enjoyable and entertaining for spectators and participants alike.

On with the lights

The rains which marred the first half of Guild Week—though without spoiling the fun for the hundreds of thousands of people who came into town to watch the processions—held off just long enough for the ceremonial switching on of the Guild illuminations. This event, which marked the beginning of the Guild Week festivities, took place outside the Harris Museum building on the evening of Friday 28 August. Preston soccer legend Tom Finney, honorary freemen of the borough and about-to-be-enrolled 1992 Guild Burgess, performed the switching-on ceremony in the presence of the Guild Mayor and Mayoress. The town centre had been fitted up with over 10,000 coloured lights, many of them thriftily reused from the previous Christmas illuminations, and some other parts of the town, such as the Lane Ends shopping centre and Plungington, were also decorated.

The switching-on ceremony was certainly not without its dramatic moments. Tom Finney spoke of his pride in being invited to perform this symbolic task in the town with which his name is so inextricably linked, and then he pulled the switch. Clouds of smoke engulfed the stage, and for several seconds nothing happened! There was a breathless hush, and then the lights flickered and came on. The crowd roared its appreciation, and all was well. Another event in the countdown to the Guild had been successfully accomplished.

Best Decorated Street Competition

The decoration of the streets of Preston to celebrate the Guild has been a popular feature of the celebrations for well over a century. The town centre has been festooned with bunting and draped with flowers, flags and banners, and special features such as triumphal arches have also been used since the early nineteenth century. The decorations in 1992 were, because of constraints of cost and safety, comparatively modest and inexpensive compared with the remarkably lavish and elaborate adornments of, for example, 1922, when every lamppost and tram standard was bedecked with artificial flowers and beautified by painted wooden panels.

Away from the town centre, however, the decorations have been of a different sort, and are in many ways more impressive. At all Guilds since the mid-nineteenth century the residents of side streets and residential roads have put in an enormous effort in time, money and patience, and have used all their creative talents and imagination to design and erect their own decorations, often in patriotic red, white and blue or—just as patriotically—the blue and white of Preston. Many streets undertake a massive communal effort at every Guild, and one of the very heartening features of the 1972 and 1992 Guilds was that where streets of houses have been replaced by flats and redevelopment schemes the same enthusiasm applied. Since 1922 the bedecking of the town has been officially encouraged by the holding of Best Decorated Street Competitions.

In 1992 Yates' Wine Lodge agreed to sponsor such a competition. It was decided that the Borough would be divided, after the entries had been received, into seven districts, together with an eighth which covered the areas outside the Preston boundary. Prizes of £100, £50, £25 and £10 were awarded for each of the eight divisions, and an overall prize of £300 was given to the Best Decorated Street in the whole of Preston. After the usual disappointing start—a feature noted at the 1952 and 1972 Guilds—almost fifty streets entered and judging (which took place in terrible weather) was arranged for Saturday and Sunday 29–30 August. The judges represented Yates', the *Lancashire Evening Post* and the Borough Council. In 1972 there had been complaints that the judging was done anonymously, so this time a high profile was achieved by the use of two vintage cars and—for some of the time—a vintage Yates' van, while streets were told in advance of the approximate time of the judges' visit. Unfortunately the timings went badly wrong in the afternoons, because too little time was allowed for visits to outlying entrants, and because the judges, to their credit, insisted on chatting with those responsible for the decorations.

The winning entry in the Best Decorated Street Competition was Marston Moor and Marston Close, Fulwood.
(Lancashire Evening Post)

The decisions were very difficult—in one area two first prizes were awarded, and when Area 8 was visited the weather was so dire that the judges awarded two £25 prizes, to Broadwood Drive and Raleigh Road, rather than trying to assess 3rd and 4th place. Mersey Street, the winner in Area 6, carried on a long Guild tradition—it had been a winner in 1952 and 1972 as well. The judges were very pleased to see entries from the outlying areas and beyond the Borough boundary, in Whittingham, Penwortham, and Walton-le-Dale.

Points were awarded for factors such as originality and novelty, colour, community involvement and relevance to the Guild, while special weight was given to areas which had serious problems of vandalism. Judging often coincided with the holding of street parties, since this was the weekend at the start of Guild Week. At Marston Moor and Marston Close in Fulwood the residents of thirty-nine houses were re-enacting the Battle of Marston Moor (1644): 'blue and white bunting decorated houses, blue and white flowers decorated bushes, hedgerows and trees and blue and white tents marked the battlefield while imposing turrets guarded the entrance'. This entry was awarded the prize for the overall winners: the residents, it was later reported, spent the £300 on a Christmas party in early December!

Street decorations were not the only adornments to the town. Many house-holders made individual efforts with garlands, bunting, flowers and flags, and some went to great lengths to make a real sensation. One of the most novel decoration schemes was that done by Joan and Lou McGurn in St George's Road. Their house was embellished with giant clowns in red, white and blue, while a clown chimney sweep emerged from the chimney pot. The house, on a busy road, was the object of much attention from startled motorists (the author of this book among them!) and Lou told the local press that 'I just hope we don't cause an accident. People in cars keep looking up at the house and not at where they are going.'

Street parties

Just as people living in side streets and suburban estates have for many years decorated their roads for the Guild, so they have also held street parties. The idea of the street party seems to have developed in tiny congested streets of terraced houses in inner urban areas during the late nineteenth century. For the great national events, such as coronations—when an extra day's holiday was granted—people would gather and hold parties in the middle of the street simply because there was nowhere else to go. There was, of course, no problem with traffic or road closures! Locally, the Guild was just such a great event, and street parties were a feature of the celebrations from 1902 and possibly earlier. By 1952 they had become a standard feature, and the idea had been carried to the newer estates and housing areas. The street parties were a practical solution to the problem of lack of space, but because they were great communal events these were times of great excitement and neighbourliness. Such parties were very enthusiastically received, and even when people had moved to more spacious surroundings the idea of a really good get-together retained its appeal.

In 1992 the street parties extended over a surprisingly long period: people were celebrating, and trying to dodge the doubtful weather, well before the Guild, during the Guild and after the Guild. During the summer the *Lancashire Evening Post* published many photographs of the merry-making in progress. Unfortunately, especially during Guild Week itself, many of the pictures and reports told a tale of deluge, dampness and destruction, as torrential rain soaked everything and everybody, and as high winds tore away at decorations. Nevertheless, with heroic determination and dedication, people carried on regardless, and some streets were fortunate in their timing and found sunshine or—at worst—showers.

There were many streets parties in areas beyond the boundary of the Borough—another indication that people who live in the wider region look to Preston as their centre and are glad to share in the excitement and spirit of the Guild. Thus, there was a party at Marina Grove, Lostock Hall, where three hundred residents 'braved torrential downpours to enjoy a treasure trail, mini-Olympics, fancy dress parade and a karaoke competition. In the evening there was a bar and disco.' At nearby Albrighton Crescent 'everything went really well

Numerous street parties were held, whatever the weather: this one was Emmanuel Street, Plungington (Lancashire Evening Post)

except for the fact that it threw it down, but nobody seemed to be put off by the rain'.

In Emmanuel Street, Plungington, a wizard, a snowman and a fairy were just some of the guests at a fancy dress party. Children and adults dressed up and enjoyed themselves, with the street decked out with flags and bunting. Sometimes a street party was held indoors: at Hargreaves Court, Ingol, dozens of pensioners celebrated with a Proud Preston cake and something good to wash it down, while at Balfour Road the rain was too heavy so the residents of the street used the nearby United Reform Church Hall. There they enjoyed the festivities until the rain stopped, at which point they went outside and had a good Lancashire hot pot supper. At Raleigh Road the position was reversed: party-goers played and danced in the rain, on the grounds that 'once they'd been soaked in one downpour they'd carry on singing in the rain', and then went indoors to the church hall for the traditional warming and filling hot pot supper.

Residents, staff and friends of the Little Sisters of the Poor Home for the Elderly enjoyed a Guild bingo competition and a party, and a barbecue rounded off the celebrations. At the Moor Lane Day Centre 160 handicapped members and visitors from Age Concern had their Guild Party on 20 August—one of the earliest parties to be held. They continued in style, however, with a 1920s' tea dance, a fashion show and the annual summer fair later in the week. On the Friday there was a special Guild Ball as the grand finale of their Guild celebrations.

The *Evening Post*'s Peter Richardson, in his irreverent diary of Guild Week events, described what happened at Cherry Close in Fulwood when the rain began: more than 100 people invaded (by invitation!) Lynn Harling's house. She was quoted as saying that 'it was an absolute riot ... All the cold food came in as well. And you should have seen the beer. Then when the band started up it was just amazing. The saxophone was terrific ... and the keyboards ... and the guitars.' The most popular number was said to be 'Bring Me Sunshine'! At Beechwood Avenue off Woodplumpton Road the rain did not matter for a different reason: one of the attractions for the children was a hosepipe fight, and everybody was soaked either by the rain or the jets of water from the hoses—and probably by both.

Markham Street, which had wonderful weather for its party, saw two hundred people celebrating for no less than thirteen hours, and at Pope Lane, Ribbleton, the party mood lasted until the early hours of the morning: one of the organisers was quoted as saying that 'We just had a really good time all day and the sun shone'. Tudor Avenue and Cairnsmore Avenue had a 'brilliant day, weather-wise and everywise', helped by the participation of a guest of honour, the Guild Mayor Harold Parker, who was revisiting the street where he was brought up. Magicians and puppet shows, fancy dress and karaoke, bagpipers and live bands, face artists and a Chippendales Contest,* commemorative mugs and George Formby impressionists ... these were just some of the street parties of '92.

---

*   Footnote for posterity: the Chippendales were a group of muscular young men, who enjoyed a considerable international popularity in the early 1990s. They provided an entertainment show which was much appreciated by (some) ladies of all ages.

The Proud Preston Exhibition (28 August–6 September)

Many events might have vied in a competition for the title 'Most Successful Feature of the 1992 Guild', and choosing the winner would have been very difficult. On the other hand, there would have been no contest in the search for the winner of the 'Most Disastrous Failure' prize: the ill-fated Proud Preston Exhibition on Moor Park, which opened, amidst much optimism, on the morning of Friday 28 August 1992, and closed, amidst much bitterness and recrimination, a week later.

The Proud Preston Exhibition was modelled on the Guild Industries Exhibition, which had been held on Moor Park during the 1972 Guild and which itself was a successor to the Trade Exhibition staged there as part of the Guild of 1952. Both of these had been extremely successful—almost 200,000 people visited the 1972 exhibition, and local industries, trade organisations and businesses found the show a very effective and rewarding way of publicising and promoting the town. The 1972 exhibition was billed as the largest event of its kind ever held outside London. On both occasions the Corporation used the event to carry out hard selling of Preston and the opportunities which it offered for investment and commercial development.

With this background it seemed obvious that a similar idea should be promoted for the 1992 Guild. As in 1972 the Borough Council did not want to manage and organise the exhibition itself. Instead, the Proud Preston event was promoted by John O'Brien Events Management Ltd of Blackpool. During the previous year handbills and advertising encouraged potential exhibitors and traders to put the date in their diaries: 'Don't Miss It! The next one doesn't take place until the year 2012'. The show, it was said, would be a major attraction—'over 300,000 visitors anticipated'. Subsequent promotional literature was even more enthusiastic: 'Over 200,000 visitors in 1972, How many in '92? Estimated at over 350,000' and 'An International Show for the Price of a Provincial One' were among the claims made.

The literature which emphasised the potential market of the exhibition pointed to Preston's centrality within the North West's motorway network, and claimed, with wild inaccuracy, that 'The population of Lancashire, Cheshire and the High Peak area of Derbyshire is almost seventy million'—it is in fact almost seven million! The exhibition, it was said, would represent all sectors of the economy—manufacturing, industrial, commercial, the utilities, wholesaling, retailing, travel, tourism and general trade. The Guild would bring many hundreds of thousands of extra visitors, beyond the numbers which would be expected at a normal exhibition of this type and, the promoters promised, 'no event in the past 20 years will compare'.

A very large number of spaces at the 25-acre Proud Preston Exhibition site were booked—almost two hundred, ranging from great multi-national firms to small family businesses. Exhibitors represented an extraordinary variety of business, from Balmoral Lingerie Ltd and Porcupine Crafts, via The Missions to

(Photo, Preston B. C.)

Not everything about the Proud Preston Exhibition was as happy as these pictures might suggest. (Lancashire Evening Post)

Seamen, Midland Bank Group, British Aerospace and British Gas North Western, to Lancashire Family Health Service Authority, Champ Chicken Co Ltd and the Dukes Theatre, Lancaster. Three huge exhibition halls, designed with large span aluminium frameworks, were imported from the Netherlands because there was none large enough in the United Kingdom. The event was to be accompanied by a great diversity of family entertainments and attractions, making it a real day out for everybody: there were to be military displays, a funfair, parachute displays, motorcycle stuntmen, an 'It's A Knock Out Contest', clowns and other circus performers, musical events and sideshows.

Almost up to the last minute there was great confidence that the show would be an outstanding success. The Guild Mayor, Harold Parker, interviewed just before the opening, said that 'The small band of medieval merchants who celebrated the first Preston Guild would be flabbergasted by what is happening here. The Proud Preston exhibition will show just how far the town has come and what has made Preston the administrative capital of Lancashire and one of the North West's biggest success stories'. Unfortunately the organisers and promoters had, it would seem, left out of their reckoning two crucial factors, one of which was outside their control, but the other of which was their own decision—the weather and the cost of admission.

As has been indicated, the weather during Guild Week was exceedingly bad, with very high winds and torrential rain. Many of the week's events in the town suffered to some extent, although the resilience of spectators was remarkable, but the weather had a disastrous effect upon the Proud Preston Exhibition. It was a calamity in two ways: first, it must have deterred many potential visitors from coming in the first place—Moor Park, although in many ways a very good venue for large-scale events, is somewhat distant from the centre, and it would appear that many people decided to stay in town, watch a procession or two, and then go home, rather than go on to the Park.

Just as serious was the combined effect of torrential and waterlogged ground after the tramping of feet and the moving of heavy machinery and vehicles. Even before the opening there were serious worries about the condition of the ground, and when the time came for the official inauguration of the exhibition some parts of the site were already becoming a quagmire. Contractors had to be brought in to dump many tons of shale, in order to create dry raised causeways through the mud. Despite this, within a day large areas had turned into thick churned-up mud, with great ruts and with their turf covering totally destroyed. The result was that visitors and exhibitors alike were splashing and squelching through a muddy sea: the damage to the ground cover in the park was very considerable.

It was, therefore, in one sense almost a blessing that so few people actually visited the exhibition. Had the anticipated crowds of a quarter of a million and more been tramping across the site for ten days, the nightmare of mud and damage can only be imagined. In the event, attendances were pitifully low in comparison with the pre-Guild estimates. There was a lengthy controversy in the local press and elsewhere about the reason for the poor attendance, and the accusing finger was most frequently pointed at the high price for admission.

In 1972 adults were charged 30p and children 15p: in 1992 the entrance price was no less than £10—which, even allowing for twenty years of inflation, was an extremely high figure for an event which depended for its success on the attracting of large numbers of ordinary visitors. Only three days after the opening the *Lancashire Evening Post* reported that the exhibition had 'been branded a disaster by furious exhibitors who are threatening to pull out ... Many of the stands outside have disappeared, one exhibitor in the main exhibition marquee packed up last night and several more are planning to cut their losses and leave'. The entrance prices were slashed, to £1 per family and 50p per adult, with free admission for children, but the damage had been done. Although the weather improved during the second half of the week, and the drastic price reductions did bring encouraging attendances from the Tuesday onwards, the very bad publicity and ill-feeling engendered by the first three days could not be erased.

In the aftermath of the failure of the exhibition, and the serious damage to parts of Moor Park, the Borough Council required the contractors to repair the damage and to pay outstanding bills. As the event had been a commercial concern and entirely the responsibility of the promoting firm, the Borough was owed money for the use of the park and for ancillary services provided. This totalled £56,000, while a further bill of tens of thousands of pounds was due for the restoration work. Unfortunately, as a direct result of the disastrous financial performance of the event, in March 1993 the promoting firms were declared insolvent: at the time of writing (May 1993) the situation regarding liability and payment has not been resolved.

The Riversway Festival

Although the 'Proud Preston' exhibition was unquestionably the biggest disaster of Guild week, the 'fire and water' events at the dock and surrounding area, billed as the Riversway Festival, came in for more than their fair share of problems. The wind and rain meant that several of the attractions were more than a little weatherbeaten, while the cancellation of the music and fireworks spectacular on the evening of Sunday 30 August provoked a good deal of criticism. The weather on that day was particularly bad, and the band of the Royal Marines Comman-

Despite some very bad weather, the Riversway Festival, with the visit of the tall ships, made good use of one of Preston's finest assets, the dock.
(Preston B. C.)

dos decided that it would not hold its planned concert. One correspondent to the *Evening Post* wrote that she and 'hundreds if not thousands of suitably dressed ticket holders assembled to participate in the first great extravaganza of Guild week ... only to discover that it had been cancelled'. She asked whether the Royal Marines had been 'deterred by a little adverse weather [or had] a few "wimps" decided that we would be afraid of a little wind and rain'.

Nevertheless, there was much to enjoy and much that was exciting at the Festival, which was intended to remind visitors of Preston's long nautical tradition, and to point to its future role as a centre of water-based leisure activities. The Festival also publicised the ongoing redevelopment and renewal of the dock estate. Tall ships, yachts, canal barges and power boats transformed the marina, and there was colour, bustle and noise. The two tall ships had come straight from Liverpool, where the 1992 Tall Ships Race (from Seville to the Mersey via Boston) had just finished. They were *Greater Manchester Challenge* and *Francis Drake*, which belong to the Ocean Youth Club and are normally used for adventure and training courses in the Irish Sea. Many people came to view them as they were moored alongside the Waterfront pub at the western end of the dock.

Another attraction was the *MV Fitzcarraldo*, the converted Norwegian ferry used for the 'Walk the Plank' performances described in a previous chapter. More than thirty canal narrow boats had been brought to the dock by low-loader and crane: they are unable to use the Ribble, because it is a tidal river, and the event had the additional benefit of publicising the Ribble Link project, which aims to make a navigable connection between the river and the Lancaster Canal. The motor launch *Preston Puffin* gave regular trips around the dock basin and along the Ribble.

The visit of the Uzorochye Folk Group in Guild Week

In July 1990 Councillor Ronald Marshall had suggested that a Russian folk dance group from the town of Tver, one hundred miles from Moscow, might be invited to Preston for the Guild celebrations. They had previously performed in Glasgow during the festivals which celebrated its term as European City of Culture, and they were well known on the continent. Making contact with the Uzorochye Folk Group was no easy task, but a formal invitation was issued in August 1991, and subsequently accepted. In February 1992, however, the Group was forced—with great regret—to cancel its acceptance because the loss in value of the rouble meant that the air fare had risen thirty times in the previous month—it now equalled five years' salary for the musical director of the group! Hurried efforts were made to try to salvage the tour, and eventually local sponsors in Russia raised the necessary sum to cover the air fares.

The visit was therefore able to go ahead. The Uzorochye Folk Group arrived in Preston, via Manchester Airport, on 28 August, and during Guild Week gave more than twenty outdoor performances in the town centre, at Riversway and at Moor Park. They also provided deeply impressive and highly acclaimed contributions to the Mayoral Ball, the Reception for Overseas Visitors and the

Carnival Ball, and took great pleasure in being part of the first ever Preston Guild Community Procession. As guests of the Council they were able to watch the International Police Bands spectacular in the Guild Hall, and the Firework and Laser and Jazz concerts in Avenham Park. Their business sponsors, who travelled with them, took the opportunity to discuss commercial matters with representatives of the Preston & District Chamber of Trade and Lancashire Enterprises Ltd. The visit was a great success, and added an unexpected and colourful dimension to an already very cosmopolitan and international event.

'My Fair Lady'

The preliminary plans for the Guild included an ambitious open-air production of the musical 'Oliver', to be performed in Avenham Park as a collaborative effort by local amateur dramatic, operatic and musical comedy societies. Among the producers were to have been some of those involved in the very successful production of 'Merrie England' at the 1972 Guild. As discussion proceeded, however, it became clear to the Borough Council that the cost of staging the project would be excessive, and the Council was therefore reluctantly compelled to drop the idea. The Preston Musical Comedy Society then came to the rescue, and decided that 'My Fair Lady', performed in the Charter Theatre, would be an excellent alternative—and the Society was proved right.

Many months were spent in planning and rehearsing the show—including the auditioning of no fewer than fourteen would-be Eliza Doolittles! The work was tiring, but well worth while, for the audience on the opening night, Saturday 29 August, was one of the warmest and most appreciative that the members of the Society had ever known. Just as rewarding was the fact that there were capacity audiences at the Charter Theatre every night throughout Guild Week.

Cliff Bell from the *Lancashire Evening Post* wrote that the audience 'loved every minute of this essentially English musical ... Every member of the cast worked hard to ensure this was a highly polished production that shone with a professional glow. The stunning costumes and sets and, of course, the wonderful score were the perfect backdrop for the action on stage'. He particularly commended Alban Dorning as Henry Higgins and Nicholas Tomlinson as Colonel Pickering, and described Pamela Heywood (Eliza Doolittle) as 'outstanding. She has a terrific singing voice and made the transition from lavender girl to lady with consummate ease'. Dean Taylor, as Eliza's coalman father, 'almost stole the show'.

Open Week at the Sessions House (31 August to 4 September)

The Sessions House is one of Preston's finest buildings, and because of its very prominent position between Lancaster Road and the Market Square, opposite the Harris Building, it is a particularly important feature of the streetscape of the town centre. It was designed by Henry Littler, the County Architect, and was completed in 1903: the present Town Hall, opened in 1933, was designed to blend in with it. As its contribution to the Guild the Preston Incorporated Law Society arranged with the administrator of the Sessions House for the opening of the building to the public during Guild Week.

The Sessions House had never before been open to the public, in all its eighty-nine-year history, and so Guild Week provided a unique opportunity to see the interior. The public were able to visit the public assembly hall, two courts, the magistrates' room, seven cells, the barristers' library and robing room, and the jury assembly room. A major exhibition of archives and artifacts had been prepared with the assistance of the staff of the Lancashire Record Office and the Harris Museum. The display contained, with many other items, fascinating documents, which included the charter of incorporation granted to Preston by Elizabeth I in 1566, and the charter granted by Elizabeth II in 1974; legal robes; the notorious 'Black Cap'; and a scold's or gossip's bridle. Conducted tours were given, and a very detailed guidesheet, in the shape of a legal brief, was produced. There were some 11,500 visitors, and £1,200 was raised in donations on behalf of the Catholic Caring Services charity. All those involved considered that opening the building had been a tremendous success, and the visitors were invariably enthusiastic.

Guild Roadshow (Monday 31 August)

One of the problems which had faced the organisers of the Guild was the choice of a major event for Avenham Park on August Bank Holiday Monday, which was the first day of the official Guild celebrations although of course well into the less formal period of festivity. Several possible options had to be ruled out, either because of cost and the difficulty of marketing them, or because they were too similar to other events which had already been scheduled. It was not until the beginning of August that the final decisions were taken, and at this point it was agreed that a free event—which would have a popular appeal, and would include some form of illumination show—would be most suitable. This meant that there would be no revenue from ticket sales, and there was no time to attract any form of sponsorship, while the period for organising and advertising the event would also be very limited.

It was only in mid-August that Intrak, a local sound and light company, were engaged to provide a roadshow-style entertainment, with live acts, prizes and give-aways. Laser Dynamics, who were scheduled to provide the laser show at the Firework and Laser Concert on 30 August, agreed to extend their contract to include a performance on the following evening. The event was then publicised by posters, handbills, press releases and some newspaper advertising, with the emphasis being on its popular character and the fact that it was free! The eventual response was very rewarding, and a sizeable crowd had gathered even before the gates opened at 6.30 p.m.

Before the main show began a roadshow DJ played music and ran competitions for children to win Guild souvenirs. The programme for the evening included Charlie Ale, a northern comedian who according to some accounts unfortunately met with a somewhat mixed response—it was felt that it was difficult for him to communicate his act to a large, widely spread and highly informal audience. The roadshow took over again until Sinitta, a nationally known singer, arrived. She sang a reprise of some of her hits, including 'So Macho', but although this was very well received she was on stage for only fifteen minutes, and this, not unexpectedly, caused a good deal of disappointment.

The laser show which followed was highly effective, and many people had turned up later in the evening specially to watch this part of the show. After this some of the crowd began to drift away, as families with children went home, but Dreamland, a popular local band, played to an enthusiastic young audience while the laser show continued. The weather remained fine throughout the evening, and the organisers were delighted with the large number of families and young people who came. Police estimates later suggested that about 12,000 people had come to the park at some stage during the event, and this was an excellent response considering the short time available for planning and publicity—undoubtedly the fact that the weather was fair and the event was free drew many people to the park to see what was going on.

Guild Concert (Monday 31 August)

The Royal Liverpool Philharmonic Orchestra has for many years held a regular Preston concert series, but on Monday 31 August the Orchestra gave a special Guild concert, which was 'a dazzling centrepiece to the Guild's classical offerings'. It was centred around Beethoven's Ninth Symphony, and surprisingly enough this was the first occasion on which this had been performed at the Guild Hall. The *Evening Post*'s reviewer, Muireall Kelt, was full of praise: 'this would have been enough to make it a special occasion, but the actuality soared over this mere historic footnote … Under the sensitive baton of Edward Warren, the RLPO musicians, the soloists Suzanne Murphy, Catherine Wyn-Rogers, Ian Caley and Robert Hayward plus the combined voices of the Preston Cecilian Choral Society and the Preston Orpheus Choir brought out the full magnificence of this work … The Tchaikovsky 1812 at the Avenham Park concert on Saturday, accompanied by fireworks, may have been voted the event of the Guild [but] Beethoven achieved the same effect without the fireworks.'

Jazz on the Park (Tuesday 1 September)

The impressive range of Guild events held in Avenham Park included two outstanding concerts—Jazz on the Park, on the Tuesday of Guild Week (1 September) and Opera on the Park on the following evening. Both brought top-quality performers to Preston, and each was a triumphant success—despite the weather! Jazz on the Park, which was managed by Performing Arts

Jazz on the Park'—the 'Best of British Jazz' entertain a rain-ished crowd, many of whom wear Guild poly-ponchos. Preston B. C.)

Management Ltd, attracted an audience of just under 3,000, and the entertainment offered was considered to be on a par with that of a major national jazz festival. The evening was divided into three segments of fifty minutes each, with short intervals between.

The first segment was entitled 'The Best of British Jazz', and the performers were a group of some of this country's leading musicians, brought together for the occasion: Kenny Baker on trumpet, Don Lusher on trombone, Lenny Bush on base, the alto saxophone of Roy Willox, the piano of Brian Lemon, and Jack Parnell on drums. They combined effortlessly to give a vigorous performance 'which belied the age of the band members'. At 8.30 p.m. Marian Montgomery, accompanied by the Laurie Holloway Trio, appeared on stage. Her warm personality and relaxed style quickly produced a close rapport with an appreciative audience, and she exhibited her famous versatility of style, from honky-tonk to mournful blues. She sang a wide range of songs including classics such as 'I've got you under my skin' and 'I've got a right to sing the blues', and the *Evening Post* reporter described her as 'the vintage wine [who] uncorked her voice which has kept her at the top of the jazz versatility stakes since her career began in the early 1960s'.

For the third section of the concert the performers were the celebrated Humphrey Lyttleton and his band, complemented by the mellow jazz singing of Helen Shapiro. Together they performed a selection of songs, many by Duke Ellington: the band comprised Kathy Stobart (saxophone), Alan Barnes (clarinet), Pete Strange (trombone), Stan Greig (piano), Paul Bridge (bass) and Adrian MacIntosh (drums). After the concert Humphrey Lyttleton and Helen Shapiro took time to autograph cassettes of their music and to meet their many fans—who had had a marvellous evening at a superb concert. John Lawrence, in the *Evening Post*, had one word for it: 'intoxicating'.

The Trades Procession (Wednesday 2 September)

To many in the past the Trades Procession has seemed the highpoint of the Guild. Although much altered in detail, it is the direct descendant of the first processions which appear in the documentary record of the Guild, for it was during those that the traders, craftsmen and merchants of the town walked through the streets, carrying symbols and emblems of their trades and accompanied by the officials and members of the Borough Council, to indicate the predominant place which the Guild exercised in the commercial life of Preston. Looking even further back into the history of the Preston Guild Merchant, it was for the trades of the town that the Guild was established over eight centuries ago, and so it can plausibly be argued that their place in the Guild celebrations is the oldest of all.

During the late eighteenth century the character of the Trades Procession began to alter. It lost its semi-civic status—the participation of the Guild Mayor and the element of civic ceremonial were gradually transferred to the opening day procession, which became an overtly civic event. Increasingly, participation in the Trades Procession was limited to the traders themselves, together with the commercial and business interests of the town. Some of the old-style traders still walked—the butchers, the bakers, the carpenters—but newer industries and crafts, such as coachmaking and printing, were also represented.

Perhaps because they now enjoyed a relatively greater prominence in the processions—they were no longer overshadowed by the Guild Mayor in his finery and the civic regalia in all its gold and silver glory—the different trades began to be more imaginative and enterprising in their contributions. Whereas hitherto there had simply been groups of men, walking or marching side by side and carrying trade badges, from 1762 onwards the tailors, then the weavers, and then the other trades of the town began to prepare tableaux, and to carry them on the distant ancestors of today's floats—wooden platforms borne on the shoulders

Watching the Trades Procession: the Ringway car park is not a beautiful building, but it certainly helped to keep some people dry! (Preston Citizen)

of several strong men. The 1762 tailors' tableau of Adam and Eve (the first people who wore clothes!) set a precedent which was quickly to transform the procession and the Guild itself.

In 1802, for the first time, the cotton industry and the mechanisation of production were represented in the Trades Procession, the great cotton magnate John Horrocks having spared no expense to ensure that his workforce and his business enterprise made the greatest possible public relations impact. The growth of the industry eventually resulted in the separation of the textile trades to form a procession in its own right, one which before long outgrew the 'all the rest of the trades procession': the spectacularly long and impressive Textile Processions of 1902 and 1922 were the culmination of this process. In 1952, after the dramatic and harrowing collapse of the cotton industry, the pattern of a single Trades Procession was resumed, and so it has remained.

The crucial role which this procession has always had in the Guild festivities is reflected in its position within Guild Week—on the morning of the Wednesday, in the middle of the week just as it has always been a central feature of the celebrations. Historically the three key events have been the Opening Court on the Monday, the Trades Procession on the Wednesday, and the Adjournment of the Court on the Saturday. The Trades Procession has also been the largest, longest and most ambitious of the processions, demonstrating the significance of the Guild in the economy of the town—and the commercial and industrial diversity and strength of Preston. In hard times as well as good times the procession has been symbolic of the resilience, enterprise and hard work of Preston and its inhabitants, and at Guild after Guild these themes have been reiterated and reinforced. During the Guild of 1992—which was held at a time of severe economic difficulty and traumatic retrenchment within Preston—the same message was emphasised.

The planning of the 1992 Trades Procession began in June 1990, when an organising committee was formed at a meeting in the Town Hall. The representatives on the committee were:

> David Rowlands, Leyland DAF and Central & West Lancashire Chamber of Commerce Chairman, 1992
> John Cooper, St George's Shopping Centre
> Robert Danielak, GMB Clothing and Textile Section (Preston and Chorley branch)
> Peter Butterworth, Building Employers' Confederation
> Gordon Eccles
> Katie Eccles (Committee Administrator)
> David Duckworth, Textile Manufacturers' Association
> Corrina Eaves, Preston Trades Council
> J. E. Evetts, N.W. Lancashire Engineering Employers Ass.
> Fred Heyworth, A.E.E.U.
> Sheila Slater, U.S.D.A.W.
> Stephen Smith, Preston Trades Council
> Susan Vendy, Preston Trades Union Council
> Peter Vickers, Preston Trades Union Council
> Supt. Gary Price, Lancashire Constabulary
> Martin Haworth, Guild Co-ordinator
> Bob Cunningham, Preston Borough Council

The closing date for applications for entry in the procession was 31 October 1991, and entry fees were set in order to defray the high cost of hiring military and other bands, an essential part of the great entertainment value of the Trades Procession. Companies with over 50 employees paid £250, employers' organisations and smaller companies paid £100, and trade unions and non-VAT registered companies paid £50. A souvenir programme was commissioned, and funded entirely by advertising revenue, and woven lapel badges were distributed free to all the 3,000 participants in the procession. By the time Guild Week began sponsorship had in fact been obtained for most of the bands in the procession, and in consequence the high costs which had been feared did not materialise. This meant that after paying for all the costs of staging the event the Committee had a considerable financial surplus, which was donated to a range of local charities at a reception held at the Town Hall on 25 November.

The Trades Procession took place in very bad weather: there was a strong wind, and at times the rain fell heavily. Nevertheless it was a great success, and the bad weather did not prevent many thousands of people from lining the streets along the processional route, and filling to capacity the grandstand seating which was provided at strategic points. A total of 123 firms and organisations took part, with 148 floats, twenty bands and 1,200 walking participants, all led by the Band of the Royal Marines. A list of the firms and organisations which participated in

...nard Watson (decorators) in the ...des Procession.
...ncashire Evening Post)

the 1992 Trades Procession is given in Appendix 12 of this book. It was estimated that between 200,000 and 250,000 people watched the procession, and the *Evening Post* reported that the 'rain-swept streets of Preston were alive with the sound of laughter and music as the Preston Guild Trades Procession snaked four miles through the town … people braved the wet to cheer on the colourful floats which represented every facet of trade and commerce in the town'.

Many of the floats produced great rounds of cheering and applause—especially those with a witty message. The staff of the Inland Revenue, Preston, were dressed in striped shirts, gloves and masks, and carried swag bags, while above their float was a banner which proclaimed 'Stop Organised Crime, Abolish the Inland Revenue': this was much applauded by the over-taxed multitude! CCA Stationery in Fulwood had a 'Christmas Comes Early' theme, with Santa Claus

Preston and District Fruit and Potato Merchants.
(Lancashire Evening Post)

British Telecom workers demonstrate other skills.
(Preston B. C.)

on a sledge with a reindeer, and a large snowman. This publicised 'Personally Printed Christmas Cards'. The float entered by HM Prison Service (Preston) included examples of old-fashioned prison uniforms, and a treadmill. Many firms chose the opportunity to publicise their international associations—Marks and Spencer, for example, had staff dressed in traditional costumes of the other countries across the world in which the company has stores. Others, proud of having survived over many decades, included 'period' costumes—with the bizarre hairstyles and strange clothes of the time of the 1972 Guild much in evidence!

Dutton Forshaw had a superb series of vintage and veteran cars, including a Rolls Royce Silver Shadow, while the fire brigade had a horse-drawn fire engine of the late nineteenth century. Two of the outstanding floats were from Plumbs, the household furnishings specialists. One was bedecked as a Roman temple lavishly provided with draperies, curtains, cushions, chairs and cloth-draped pillars. Toga-clad ladies were escorted by legionaries. In the other float a fairground scene was shown, with a merry-go-round for children, and people clad from head to foot in furnishing fabrics!

The range of industries, commercial concerns and public services represented was remarkable. The County Council, the University of Central Lancashire and the Royal Mail, the armed forces, window and double-glazing firms, retailers such as Marks and Spencer and C&A, building societies and trade unions, GEC Alsthom and the Carlova School of Dancing, the Forte Crest Hotel and the Prison Service, Peter Craig catalogue shopping and Red Rose Radio, UCI cinemas and Lanfina Bitumen: heavy industries to small firms, international retailers to local stores—the variety was impressive, the ingenuity and cleverness of the float themes equally so. The rain, wind and dullness of the day could not dampen the spirits of those watching and those participating. As always, the bands and musicians between and on the floats attracted much attention, while sometimes there were singers. The *Evening Post* interviewed eighty-three-year-old Bob Anderton, of Avenham Court, who had been to four Guilds: 'I was a stiltwalker at the 1922 Guild as a boy—but I'm just as excited about today's procession as I was all those years ago'.

Opera on the Park (Wednesday 2 September)

The final concert in the Avenham Park series was Opera on the Park, held on Wednesday 2 September. This, too, was managed by Performing Arts Management Ltd, and they conducted all the negotiations with the orchestra, soloists and choir. The aim was to provide a varied and interesting programme of favourite pieces from opera, including arias, tenor solos and choruses, against the background of special illuminations and lighting effects in a magnificent natural arena.

The orchestra was the Royal Liverpool Philharmonic, which has for many years been a regular visitor to Preston, and whose Guild Hall concert season is a highlight of the local musical calendar. The 'Liverpool Phil' has a growing international stature, and it proved to be the ideal choice for the event, and very popular with the large audience. The choir of over 200 singers was made up primarily of the members of the Preston Opera Group, supported by other local singers recruited for the occasion. The boys' chorus was provided by pupils of Kirkham Grammar School and choristers from Broughton parish church. The chorus conductors were F. W. Salter and J. Catterall, LRAM.

All the soloists were professional singers, and two of them—the tenors John Winfield and Ian Caley—were born in Preston, which was particularly appropriate for this very special occasion. The third tenor was the Finn, Seppo Ruohonen. The fourth soloist was the world-famous soprano Sarah Walker, CBE, a singer with immense experience and a vast repertoire, who enjoys great critical acclaim, and is now nationally celebrated for her sensational theatrical performance at the Last Night of the Proms. Criticism was levelled at the organisers for their choice of soloists: Muireall Kelt, reviewing the event in the *Lancashire Evening Post*, said that 'there seemed to be an imbalance ... one female to three men, and all the latter tenors. One longed for a baritone or bass for contrast'. She did admit that it might have been something other than the singers which detracted from her pleasure—'I know that the three famous tenors, Pavarotti, Carreras and Domingo, did brilliantly at that famous Roman concert, so perhaps the lack of that balmy Italian weather dampened one's enjoyment'.

The programme is given below:

Bizet	*March* from Carmen (Orchestra, Chorus, Children's Chorus)
Bizet	*Habanera* from Carmen (Sarah Walker and Chorus)
Bizet	*Flower Song* from Carmen (Ian Caley)
Bizet	*Danse Boheme* from Carmen (Sarah Walker)
Puccini	*Recondita Armonia* from Tosca (Seppo Ruohonen)
Puccini	*E Lucenvan le Stelle* from Tosca (Seppo Ruohonen)
Puccini	*Agnus Dei* from Messi di Gloria (Children's Chorus)
Verdi	*Act IV, Scene 1* from Macbeth (Ian Caley and Chorus)
Verdi	*Act IV, Finale* from Macbeth (John Winfield, Ian Caley and Chorus)
Interval	
Verdi	*Overture* from Sicilian Vespers (Orchestra)
Verdi	*Prologue Finale* from Attila (John Winfield and Chorus)
Verdi	*Hebrew Slaves Chorus* from Nabucco (Chorus)
Saint-Saens	*Softly Awakes* from Samson and Delilah (Sarah Walker)
Mozart	*Dies Bildnis ist Bezaubernd Schön* from The Magic Flute (Ian Caley)
Mascagni	*Intermezzo* from Cavalleria Rusticana (Chorus)
Puccini	*Nessun Dorma* from Turandot (Seppo Ruohonen)
Lehar	*Romance* from Merry Widow (John Winfield)
Lehar	*Vilja's Aria* from Merry Widow (Sarah Walker and Chorus)

Lehar　　　*Waltz* from Merry Widow (Seppo Ruohonen, Sarah Walker and Chorus).

The event required an exceptional level of organisation, because there were over three hundred participants, and backstage facilities were therefore heavily congested. The instruments arrived by truck during the morning, and were set out, with the stage furniture, as quickly as possible, before the arrival of the performers which began in mid-afternoon. Rehearsals began at 3.00 p.m. and continued with only a short break for three hours, the gates opened at 7.00 p.m., and the performance began at 8.00 p.m.

The soloists were all in outstanding form, and the lighting was used to dramatic effect—for example in 'Nessun Dorma', when skytracker lighting lit up the heavens. During his scene from 'Macbeth', Ian Caley was joined by his brother Stuart, a member of the chorus, emphasising the Preston connection, while Sarah Walker's celebrated rendering of 'Rule Britannia' brought the flavour of the Royal Albert Hall and the Proms to the evening.

The audience—2,833 people— was, unfortunately, rather smaller than had been expected, although still a very satisfactory number. The reason for the reduced attendance was probably the terrible weather which had afflicted the Wednesday of Guild Week. It had rained heavily for much of the morning, while the Trades Procession was in progress and, although the afternoon had seen an improvement, conditions began to deteriorate during the evening. At times the combination of heavy rain and strong blustery winds had such a deleterious effect that the concert was in danger of being halted. The wind drove the rain across the stage, and the musicians became concerned in case water damaged their instruments. In the event, the concert was completed as planned but by the end

A rainswept audience enjoy the performance of internationally known opera singer, Sarah Walker. (Lancashire Evening Post)

the weather was so appalling that the conductor decided against performing an encore. The orchestra, soloists and chorus received enthusiastic applause from a weather-beaten and battered audience, and the evening was generally regarded as a musical triumph, as well as a triumph over adversity!

The Guild Community Procession (3 September)

Of all the new features of the 1992 Guild the most important—and the one which, because of its success, is certain to be repeated in the Guild of 2012 and its successors—was the Guild Community Procession, held on Thursday 3 September. Just as the Guild of 1842 saw the first procession by schoolchildren and the churches, and so dramatically widened the role and relevance of the Guild, so the 1992 Guild will be seen as the one in which the community as a whole, and in particular its many voluntary, charitable and 'grassroots' organisations had a chance to participate in one of the formal public events.

In 1990, during the early stages of the planning of the Guild, the Preston Consultative Committee for Ethnic Minority Groups met Guild officials at the Town Hall. The Senior Guild Co-ordinator emphasised that the Borough Council wanted to see the ethnic minorities within the town play a full part in the Guild celebrations, and he mentioned in particular the Ethnic Minority Communities Procession, which was already being planned for 3 September. It was decided that a Guild (Ethnic Minorities) Advisory Group should be formed, to develop ideas and help to arrange participation of the ethnic communities in

The first-ever Community Procession was an occasion of colour, noise, fun and excitement, with Preston's ethnic minority communities participating fully. (Preston B. C.)

*The Community Procession also demonstrated the marvellous community spirit which was typical of the Guild.
(Lancashire Evening Post)*

the Guild events. Dr A. K. Chatterjee was elected chairman, Mr R. Thomas vice-chairman, and Miss I. Merrifield as Secretary.

There was extensive discussion over the next few weeks, and it became clear that the ethnic minority communities within the town did not wish to be 'segregated' in this special way but, rather, wanted to be seen as an integral part of the community as a whole. The decision was therefore taken to change the title, and the emphasis, of the planned procession: it was renamed the Guild Community Procession, and all community groups and organisations were invited to participate. The response was enthusiastic and encouraging. Many local organisations expressed a willingness to join in, and they were drawn from a very wide range of backgrounds and had a great diversity of roles and functions. This variety was seen as a particularly strong point in the planning of the procession.

The essence of the Community Procession was to be colour, fun, music and drama, with the participants invited to show as much imagination and make as much of an impact as possible. Over 2,000 people took part in the procession itself, led by the Mounted Police, the Town Crier (Mike Chapman), Miss Preston Guild 1972 (Karen Mortenson Fowler), Miss Preston Guild 1992 (Hazel Taylor) and Little Miss Preston Guild (Rachael Burke). To add to the noise and excitement, eleven bands were involved: the King's Own Scottish Borderers, the St Anne's Pipe Band, the Longridge Band, the Nat West Jazz Band, the Red Rose Band, the Freckleton Band, the Cologne Military Band, the Blackpool Brass Band, the Uzorochye Folk Group, the St Matthew's Church Lads Brigade Band, and the Preston District Scout Band.

Some commercial firms and businesses asked if they might participate in the procession, and this was resisted by the organising committee at first. Subsequently such applicants were admitted on the understanding that they would have to pay entry charges, which were the same as those levied upon participants in the Trades Procession. In all, seventy-eight organisations participated, involving eighty-two vehicles and 1,766 walkers, together with horses and cyclists. The Guild Queens travelled in an open carriage loaned by the Lancashire Carriage Collection from Rochdale. Sponsors for the event were Preston Bus, Radio Lancashire and Post Office Counters Ltd. A special medal, showing the lamb and flag crest and legend 'Preston Guild 1992' on one side, and inscribed 'Participant in the Inaugural Community Procession 3rd September 1992' on the other, was produced to mark the historic event, and was sold to subscribers.

The Guild Mayor, in his introductory message printed in the programmes for the Community Procession, noted the way in which the event represented, 'probably more than any other … you, the people of Preston'. He was heartened to see so many people participating, and looked forward to 'that uniquely colourful carnival atmosphere with members of the Asian, African, Afro-Caribbean and Chinese communities taking part'. The organisations which joined included, taking a random sample, the National Childbirth Trust, Woodcraft Folk, Preston Stroke Club, Ribbleton Hall High School, Tokyo Jo's Discotheque, Preston Muslim Forum, Ristorante Fossalto, Chinese Community, Preston and District Samaritans, and Heartbeat NW Cardiac Centre.

The range of themes and styles, of costumes, float decorations, dancing, music and entertainment, was immense. There were Hare Krishna followers playing traditional cymbals, Hindu Stick Dancers, nursery children dressed as teddy bears, brilliantly painted Chinese banners, Scottish pipers in full regalia, penny-farthing riders and baton-twirling majorettes. Women from the Hindu community, dressed in the finest saris, carried silver jars (specially imported from India) on their heads—one of the women, Pusspa Patel, explained that the jars were a symbol of good luck, and that by carrying them in the procession they hoped to bring good fortune to all the people of Preston.

A remarkable feature of the Community Procession was the interest—and the participants—which it attracted from outside the Borough of Preston. Organisations from 'outside' which were present included Chorley and South Ribble Health Authority, Leyland Cricketers Morris Dancers, Brownedge St Mary's High School, Bamber Bridge Girl Guides and South Ribble Borough Council, as that much-less-historic authority from across the river carried its message into the heart of enemy territory! The way in which the Guild drew interest, enthusiasm and participation from beyond the boundaries of the Borough is a clear reflection of Preston's place as a sub-regional capital, and of the way in which citizens of neighbouring districts look to Preston as the natural focus for the area. Their involvement in so many Guild activities was particularly welcome.

The development of a completely new procession was a major triumph of organisation, and it is certain that future Preston Guilds will include this feature. It was a huge success, and thoroughly enjoyed by participants and spectators alike. The procession was colourful, entertaining and attractive, and successfully allowed many sections of the town's community who did not fit into the other, traditional, Guild events to be full participants. That does not mean that it was a 'second-best'—rather, it was the logical culmination of a century and a half of evolution, in which the scope of the Guild had progressively been widened to include new and different elements of Preston and its people. In this way it fits perfectly into the long historical development of the Guild, and 1992 will be seen, by future historians, as the year when that development reached a new stage.

Military Open Day (5 September)

A Military Open Day and Beating the Retreat Ceremony was held at Fulwood Barracks on Saturday 5 September. The attractions included six bands, helicopter and parachute displays, and aerial slide and assault course, and—the weather being bright and sunny—over 16,000 people visited the Barracks. Some of the latest British Army equipment and weaponry was on display, and there was a Search and Rescue Helicopter display, a demonstration of martial prowess by the Royal Marines Unarmed Combat team, flight simulators, a Scorpion Armoured Reconnaisance Vehicle, and—in a rather less military vein—morris dancers and a children's funfair.

The highlight of the day was the hour-long Beating the Retreat ceremony, with the massed bands of the 14th/20th King's Hussars, the King's Own Royal Border Regiment, the Royal Regiment of Fusiliers, the King's Own Scottish Borderers, the Queen's Lancashire Regiment, and the Parachute Regiment, together with two corps of drums. The programme featured many old military band favourites, including 'The Lancashire Lass' and 'Rawtenstall Annual Fair' to give a special Lancashire flavour. The salute was taken by the Guild Mayor. During the day, which was most ably compered by Mike Chapman, the Preston town crier, over £3,000 was raised for Services charities.

Sporting Events during Guild Week

The Preston and District Vintage Car Club organised a Guild Car Rally, which started at Cicely's Garage in Preston and involved a round trip of sixty miles, ending at Hoghton Tower. The 101 cars which entered, dating from between 1904 and 1939, were sponsored for up to £100 each, and the money raised was to be given to the Derian House Appeal. At Hoghton Tower there was a rally, with picnic, and many visitors to the Tower took the opportunity to inspect the cars.

In the world of golf, it was decided that in addition to the 'open to all' competition for the Guild Trophy, two further tournaments—one for ladies and one for men—should be held to commemorate the Guild. Entry would be restricted to the members of seven designated local clubs—Ashton & Lea, Fishwick Hall, Ingol, Leyland, Longridge, Penwortham and Preston. After preliminary rounds at each club the leading qualifiers were invited to participate in a prestigious final competition, which was held at Preston Golf Club on 30 August for the ladies and 6 September for the men.

Approximately 230 ladies and more than 800 men entered the qualifying rounds, a very impressive figure which reflected the popularity both of the sport and of the Guild. The competition was sponsored by British Aerospace (Military Aircraft) Ltd, and the firm generously provided prizes for the qualifying rounds, with superb crystal as the prize for the overall winners, and all finalists received a pack of golf balls, tee pegs and a pitch mark fork. The finals were played in a spirit of keen but friendly rivalry—the ladies' final was also played in torrential rain! After presentation of prizes a cheque, representing all the entrance fees, which were to be given to charity, was handed to the *Lancashire Evening Post* to be put towards its MRI Scanner Appeal.

On 31 August Penwortham Cricket club, which was celebrating not only the Guild but also the centenary of its residence at the ground at Middleforth Green, played host to some international celebrity cricketers. In a special celebratory match, which fortunately and honourably ended in a draw, the International XI featured West Indies skipper Ritchie Richardson, New Zealand all-rounder Mark Greatbatch and, the favourite with the crowds, Alvin Kalicharran.

The North Lancashire Hockey Development Committee, on which Preston Borough Council is represented, organised a major event, 'Hockey For All Ages', at Preston North End stadium on Sunday 6 September. Between 10 a.m. and 2 p.m. a series of seven-a-side matches was held, for under-11, under-13 and under-16 teams from all over the North West. This was followed by two under-16 eleven-a-side matches, for boys and girls respectively, and the climax was two superb matches between a Ladies' Preston Guild Select Eleven and a Wales International Eleven, and a Men's Preston Guild Select Eleven against an England International Eleven. The two international teams won narrowly, but a feast of hockey was provided for a small but very appreciative crowd.

Guild Week saw a ladies' bowling competition, organised by the Preston and District Ladies Night Bowling Team, which has over 900 members. More than 125 women from local clubs took part in four days of heats, and the overall winner was Barbara Coupe, who plays for Longridge Conservative Club. The event was a great success, and the participants thoroughly enjoyed themselves—helped by the good weather, for they had very cleverly avoided the torrential rains at the start of the week and had a dry time. The rain began again just after the competition had finished on Sunday 7 September.

The Torchlight Procession (Saturday 5 September)

In 1882 something sensational happened at the Guild—the first ever Torchlight Procession was held. On the Saturday night at the end of Guild Week, hundreds of masked and costumed people, with grotesque faces and fanciful garb, wound their way through the streets, their route illuminated by flaming torches. Nothing remotely like it had been seen in Preston before, but it has been repeated at every Guild since, and at each its immense popularity has grown. In 1992 the Torchlight Procession drew by far the biggest crowds of any event—the police estimated that half a million people crammed into the town centre to watch the

dazzling and sensational spectacle, and everybody agreed that it was 'the best ever'. Although in the past the estimates of the size of crowds were often unreliable, it seems likely that numbers present for the 1992 Torchlight Procession make it at least as large as any Guild event which has ever taken place, and it is probable that it in fact broke all the records in the Guild's 823-year history.

Guild Week 1992 ended with what was probably the best-attended event in the eight centuries of Preston Guild—the Torchlight Procession, watched by perhaps as many as 300,000 people. (Lancashire Evening Post)

The Procession was organised by the Preston and District Chamber of Trade, which had undertaken the work in 1972 with great skill and efficiency. An organising committee was established in 1990, initially under the chairmanship of Michael Ormerod and subsequently of David Benson. Other members were David James (Chamber President 1991/2) and Tony Billington (President 1992/3), P. Johnson, S. Hall, R. Evans, A. Croft, E. Post, A. Sharp, L. Redmayne, Heather Whittaker, Heather Taylor and D. Hills. Marie Abbey was the Administrative Secretary, and Preston Borough Council was represented by Bob Cunningham and Harry Walker. Police representatives attended as required, and Keith Hughes of the Midland Bank, which was the event's main sponsor, was available in an advisory capacity.

In all previous Torchlight Processions the participants had not been charged an entrance fee, but it was considered that for the 1992 Procession a charge had to be made. This would help to cover the very considerable costs, and was in accordance with the policy of the Borough Council to reduce direct charges to the community charge payers of Preston as much as possible. Set against this financial need was the desire on the part of the Committee to make the Procession available to everybody who might want to join in, no matter how small or under-funded the organisation. They therefore set the charge at the minimum possible—£10. Such a sum was not expected to cover the costs, and so sponsorship was also sought for specific items such as bands, and this initiative was very successful. The Midland Bank was especially generous in its financial and practical assistance, and many other firms and individuals helped with sponsorship.

The theme of the procession was, as it has been since 1882, fun, entertainment, carnival and excitement. There was a vast amount of noise, colour and drama, and many magnificent floats were entered. The music played by the bands ranged from military to jazz, and from swing and calypso to brass and pipe. Over 500 torches were provided by the Chamber of Trade, separately sponsored by the Frank Whittle Partnership. In all there were twenty bands to accompany 96 floats and 1,650 walkers, representing 178 entrants. The pavements of the entire processional route were packed from barrier to wall, and every available vantage point was crowded with spectators. It was a huge success, and everything was accomplished without serious incident and with the greatest enjoyment and good humour—what more could Preston have asked!

The imaginations of Prestonians had run riot in designing and decorating their floats and themselves. Some followed the theme of ghosts and ghouls and eerie creatures of the dark, a motif which has been prominent in the Torchlight Procession ever since it began in 1882. The staff from the Royal Preston Hospital's X-Ray department were dressed as luminous skeletons, and those from the Midland Bank appeared as ghosts. There were witches and highwaymen, spooks and spirits. Starting off the procession were representatives of the Veteran Car Club, driving ancient vehicles to roars of applause, and cyclists riding penny-farthings who were also very popular. The Preston Hairdressers Association had a hilarious 'Hairstyles Through The Years' theme, while Pontins Ltd had, as the *Evening Post* put it 'moustachioed musclemen [who] put on an impressive display of synchronised swimming'. Elvis Presley came, complete with elaborate stage costume … although on reflection it may have been his double. The 5th Penwortham Scouts rode on a magnificently fierce Chinese dragon, members of the Boys Brigade paddled canoes, Preston Headway Group sat wearing exotic kimonos in a sumptuously decorated Japanese garden, and wild animals, clowns, grotesques and the Prime Minister joined in the revelry.

The sensation and excitement of the Torchlight Procession led straight on to the Great Firework Display which was held in Avenham Park later in the evening. This was perhaps the most magnificent of a whole series of Guild firework events, and it could be seen and heard over much of the town and surrounding area. The holding of a firework spectacular on the Saturday of Guild Week has gradually become a tradition—with the century-old tradition of the Torchlight Procession as its prelude it ensures that the official celebrations end not with a whimper but with a bang.

The organisers had decided that because of the huge crowds which were expected, and since the event was entirely free, there should be no seating. Originally it had been suggested that a limited number of seats might remain, to be used for civic purposes, but the police and fire service had recommended against this on safety grounds. Therefore, as soon as the last performance of the Children's Pageant had ended, the removal of all seats and most other fixtures was started. Workmen laboured throughout the Friday and Saturday to dismantle everything—it had taken almost a week to construct the seating and associated fittings, and the removal was hampered by the wet ground, so the effort was a race against time. Crowd safety was an essential consideration, and as much as possible of the security fencing was removed, to prevent potential dangers from the crush, while crowd control barriers were used to cordon off the display and fall-out area.

Matthew Brown plc sponsored the firework display, and used the event to promote a new product, 'Coors Extra Gold'. The Red Rose Rock FM Roadshow

was hired to provide live entertainment on stage during the evening, and this began at about 8 p.m. when small groups of people began to gather in the park. Gradually the crowds swelled, but the main influx did not come until the great Torchlight Procession had passed through the nearby town centre. The procession attracted enormous crowds—as noted above, at least half a million people were thought to have lined the streets—and many of these immediately began to make their way to the Park for the firework display. By 10 p.m. the Park was almost filled with a good-natured and festive crowd, while the adjacent streets were completely blocked with people trying to reach the Park.

All access to vehicles was prevented because of the numbers of people. The civic party, which had been due to travel to the Park in three double-decker buses, was forced to return to the Harris Building, and had to abandon plans to watch the fireworks. By 10.30 p.m. the police advised that it would be impossible for any more people to enter the Park or the surrounding parts of the town, and Neville Bridge, the Senior Guild Co-ordinator instructed that the fireworks should therefore begin as soon as possible. Later estimates suggest that there were about 150,000 people in Avenham Park itself, and probably another 100–150,000 in the streets around, and it is probable that the Torchlight Procession and the Firework Display which followed attracted a larger crowd than any Guild event in history. Everyone remained good-humoured and friendly throughout, and the

Above and opposite:
'Not with a whimper, but with a bang'—a wonderful firework display concludes the 1992 Guild, as crowds throng the Market Place. (Preston B. C.)

police were full of praise for the behaviour of the crowd, which had almost completely disappeared, without incident, by midnight. Many went back to the Market Square and danced and enjoyed themselves until, at midnight, the Guild Mayor came out onto the steps of the Harris Museum and addressed the throng. This, the official end to Guild Week, has already been described, in Chapter 5.

The firework display, which was provided by Kimbolton Fireworks Ltd, cost £20,000 and lasted thirty minutes. It was of quite exceptional quality—the titles of some of the many different sequences perhaps give a flavour: Golden Glory, Green Devils, Glittering Bombettes, Golden Mosaic: A Speciality, Rhapsody in Blue, Glow Worm, Kimbolton Violet, Yellow and Blue Butterflies, Silver Comet Candles, Scarlet Pimpernel, White Butterflies and Green Candles, Silver Mosaic, Silver and Red Magnesium, Golden Rain, Silver Titanium, Patriotic Salute in Red, White and Blue, Thunder and Lightning, Oriental Interlude (Chrysanthemum Shells), Exploding Stars and, the Grand Finale.

The firework display was the perfect finale to Guild Week. Seen from close at hand the display was breathtaking—seen from a mile away, in Ashton, it was breathtaking too. The sky was so brightly lit by some sequences that it seemed as if daylight had come, while at other times the vivid greens, crimsons, golds and silvers glowed across the whole of the town. Countless glittering stars rained down, bursts of colour banished the night, and for half an hour Preston thrilled to the magical spectacle. As always with that quality peculiar to fireworks, even as their sensational impact was being appreciated, the scene was changing and they were proving themselves ephemeral—but the memories of what was certainly the greatest firework display that the author of this book has witnessed will remain for a very long time.

Chapter 8

Endings

NOT WITH A WHIMPER BUT WITH A BANG ... That was how it should be, and that was how it was. With events spread over such a long period there was a danger that the Guild activities might have carried on beyond the end of Guild Week, and that would have been a serious mistake—the Guild would have petered out in a desultory fashion, as indeed it showed some signs of doing in 1972. But instead the 1992 Guild ended in spectacular and memorable fashion, in a brilliant display of light, noise and colour. After that, quietness fell and peace reigned. The Guild, which had occupied so much of the thinking of Preston people for several months, and had been so carefully designed and planned over several years, was finished, and would not begin again until the Monday after the Feast of the Decollation of St John the Baptist in the year 2012. There was much sadness and nostalgia, a great deal of retrospection and thinking about the exciting, rain-battered, uplifting, windswept, glorious, mud-spattered, triumphant Guild which had just gone. History had been made, new features added, new traditions created. Thus it is at all Guilds.

Later on, when the memories were being stored away and there was a little more time to pause and think, it was possible to reflect on what had gone on during the year, and how the 1992 Guild would make its mark upon the town and its people. Some assessed the Guild in the prosaic and unromantic terms of money, incomings and outgoings, and cash balances. The cost of the Guild to Preston Borough Council, and hence to the community charge payers of the town of Preston was estimated in January 1993 to have been £1,587,530. This figure included £350,000 for the support of non-commercial fringe activities, an area which is an essential feature of the Guild but one which could not have been so ambitious or so varied without financial assistance from the Borough. The provision of illuminations, temporary car parks, engineering works, park and ride facilities, and transport arrangements for the disabled together cost £240,000. The activities of the Works Department cost about £100,000, transport for children to and from the Pageant and other transport costs came, in total, to another £150,000. All these, together with other Guild expenses, produced the final figure of £1.5 million.

The Senior Guild Coordinator, Neville Bridge, pointed out that the cost of the 1972 Guild, adjusted to 1992 prices, would have been approximately the same, but that in 1972 a range of activities and costs were concealed because they were counted as part of the normal budgets and accounts of the relevant departments, rather than being separately identified and costed. The true figure for 1972—in terms of direct costs to the Borough—was therefore significantly higher than that for 1992.

In 1992, however, there were major funds which helped to offset the costs of approximately £1.5 million. For fifteen years the Council, with great care and foresight, had been accumulating money in a special Guild fund. The amounts added each year had been comparatively small in relation to the overall Borough Council budget, but they had cumulatively produced no less than £752,000, all of which was available to part-fund the celebrations. A second source of money— which was of little significance in 1972 but of major value and benefit in 1992—was commercial sponsorship of events and activities. Finally, the Council had a very effective marketing campaign for Guild goods and souvenirs, and this had brought valuable additional income. The total of sales and sponsorship money was therefore approximately £235,000, which with the Guild Reserve Fund meant that almost £800,000 had been available to offset the costs. The balance—the 'final bill' for the Guild of 1992—was therefore approximately £600,000.

The cost was higher than had been hoped because there were unforeseen liabilities. The main problem, it was suggested, was the weather, which had led to lower than expected takings at several of the events and had forced the cancellation of part of the Riversway extravaganza. Nevertheless, to balance this was the fact that in 1992 the number, scale and ambitiousness of the events was much greater than in 1972. Guild Year had lasted for a whole year, and so the cost had been much better value for money.

These figures all refer to the cost to the Borough Council and the community charge payers of Preston. They do not include the costs and receipts of the many events which were entirely funded by the private sector or covered by sponsorship. The overall level of sponsorship, for example, was estimated at £800,000, of which less than one fifth went to the Council. There was also a very significant generation of income for charities, both local and national. Many of the sponsorship agreements for individual events had an arrangement whereby profits, or a proportion of profits, were given to selected charities, and in January 1993 it was calculated that about £100,000 was raised in this way—a major tangible benefit of the Guild and one which, for the smaller local charities which did not have long-term funding or large-scale national advertising, was of immense importance.

Would the 1992 Guild leave a permanent legacy in the form of buildings or public works? Some previous Guilds had indeed left large and very tangible physical reminders, because it became an unofficial custom to start or finish an important building during Guild Year. Thus, in 1761 a new Guild Hall was completed in the Market Square in readiness for the Guild of 1762; in 1782 a new Town Hall was finished; in 1862 work began on the superb Victorian Gothic Town Hall which burned down in 1947; in 1882 the foundation stone of the Harris Museum and Library was laid; and, nearer our own time, the 1972 Guild should have been marked by the completion of the Guild Hall—but unfortunately the work was delayed, and it was not opened until after the Guild had ended.

There had been a considerable debate about whether it would be feasible to carry out a similar project in readiness for the Guild of 1992. In 1990 it was suggested that a major building scheme, or a project to provide some form of 'monument', should be undertaken, but the Borough Council decided that it did not have sufficient financial resources to make a large-scale memorial to the 1992 Guild. During the autumn of 1991 there were ambitious private plans to raise £100,000 to provide a thirty-foot-high animated clock in the market place. A consortium of local businessmen, led by architect David Bennett, proposed that the design for the clock tower should be based on the tower of the former Town Hall. The animated clock would have a town crier who would appear on the quarter and half hours to proclaim the Guild, while on the hour a procession of model figures would form a 'trades procession' rotating around a balcony. Although the scheme received substantial local support—as well as some strong criticism on aesthetic and amenity grounds—it eventually faded away.

So what record does 1992 leave on the face of Preston? Although there was no specific Guild project, there were several important improvements and building projects. Perhaps the most notable was the completion of the pedestrian-isation of much of the town centre, including the Friargate area. This scheme, with its planting of trees and shrubs and its attractive paving, was publicised by the Borough Council ahead of Guild Year as something which would be a project for the Guild. Another very important change was the demolition of the old Public Hall and the very impressive refurbishment and restoration of the Corn Exchange to provide a new pub and restaurant. Whatever the impassioned feelings which the demolition of the Hall roused, few would disagree that the Corn Exchange looks superb in its new guise, and is a very valuable visual asset. Many would not share that view about the highly controversial statues, com-memorating the Lune Street shootings of 1842, which stand outside the Corn Exchange—but, like them or not, they are another monument to Guild Year.

Another monument for which the Council and citizens had been hoping, but which came to nothing, was the elevation of Preston to the status of a city. Guild Year, 1992, was also the fortieth anniversary of the accession of Queen Elizabeth II, and to mark the anniversary the Queen had agreed to give royal approval for the creation of a new city. Towns throughout the United Kingdom were eligible to make applications, and some twenty submitted their case to a Privy Council committee which would make the decision. Preston was one of these, and early in 1990 work on the application began. It was submitted at the start of Guild Year, and hopes were high that the Guild would be crowned by the granting of the title 'City of Preston'. It was not to be. Despite a strong belief in the town that Preston had an excellent case, in the event the Queen granted the coveted title to Sunderland.

A permanent Guild record of a different sort will be hung in the Harris Museum, and will—all being well—represent a major new acquisition for the borough's art collection. This is the official Guild portrait showing Councillor Harold Parker, and commemorating his place as the twenty-sixth Guild Mayor since reliable records began. For over 150 years portraits of Guild Mayors have been commissioned by, or presented to, the Borough Council, and in January 1993 the opportunity was taken to ask a leading contemporary artist to undertake the work. The artist, Maggie Hambling, was a controversial choice—'her loose, lavish style will be in stark contrast to the more formal portraits of previous Guild years'. Some councillors raised objections, on the basis of the style of her earlier works.

However, the subject of the portrait was not bothered: Councillor Parker said that he had not been involved in the consultations about the painting and the choice of artist but, with characteristically dry humour, he added that 'I wanted to get away from bland portrait painting and judging from some of her previous portraits she will certainly achieve that. If the painting turns out to be a work of quality and importance I can say it will have been in no way due to the subject matter. If it turns out to be controversial at least it will bring more people into the museum.' A possible foretaste of the reaction occurred in June 1993, when a framed photograph of the Guild Mayor disappeared from outside the council chamber in the Town Hall. Councillor Parker told the *Lancashire Evening Post* that 'I must have a secret admirer, which could be unique and most unlikely. On the other hand it could be the opposite, and someone is sticking darts or pins in it as we speak.'

The good humour of the Guild Mayor, and his friendly, witty and dignified enjoyment of the role, were two features of Guild Year and its multitude of events which were most often commented upon at the time. There was a universal admiration, in reports of events, in eye-witness descriptions, and in the summings-up made by Guild officials and stewards, for the work of Councillor Parker, and his wife and Guild Mayoress, Mrs Enid Parker. It was for them a very exacting and difficult year, a time of immense hard work and dedication, as well as a year which brought outstanding pleasure and achievement.

There can be no doubt that Harold and Enid Parker brought to the time-honoured positions of Guild Mayor and Mayoress a very special quality. The Guild Mayor always attracts particular attention and has a central role, and over the centuries many illustrious people have had the rare honour of being Guild Mayor of Preston, but it is true to say that few can have carried out the task so well, so enthusiastically and with such professionalism as Councillor Parker. On Monday 7 September, after the end of Guild Week, the *Lancashire Evening Post* paid a glowing tribute to the Guild Mayor and Mayoress, and in doing so echoed the tributes made by the Guild Mayor's colleagues during the ceremonies for the adjournment of the Guild Court two days earlier: 'Over the course of the week, their dedication to the cause has been total; between them they have epitomised warmth, friendship and hospitality. For them it has been a personal triumph, and one which is fully deserved.'

Assisting the Guild Mayor and Mayoress were the Deputy Mayor, Miss Mary Rawcliffe, and the Deputy Mayoress, Jacqui Nagy. Until the installation of the Guild Mayor in May 1992 Miss Rawcliffe was the town's chief citizen, and she therefore had the honour of initiating many of the early activities during the first half of the year. The sterling work of the Deputy Mayor and Mayoress was very much appreciated.

A sad note was the death of the Honorary Recorder of the Guild, Judge Anthony Jolly, on 26 September 1992—less than three weeks after he had played such a prominent part in the formal ceremonies which opened and closed Guild Week. Judge Jolly had been made Honorary Recorder by the Council's resolution of 3 May 1989, and during his three years in office he had committed himself totally to his civic and ceremonial duties. Less than four weeks earlier he had delivered the traditional Latin oration, notable for its wit and eloquence. His conscientious, jovial and entertaining contribution to the civic life of Preston will be greatly missed.

The Borough Council, at its meeting on 23 September, passed a series of resolutions which expressed the thanks which it, and the people of the town, felt towards those who had worked so hard and so long to make the Guild a success. The members of the Council's own staff and the Guild team were praised for their efficiency and dedication, and the special gratitude felt towards the Guild Mayor and Mayoress was given in a separate resolution. The Council also thanked all the private individuals, other public bodies, and the many commercial and industrial concerns which had given so freely of time, money, initiative and manpower during 1992. The full text of the resolutions is given in Appendix 13, while Appendix 14 lists the specific contributions of the Lancashire County Council, which was extremely co-operative and helpful throughout the planning and holding of the Guild.

Before every Guild there are many doubts, many uncertainties, and many who say that the event is doomed to fail. Predictions that 'it won't be as good as last time' or that 'nobody will want to go to it now' are made, and there are rumblings and grumblings about the cost of it all, the commercialism which is said to have appeared since the last time, the inefficiency of the management and the unsuitability of the events and activities. Such prognostications of gloom and failure have been a part of the Guild for at least a century and a half: comparable doubts and similar dire warnings can be seen in the letters written to the Preston newspapers in advance of the Guilds of 1822 and 1842.

Yet, at every Guild, the event itself is hailed as a triumphant success, and there is an abundance of people who gladly say that it is 'the best ever', that they were at previous Guilds and found the latest one 'even more enjoyable', and that the Guild has restored their faith in humanity and reinforced their pride in Preston. The quiet murmurings that all was not well are drowned out by the volume of praise, enthusiasm and excitement. Inevitably there are some specific complaints—costs, timings, events which did not live up to expectations—but overall the support, and the view that the Guild has been a success, are overwhelming.

The Guild of 1992 was no exception. There were all the same grumbles and doubts beforehand, and all the same worries and uncertainties about the financial and logistical arrangements, but the response to the Guild was almost unanimously favourable. There was great enthusiasm, remarkable community spirit, and extraordinary fortitude on the part of the thousands of people who braved wind and rain to watch events or participate in them. Perhaps the greatest legacy of the 1992 Guild is this community spirit: at a time of acute economic depression and gloom, rapidly rising crime, terrorism and civil disturbance, international distress and domestic cynicism, it was possible for hundreds of thousands of people to enjoy themselves spontaneously in complete peace and with the best of behaviour, to help their neighbours and feel pride in their town and its achievements.

Often, in the past, a local newspaper has effectively summed up the Guild. In 1992 the *Evening Post*, in its final issue of Guild Year, gave its verdict: 'the gloom of the recession was at least pierced for a while ... by the extraordinary Preston Guild celebrations. For those who had never experienced a Guild, 1992 will long

live in the memory. Full credit for that must go to the council which set about organising a year-long programme of events with vigour. In doing so, it attracted significant amounts of sponsorship from private enterprise and was thus able to stage the sort of top-rate entertainment which had never before been viable ... Guild Week itself was a revelation in that it united the various religious groups, ethnic and cultural organisations in a way which many would not have believed possible. The weather was unimaginably awful but the processions, the pageants and the street parties were a triumph for community spirit.'

Ready for the Guild of 2012—the children of Preston.
(Preston Citizen)

Much of what was said in this context might be interpreted by cynics as simply the use of cliches and trite phrases, but to those who were there, and who experienced the sights, sounds, feelings and sensations of the Guild, its success and appeal were a reality. Nobody who watched the colourful processions, or witnessed the great gatherings and concerts, or was enchanted by the fireworks, or joined in community singing in the pouring rain while sitting huddled under a plastic poncho, or felt pride in the splendour and solemnity of Preston's pageantry, would have any real doubt that the Guild was a unique and historic event, and one which was indeed a triumph. Many of those present must have sensed, and been thrilled by, the continuity of tradition and civic pride which the Guild represented, and many will have agreed with the Guild Mayor when he looked forward with optimism and confidence, beyond the Guild of 1992.

Until 2012 ...

On 31 December 1992 the Guild Year came to an end. It has become a tradition for the Market Square to fill with merrymakers on New Year's Eve, but of course this was a particularly special event. During the evening thousands of revellers saw fireworks, were entertained by dancers, morris men, the rock and roll band Curfew Breakers, and a New Years Eve disco. The police kept a low profile despite the large crowds and the unruliness often associated with New Year's Eve celebrations. Superintendent Derek Taylor said that 'Everyone likes to let their hair down at New Year and the last thing that those officers who are on duty want is to be sorting out punch-ups and arresting people. We have enjoyed an excellent relationship with the public during this special year and see no reason why that should change tonight.'

The crowds sang 'We'll meet again' before the Guild Mayor addressed the crowds. He spoke of the success of the Guild, and the pride which the town should feel in the spirit and conduct of the celebrations. 'As long as you live, wherever you go in life, you will never witness the likes of the community spirit which existed in Preston, particularly during Guild week. Your good behaviour and your kindness and concern for others told the world why this town is called Proud Preston. It is you, the people of Preston, who put the pride in Proud Preston, and if at any time you are asked which town you come from tell them Preston, in the Red Rose County of Lancashire, and tell them it with pride.'

Appendices

Appendix 1

Members of the Guild Committee

The Guild Committee of Preston Borough Council was constituted in 1988, and functioned until early 1993. It therefore had numerous changes of membership, and these are listed below. The councillors who served during the time of the Guild itself (i.e. from May 1992) are named in capital letters.

Councillors:
Afrin (from May 1989 to May 1991)
ATKINSON [Chairman]
BAINES (from May 1992)
BALL
BLACK (to May 1991; from May 1992)
W. N. Borrow (to May 1992)
BURNS (to May 1991; from May 1992)
Chaloner (to May 1990)
EVANS (from May 1990)
A. A. GREEN (from May 1992)
HALL
Heatley (to May 1990)
Hodge (to May 1990)
HOOD
HUDSON (from May 1989)
JACKSON (from May 1990)
Johnson (to May 1989)
KEHOE (from May 1989)
KINSELLA (from May 1991)
MARSHALL
McGrath (to May 1992)
MILNE (from May 1990)
Nagy (from May 1991 to May 1992)
PARKER
PATEL (from May 1990)
RATCLIFFE (from May 1991)
RAWCLIFFE (to May 1990; from May 1991)
Mrs Robinson (from May 1991 to May 1992)
D. C. Robinson (to May 1992)
Scott (from June 1988 to May 1990)
Walmsley (from May 1990 to May 1991)
J. WARD (to May 1991; from May 1992)
P. R. Ward (from June 1988 to May 1992)

Appendix 2

Members of Preston Borough Council 1992

The Right Worshipful the Guild Mayor (Harold PARKER)
The Deputy Mayor (Mary RAWCLIFFE)
AFRIN, Veronica Mary
ATKINS, Ronald Henry
ATKINSON, Richard
BAINES, Stanley
BALL, Ronald
BENTHAM, Stephen
BLACK, Irene, JP
BORROW, David Stanley
BOSWELL, Robert Philip
BROWNE, John William
BUCKLEY, Mark Edward
BURNS, David Robert
CARTWRIGHT, Lawrence Neil Henderson
CARTWRIGHT, Terence
CHADWICK, William David
CHALONER, Dorothy Eileen, JP
CLARKSON, Elizabeth
De MOLFETTA, Francesco
EVANS, Henry Richard, JP
GORNALL, Anthony
GREEN, Amelia Ann
GREEN, Hayley Jane
GREENHALGH, Jennifer Elaine
HACKETT, Alan Lester
HALL, Ian Whyte, JP
HAYNES, Geoffrey Arthur
HEATLEY, John
HILL, Stephen Christopher
HOOD, Joseph, CBE, JP
HUDSON, Kenneth James, JP
JACKSON, Dorothy
KEHOE, Dennis
KINSELLA, Rose
MARSHALL, Ronald Philip
MILNE, Marie Francoise Therese
MONK, John
NAGY, Sandra Jacqueline
ONYON, Michael Edward
PARRY, Brian Joseph
PATEL, Bhikhu
PEET, Kenneth
RANKIN, Peter John
RATCLIFFE, Blodwen Mair
REID, Anthony David
RICHARDSON, Albert James
ROBINSON, David Charles
SAKSENA, Jonathan Harish Chandra
SCOTT, Audrey, JP

SWARBRICK, Geoffrey Threlfall
TAYLOR, Nancy
TYSON, William Frederick
WALMSLEY, Gerard
WARD, Joseph
WARD, Peter Rimmer
WISE, Valerie

Appendix 3

Initiatory resolutions and formal notices

On 26 March 1992 the Council, on the recommendation of the Guild Committee, passed, pursuant to ancient custom, the following resolutions:

RESOLVED

That the Guild Merchant of this Borough be held according to ancient custom in the week commencing Monday, the 31st day of August, 1992 being the Monday next after the Feast of the Decollation of St John the Baptist.

RESOLVED

That notice of the celebration of the forthcoming Guild Merchant be issued by the Clerk of the Guild and inserted in appropriate national and local publications and newspapers.

RESOLVED

That Proclamation of the holding of the Guild Merchant be made in the Market Place on three successive Market Days immediately preceding the celebration of the Guild Merchant (Saturdays, 15th, 22nd, and 29th August, 1992).

RESOLVED

That the Guild Merchant of this Borough be opened and held, according to ancient custom, in the Guild Hall in Preston on Monday, the 31st day of August, 1992 and that one student each from Preston College and Newman College deliver a Latin Oration at this Guild Court Ceremony, to which the Honorary Recorder be invited to reply.

RESOLVED

That the Clerk of the Guild be authorised to issue appropriate notices to invite Guild Burgesses to renew their franchise and other persons so qualified to apply for admission to the Roll of Guild Burgesses.

RESOLVED *

That the Council appoint Councillors Richard Atkinson, Ian Whyte Hall, Joseph Hood, Dennis Kehoe and Ronald Philip Marshall to be Stewards of the Guild Merchant.

RESOLVED

That the Council appoint Judge Anthony Jolly to be Honorary Recorder of the Guild Merchant.

---

* The appointment of five Guild Stewards ended a tradition dating back several centuries, whereby the number of Guild Stewards had been limited to three. No statutory authority or charter right could be found to warrant this limitation. Since there was a desire to appoint five Stewards for the 1992 Guild this was put into effect.

RESOLVED

That the Council appoint Mr Antony Owens, Town Clerk/Chief Executive of the Borough, to be Clerk of the Guild Merchant.

RESOLVED *

That the Council appoint Mr Ian P. Threlfall, Director of Finance of the Borough, to be Treasurer of the Guild Funds.

The Guild Mayor (Councillor Harold Parker) was formally installed in office at the Annual Meeting of the Council on 21 May 1992, when he agreed to preside and act in the Guild Merchant according to ancient custom.

In accordance with the foregoing resolutions the following Notice was published in *The Times* and the *Lancashire Evening Post* on 5 August 1992.

NOTICE
PRESTON BOROUGH COUNCIL
GUILD MERCHANT 1992

NOTICE IS HEREBY GIVEN that the Guild Merchant of and for the said Borough will be opened and held, according to Ancient Custom, in the Guild Hall in Preston aforesaid on Monday, the thirty-first day of August next ensuing, being the Monday next after the Feast of the Decollation of St John the Baptist, whereof all persons concerned are required to appear at the day and place above-mentioned and give such attendance and service as to them shall appertain.

FURTHER NOTICE IS HEREBY GIVEN that applications for the renewal of Guild Burgess rights and for admissions of persons qualified for such rights, may be made to the Town Clerk/Chief Executive's office, Town Hall, Preston, PR1 2RL, where any information relating thereto may be obtained.

A. OWENS,
Town Clerk/Chief Executive and Clerk of the Guild
5th August, 1992

At previous Guilds during the past century, notices with a similar wording to the above had been printed and posted throughout the town. This practice was discontinued for the Guild of 1992, as it was felt that general publicity and advertising would be sufficient.

Appendix 4

The patrons of the Preston Guild 1992

Her Majesty the Queen
The Lord Lieutenant of Lancashire (Simon Towneley JP)
The High Sheriff of Lancashire (Keith A. Gledhill, DL)
The Lord High Chancellor (The Rt. Hon. the Lord Mackay of Clashfern)
The Prime Minister (The Rt. Hon. John Major MP)
The Leader of the Labour Party (The Rt. Hon. R. Neil Kinnock MP)

---

* Following the retirement of Mr Threlfall in June 1992, the Deputy Director of Finance, Mr D. W. Clarke, was appointed Treasurer of the Guild.

The Leader of the Liberal Democrat Party (The Rt. Hon. J. J. D. Ashdown MP)

His Grace the Duke of Hamilton and Brandon

The Rt. Hon. the Earl of Derby MC

The Rt. Revd the Lord Bishop of Blackburn (The Rt. Revd Alan Chesters)

The Rt. Revd the Roman Catholic Bishop of Lancaster (The Rt. Revd John Brewer)

The Moderator of the Free Church Federal Council (Preston District) (Revd Fred Wilson)

Appendix 5

A complete list of the 1992 Guild Burgesses

AINSCOUGH

JOAN of Penwortham, Personal Assistant, N.S.P.C.C., former Mayor of the Borough

ROSAMUND ANNE (GORDON) of Pennington, Manager, daughter of Joan, former Mayor of the Borough

NOEL JOHN of Bamber Bridge, Technician, son of Joan, former Mayor of the Borough

ALKER

RALPH of Iowa, USA, Retired Millwright, son of Ralph Salisbury deceased

MARCUS of California, USA, Forrester, (described as Ralph Marcus in the Guild Roll of 1972), son of Ralph

RODNEY of Penwortham, Retired Journalist, another son of Ralph Salisbury deceased

NEIL of Bamber Bridge, Engineer, son of Rodney

RACHEL LOUISE, daughter of Neil

LYNN of Lostock Hall, Finance Controller, daughter of Rodney

JEREMY MICHAEL of Longton, Aerospace Design Consultant, son of Frederick deceased

NICOLE MICHELLE, daughter of Jeremy Michael

ANDREW MICHAEL, son of Jeremy Michael

SIMON JAMES of Penwortham, Engineer, another son of Frederick deceased

ASHCROFT

THOMAS of Rufford, Haulage Contractor, son of John deceased

JOHN THOMAS of Rufford, Driver, son of Thomas

STEPHEN JOHN, son of John Thomas

SUZANNE LOUISE, daughter of John Thomas

DAVID PHILIP of Nateby, Haulage Contractor, another son of Thomas

DANIEL JOSEPH, son of David Philip

MEGAN SUSAN, daughter of David Philip

GILLIAN, another daughter of David Philip

MICHAEL BRIAN of Tarleton, Driver, another son of Thomas

LEE MICHAEL, son of Michael Brian

THOMAS JAMES of Croston, Driver, another son of Thomas

STEVEN, son of Thomas James

MARK, another son of Thomas James

JENNIFER, daughter of Thomas James

SUSAN (HARRISON) of Westhoughton, daughter of Thomas

THOMAS DANIEL, son of Joseph Austen deceased

Assheton

RALPH JOHN of Downham Hall, Clitheroe, The Right Honourable Lord Clitheroe, Peer of the Realm, son of Ralph, Baronet deceased

RALPH CHRISTOPHER of Downham Hall, Clitheroe, Army Officer, son of Ralph John

JOHN HOTHAM of Banbury, Printer, another son of Ralph John

ELIZABETH JANE of Downham Hall, Clitheroe, daughter of Ralph John

NICHOLAS of London, Banker, another son of Ralph, Baronet deceased

THOMAS of Moreton-in-Marsh, son of Nicholas

NOAH FREDERICK, son of Thomas

CAROLINE of Skipton, daughter of Nicholas

MARY THERESE of County Galway, Ireland, another daughter of Nicholas

NICHOLAS MASTER of Shaftesbury, Dorset, Retired Colonial Civil Servant, son of the Revd Canon William Orme deceased

WILLIAM FRANCIS of London, Architect, son of Nicholas Master

EMILY NEST, daughter of William Francis

DAVID NICHOLAS of Rugby, Local Government Officer, another son of Nicholas Master

CECILIA MARY (HAWKES) of Dunmow, Essex, daughter of Nicholas Master

JOHN RICHARD of Malmesbury, Wiltshire, Retired Solicitor, son of Richard Thomas deceased

Atkinson

JAMES PETER of Preston, Planning Manager, son of James of Preston, Printer, Alderman, Mayor of the Borough and a Steward of the Guild of 1972 deceased

PETER JAMES of Lostock Hall, Mobile Crane Driver, son of James Peter

STEPHEN JAMES, son of Peter James

DAVID CHARLES, another son of Peter James

SUSAN MARIE (McMANUS) of Preston, Computer Operator, daughter of James Peter

DENISE MARY (RISHTON) of Preston, another daughter of James Peter

RICHARD of Preston, Retired Engineer, Councillor, former Mayor of the Borough and one of the Stewards of this Guild

JOYCE (CARLIN) of Victoria, Australia, daughter of Richard, former Mayor of the Borough and one of the Stewards of this Guild

GLYNIS (ALTY) of Preston, Senior Drawing Office Assistant, another daughter of Richard, former Mayor of the Borough and one of the Stewards of this Guild

IAN RICHARD of Victoria, Australia, Works Officer, son of Richard, former Mayor of the Borough and one of the Stewards of this Guild

Ball

RONALD of Preston, Retired Painter and Decorator, Councillor and former Mayor of the Borough

CHRISTINE MARGARET (JOHNSTON) of Preston, Teacher, daughter of Ronald, former Mayor of the Borough

KATHRYN MARY (MACKIN) of Thornton-in-Lonsdale, another daughter of Ronald, former Mayor of the Borough

ALISON JEAN (SHAW) of Preston, Secretary, another daughter of Ronald, former Mayor of the Borough

HILARY RUTH (SCHWARTZ) of Clearwater Bay, Hong Kong, another daughter of Ronald, former Mayor of the Borough

ALAN RONALD of Preston, Sales Executive, son of Ronald, former Mayor of the Borough

Bamber

WILLIAM ANDREW of Walmer Bridge, Retired Engineer, son of William Henry deceased

WILLIAM ANTHONY of Penwortham, Manager, son of William Andrew

KATHRYN AMY, daughter of William Anthony
ANTHONY GREGORY, son of William Anthony
TIMOTHY RICHARD, another son of William Anthony
RICHARD NOEL of Garstang, Retired Librarian, son of Richard James deceased
NANCY JANE (CROWTHER) of Garstang, Nurse, daughter of Richard Noel
ANN MARGARET (BELCHER) of Sutton, Solicitor, another daughter of Richard Noel
JOHN of Preston, Retired Industrial Relations Officer, another son of Richard James
    deceased
ANDREW WILLIAM JOHN of London, Solicitor, son of John
ROBERT of Chipping, Builder (a Burgess of the Guild of 1952), son of Robert deceased
ROBERT DAMIAN, son of Robert
LOUISE JANE, daughter of Robert
PETER ANTHONY, another son of Robert
STEPHEN JOHN, another son of Robert

BEAUMONT

JOHN ERIC of Southport, Retired Architect, son of Harry, Alderman of Preston deceased
WINIFRED MARY (MILES) of Pinner, Middlesex, Manager, daughter of John Eric
EDWARD ALAN of East London, South Africa, Chartered Accountant, another son of
    Harry, Alderman of Preston deceased
KAREN ELIZABETH of East London, South Africa, daughter of Edward Alan
STEPHEN ANDREW of East London, South Africa, Printer, son of Edward Alan
GARY MARK of East London, South Africa, Businessman, another son of Edward Alan
DEBORAH ANN of East London, South Africa, Student, another daughter of Edward Alan

BECKETT

EDMUND of Lostock Hall, Retired Local Government Officer, son of William of Preston,
    Honorary Freeman, Alderman, Former Mayor of the Borough and a Steward of the
    Guild of 1972, deceased
WILLIAM GREGORY of Chorley, Gardener, son of Edmund deceased
KAREN ANNE (THOMPSON) of Chorley, daughter of Edmund deceased
CATHERINE ROSE (LANGTREE) of Rufford, Manager, another daughter of Edmund
    deceased

BLACKHURST

JOHN BERNARD of Matlock, Land Agent, son of Alfred Bernard deceased
JANE LOUISE, daughter of John Bernard
HELEN RACHEL, another daughter of John Bernard
GEOFFREY CHARLES of Hanover, Germany, Retired Chief Clerk, son of Albert Edward
    deceased

BRADLEY

WILLIAM of Preston, Retired Recreational Officer, son of William Henry deceased
WILLIAM CLINTON of Leyland, Joiner, son of William
ZOE DAWN, daughter of William Clinton
JANIS (FAIRHURST) of Western Australia, Hairdresser, daughter of William
JOHN THOMAS of Rhyl, Grocer, son of Harry Chamberlain deceased
IAN SIMON, son of John Thomas
ZOE LOUISE, daughter of John Thomas

BRANDRETH

GEORGE ANTHONY WILSON of Weybridge, Surrey, Retired Architect, son of John Moss
    deceased

MARK of Malvern, Civil Servant, son of George Anthony Wilson

FREDERICK PETER of Grantham, Retired Engineer, son of Frederick Herbert deceased

NICHOLAS PETER of Tenterden, Kent, Chartered Surveyor, son of Frederick Peter

THOMAS PETER, son of Nicholas Peter

WILLIAM JAMES, another son of Nicholas Peter

BENJAMIN CHARLES, another son of Nicholas Peter

MARK WILLIAM CHARLES of Grantham, Retailer, another son of Frederick Peter

PETER JOHNATHAN, son of Mark William Charles

LISA MARIE, daughter of Mark William Charles

ANTHONY HUGH of Tetney, Retired Hardware Retailer, another son of Frederick Herbert deceased

TIMOTHY JAMES of Tytherington, Planning Executive, son of Anthony Hugh

DIANA LYNNE (DONOVAN) of Tetney, Dietician, daughter of Anthony Hugh

BRIGG

RICHARD of Blackpool, Retailer, son of John, Alderman and former Mayor of the Borough deceased

MARTIN NEIL of Blackpool, Company Director, son of Richard

BUNKER

ANTHONY JOHN of Penwortham, Retired Local Government Officer, son of Ernest William, former Mayor of the Borough deceased

PAULINE ELIZABETH (THOMSON) of Longton, Furniture Restorer, daughter of Anthony John

JANE HEATHER MARJORIE (COOK) of Chorley, another daughter of Anthony John

BUTCHER

ROBERT EDWARD of Preston, Coach Painter and former Mayor of the Borough

CARTMELL

HARRY LESLIE of St Annes-on-Sea, Solicitor, son of Cyril deceased

BARRIE MAXWELL of Sedgeberrow, Evesham, Company Director, son of Harry Leslie

CLAIRE LOUISE, daughter of Barrie Maxwell

ROBERT JAMES, son of Barrie Maxwell

PHILIPPA ANN (CAWLEY) of Eccleston, daughter of Harry Leslie

CHALONER

DOROTHY EILEEN of Preston, Councillor and former Mayor of the Borough

PENELOPE ANN of Hassocks, West Sussex, Lecturer, daughter of Dorothy Eileen, former Mayor of the Borough

COOK

ALBERT EDWARD of Lytham, Retired Company Director, son of Thomas deceased

EDWARD of Lytham, Casino Director, son of Albert Edward

FIONA CLARE, daughter of Edward

REBECCA EMILY, another daughter of Edward

JENNIFER ANNE (FULFORD-BROWN) of Blackpool, daughter of Albert Edward

CHRISTINE MARY (MION) of Langley, Canada, Physiotherapist, another daughter of Albert Edward

THOMAS PARKINSON of Kendal, Gardener, (a Burgess of the Guild of 1952), son of Richard deceased

CHRISTOPHER PARKINSON of Kendal, Foreman, son of Thomas Parkinson

JACQUELINE (WOOF) of Kendal, daughter of Thomas Parkinson

DAVID RICHARD of Lumb-in-Rossendale, Accountant, (a Burgess of the Guild of 1952), another son of Richard deceased

JANE YVONNE (BLANDFORD) of London, Secretary, daughter of David Richard

JOHN DAVID of Walton-le-Dale, Waste Disposal Officer, son of David Richard

SIMON ROBERT, son of John David

ROGER DAVID of Lumb-in-Rossendale, Store Manager, another son of David Richard

CATHERINE, daughter of Roger David

DIANNE, another daughter of Roger David

CHERYL LOUISE of Lumb-in-Rossendale, Nursing Auxillary, another daughter of David Richard

COOKE

FLORENCE of Preston, Retired Shopworker

LYNDA MERRILL (WHITTLE) of Preston, daughter of Florence

ARTHUR of Leyland, Chauffeur, son of Florence

CROSS

ASSHETON HENRY of Wells, Somerset, The Right Honourable 3rd Viscount Cross, Peer of the Realm (a Burgess of the Guild of 1952), son of Richard Assheton, 2nd Viscount Cross deceased

VENETIA CLARE (HILL) of Walsingham, Norfolk, daughter of Assheton Henry

NICOLA of London, Solicitor, another daughter of Assheton Henry

ANTHONY ASSHETON of Tiverton, Devon, Farmer (a Burgess of the Guild of 1952), son of Geoffrey John Assheton deceased

RICHARD ASSHETON of Tiverton, Devon, Farmer, son of Anthony Assheton

WILLIAM JOHN ASSHETON of Tiverton, Devon, Farmer, another son of Anthony Assheton

CUERDEN

JOHN of Preston, Retired Civil Servant, son of Henry deceased

PHILIP HENRY of Preston, Solicitor, son of John

ANNE PATRICIA (MACFARLANE) of Blandford, Dorset, Personnel Officer, daughter of John

FRANK of East Preston, W. Sussex, Retired Civil Servant, another son of Henry deceased

MICHAEL JOHN of Harrietsham, Kent, Computer Consultant, son of Frank

RUTH ELIZABETH, daughter of Michael John

HEATHER ANN, another daughter of Michael John

JAMES MICHAEL, son of Michael John

ELIZABETH JANE (FULLER) of Den Haag, Holland, daughter of Frank

HAROLD of Natal, South Africa, Retired Structural Engineer, son of George deceased

DIANE ELIZABETH (GRIGGS) of Natal, South Africa, Sales Executive, daughter of Harold

DEWHURST

THOMAS of Warrington, Civil Engineer, son of Thomas, Alderman and former Deputy Mayor of the Borough deceased

JANE ELIZABETH, daughter of Thomas

KATHERINE LOUISE, another daughter of Thomas

ECCLESTON

HENRY of Preston, Retired Sheet Metal Worker, son of James deceased

WILLIAM of Formby, University Professor, son of Henry

JOHN of Formby, Marketing Executive, son of William

DANIEL of Formby, Engineer, another son of William

EMETT

THOMAS LADYMAN of Kingsbridge, Devon, Retired Chartered Surveyor (a Burgess of the Guild of 1952), son of Thomas deceased

MICHAEL ROBERT of Victoria, Australia, Manager, (a Burgess of the Guild of 1952), son of Thomas Ladyman

CHRISTOPHER MICHAEL, son of Michael Robert

FINNEY

THOMAS of Preston, Company Director and Honorary Freeman of the Borough

BRIAN THOMAS, Company Director, son of Thomas

BARBARA ANNE (HERBERT) of Preston, daughter of Thomas

GARNER-GRAY

PETER FREDERICK of Preston, Scientist, nephew of the Mayor of the Guild of 1972

GARRATT

JOHN TAYLOR of Preston, Insurance Broker, son of Charles Jamieson deceased

CLIFFORD JOHN of Preston, Doctor, son of John Taylor

RICHARD MARK of Preston, Insurance Broker, another son of John Taylor

JAMES DAVID of Preston, Insurance Broker, another son of John Taylor

GEE

MICHAEL ATKINSON of New Longton, Retired Sales Manager, son of Stanley Walsh deceased

DEBORAH ANN (WILSON) of Reading, Consultant, daughter of Michael Atkinson

CATHERINE ELIZABETH of Birmingham, Reception Manager, another daughter of Michael Atkinson

PATRICK DAVID of Heswall, Wirrall, Local Government Officer, another son of Stanley Walsh deceased

ANDREW MARK of Warrington, Teacher, son of Patrick David

DAVID JAMES STANLEY of Heswall, Wirrall, Engineer, another son of Patrick David

JOANNA HILARY (WEINER) of Romford, Essex, Nurse, daughter of Patrick David

GRAY

REGINALD STANLEY of Askam-in-Furness, brother of Joseph Frederick, Alderman and Mayor of the Guild of 1972 deceased

LINDA JOAN (CONROY) of Rushdon, Northants, daughter of Reginald Stanley

GREEN

RAYMOND of Preston, Data Processing Manager, son of Thomas deceased

STEPHEN of Congleton, Research Scientist, son of Raymond

CAROLINE ROSE, daughter of Stephen

STUART of Freckleton, Engineer, another son of Raymond

RACHEL LOUISE, daughter of Stuart

JOSEPH LEO of Bournemouth, Retired Dental Surgeon, son of Leo deceased

DAVID BERNARD of Bournemouth, son of Joseph Leo

STEPHEN JOHN of Bournemouth, Physiotherapist, another son of Joseph Leo

SUSAN MARY (JOHNSON) of Poole, Nurse, daughter of Joseph Leo

PAULA MARIA (JOHNSTONE) of Bournemouth, Nurse, another daughter of Joseph Leo

GREGSON

ALAN of Ontario, Canada, Retired College Administrator, son of Robert deceased

SIMON JOHN of Aberdeen, Diver, son of Alan
RICHARD PAUL of Calgary, Canada, Theatre Consultant, another son of Alan
KENDRA JANE of Ontario, Canada, Social Worker, daughter of Alan

GUEST GORNALL

JOHN FOSTER of Tattenhall, Cheshire, Retired Solicitor, son of Richard deceased
ANTHONY RICHARD of Sunningdale, Berkshire, Literary Agent, another son of Richard
    deceased
RICHARD FOSTER DAWSON of Sunningdale, Berkshire, Student, son of Anthony Richard
LUCY of London, Management Consultant, daughter of Anthony Richard

HALL

IAN WHYTE of Preston, Retired Railway Traffic Controller, Honorary Freeman, Coun-
    cillor, former Mayor of the Borough and one of the Stewards of this Guild
CATHERINE MARY (COTTON) of Blackburn, daughter of Ian Whyte, Freeman and former
    Mayor of the Borough and one of the Stewards of this Guild

HARRISON

JAMES WARD of Penrith, Solicitor, son of Thomas deceased
THOMAS ALLAN of Ulverston, Gentleman, son of Allan deceased
ROBIN ALLAN GILL of Preston, Chartered Surveyor, son of Thomas Allan
ANNA PATRICIA, daughter of Robin Allan Gill

HENERY

RONALD JAMES of Preston, Engineer, son of James, former Mayor of the Borough,
    deceased
PETER JAMES of Lytham, Engineer, son of Ronald James
PAMELA JEAN (CLEATOR) of Manchester, General Practitioner, daughter of Ronald James
ELSIE KATHRYN (HARTH) of Preston, Teacher, another daughter of Ronald James
WALTER CYRIL of Preston, Gentleman, another son of James, former Mayor of the
    Borough, deceased
JUNE MARGARET (WAND) of Preston, Secretary, daughter of Walter Cyril
CAROLE ANNE (MATTA) of Montreal, Canada, Accountant, another daughter of Walter Cyril

HESKETH

ROBERT FLEETWOOD of Meols Hall, Southport, Company Director, son of Roger
    Fleetwood deceased and grandson of Charles Fleetwood deceased

de HOGHTON

RICHARD BERNARD CUTHBERT, Baronet, of Hoghton Tower, Landowner, son of Cuthbert,
    Baronet, deceased
ELENA SUSANNA ISABELLA, daughter of Richard Bernard Cuthbert
THOMAS JAMES DANIEL, son of Richard Bernard Cuthbert

HOOD

JOSEPH of Preston, Chairman of Preston Health Authority, Honorary Freeman, Council-
    lor, former Mayor of the Borough and one of the Stewards of this Guild
MARILYN VIVIENNE (SALTER) of Preston, Teacher, daughter of Joseph, Freeman and
    former Mayor of the Borough and one of the Stewards of this Guild
WINSTON JOSEPH HARRIS of Kirkham, Solicitor, son of Joseph, Freeman and former
    Mayor of the Borough and one of the Stewards of this Guild

KAREN ANGELA (SENIOR) of Preston, Civil Servant, another daughter of Joseph, Freeman
and former Mayor of the Borough and one of the Stewards of this Guild

HOSKIN

GEORGE of Minchinhampton, Accountant, son of Florrie, former Mayor of Preston,
deceased

STEPHEN GEORGE of Minchinhampton, Salesman, son of George

ANDREW GEORGE, son of Stephen George

EMMA LOUISE, daughter of Stephen George

MICHAEL KEITH of Wokingham, Manager, another son of George

ROBERT IAN of Birmingham, Manager, another son of George

DAVID JAMES of Bristol, Student, another son of George

HANNAH RUTH, daughter of David James

HUMPHREYS

RICHARD FOSTER of Preston, Company Chairman, son of John Foster, Alderman of the
Borough, deceased

GORDON JAMES FOSTER of Preston, Managing Director, son of Richard Foster

NATALIE JAYNE, daughter of Gordon James Foster

ANNETTE KATHLEEN (FEARN) of Scarborough, Teacher, daughter of Richard Foster

HUNTER

ROBERT of Southport, Retired Market Gardener, son of Richard deceased

PHILIP ROBERT of Southport, Driver, son of Peter deceased and grandson of Richard
deceased

CATHERINE LOUISE, daughter of Philip Robert

DIANE MARGARET, another daughter of Philip Robert

KEVIN BRIAN of Southport, Joiner, another son of Peter deceased and grandson of
Richard deceased

PAUL KENWYN of Southport, Company Director, son of John Richard deceased and
grandson of Richard deceased

STEPHEN BRIAN RICHARD, son of Paul Kenwyn

DAVID JOHN of Southport, Taxi Driver, another son of John Richard deceased and
grandson of Richard deceased

LUCY JADE, daughter of David John

DAVID JAMES, son of David John

SOPHIE ALICE AMANDA, another daughter of David John

JOSHUA DANIEL, another son of David John

EILIS KATHERINE, another daughter of David John

TREVOR RICHARD of Swanage, Dorset, Social Organiser, another son of John Richard
deceased and grandson of Richard deceased

JOHN of Banks, Haulage Contractor, son of John deceased

JANET MARY (WILDING) of Banks, daughter of John

JACKSON

JOHN WILLIAM of Alton, son of William George deceased

MICHAEL ANTHONY of Alton, Commercial Manager, another son of William George
deceased

CATHERINE ANNE MARGARET, daughter of Michael Anthony

GERARD VINCENT of Durban, South Africa, Hotelier, son of Francis Edward deceased

EDMUND STEPHEN, son of Gerard Vincent

NUALA YVETTE, daughter of Gerard Vincent

PETER JOHN of Sandton, South Africa, Director, another son of Francis Edward deceased

ROGER ANTHONY of Durban, South Africa, another son of Francis Edward deceased

FRANCIS PAUL of Warsaw, Poland, Company Secretary, another son of Francis Edward deceased

JAMES DUNSTAN, son of Francis Paul

CATHERINE RUTH, daughter of Francis Paul

JAMIESON

GORDON JAMES of Nottingham, Headteacher, son of Norman deceased

ANDREW JAMES of Leeds, Archivist, son of Gordon James

JOLLY

ANTHONY CHARLES of Freckleton, Circuit Court Judge and Honorary Recorder of the Borough

MATTHEW CHARLES of London, Doctor of Medicine, son of Anthony Charles, Honorary Recorder of the Borough

PATRICK EDMUND of Leeds, Solicitor, another son of Anthony Charles, Honorary Recorder of the Borough

CHARLOTTE ELIZABETH of Freckleton, Student, daughter of Anthony Charles, Honorary Recorder of the Borough

JONES

RAYMOND HENRY GREENWOOD of Preston, Retired Process Worker and Honorary Alderman of the Borough

KAY-SHUTTLEWORTH

CHARLES GEOFFREY NICHOLAS of Leck Hall, Carnforth, Peer of the Realm, son of Charles Ughtred John deceased

THOMAS EDWARD, son of Charles Geoffrey Nicholas

DAVID CHARLES, another son of Charles Geoffrey Nicholas

WILLIAM JAMES, another son of Charles Geoffrey Nicholas

ROBERT JAMES of London, Company Director, another son of Charles Ughtred John deceased

KEHOE

DENNIS of Preston, Retired Company Director, Councillor, former Mayor of the Borough and one of the Stewards of this Guild

DENNIS PAUL of Elswick, Chief Officer, Royal Fleet Auxiliary, son of Dennis, former Mayor of the Borough and one of the Stewards of this Guild

JOHN MARK of Preston, Company Managing Director, another son of Dennis, former Mayor of the Borough and one of the Stewards of this Guild

MARK SIMON of Preston, Electronics Engineer, another son of Dennis, former Mayor of the Borough and one of the Stewards of this Guild

DAMIAN PETER of Preston, Company Director, another son of Dennis, former Mayor of the Borough and one of the Stewards of this Guild

KATHRYN MARIA (WILD) of Preston, daughter of Dennis, former Mayor of the Borough and one of the Stewards of this Guild

LIVESEY

ROBERT EDWARD of Penwortham, Decorator, son of Richard deceased

LUND

JOSEPH of Preston, Retired Engineer, Former Councillor and Mayor of the Borough

ANTHONY MARTIN of Preston, Builder, son of Joseph, former Mayor of the Borough

MARK ANTHONY of Walton-le-Dale, Postman, son of Anthony Martin

AARON JAMES, son of Mark Anthony

RAYMOND JOSEPH of Preston, another son of Joseph, former Mayor of the Borough

MARLENE ELIZABETH (SHERLIKER) of Preston, Shop Assistant, daughter of Joseph, former Mayor of the Borough

LYTTON

RITA of Jersey, Housewife, Alderman and former Mayor of the Borough

GRAHAM JEFFREY of Worplesden, Medical Practictioner, son of Rita, Alderman and former Mayor of the Borough

MARSHALL

RONALD PHILIP of Preston, Retired College Vice-Principal, Councillor and one of the Stewards of this Guild

KAREN REBEKAH (MARSHALL EVANS) of Shipley, Teacher, daughter of Ronald Philip, one of the Stewards of this Guild

SARAH KIRSTIE (SCHILLING) of Recklinghausen, Germany, Teacher, another daughter of Ronald Philip, one of the Stewards of this Guild

MILLER

JAMES EDGAR of York, Monk and Priest, son of Gerard Joseph Ignatius deceased

HUGH of Golborne, Retired Woodmachinist, son of George White deceased

JOHN BRIAN of Lostock Hall, Toolmaker, son of John Joseph deceased

ALAN JOHN, son of John Brian

DIANE ELIZABETH, daughter of John Brian

JANET MARIE (NICHOLSON) of Lostock Hall, Shop Supervisor, another daughter of John Brian

THOMAS NIGEL of Repton, Consultant Physician, son of Nathaniel Allan deceased

MATTHEW THOMAS VIVIAN of Repton, Medical Student, son of Thomas Nigel

AURIOL JANE VERONA, daughter of Thomas Nigel

ELENA FRANCES LOVEDAY, another daughter of Thomas Nigel

DAVID EDWARD BEYNON, another son of Thomas Nigel

ALEXANDER HENRY JULIAN, another son of Thomas Nigel

MICHAEL JULIAN RUNCIMAN of London, Solicitor, another son of Nathaniel Allan deceased

CHRISTOPHER JAMES NATHANIEL, son of Michael Julian Runciman

THOMAS HENRY WORSLEY, another son of Michael Julian Runciman

THOMAS PARKINSON of Hoscar, Farmer, son of Thomas deceased

THOMAS EDWIN of Mawdesley, Farmer, son of Thomas Parkinson

JANE LOUISE, daughter of Thomas Edwin

STUART EDWIN, son of Thomas Edwin

CAROLINE RUTH (WEBSTER), daughter of Thomas Parkinson

LEO BERNARD of Blackpool, Retired Painter, son of Joseph deceased

BRIAN JOHN of Blackpool, Ride Operator, son of Leo Bernard

DAVID of Blackpool, Shop Assistant, another son of Leo Bernard

ANDREW PAUL of Blackpool, Warehouseman, another son of Leo Bernard

STEVEN of Blackpool, another son of Leo Bernard

CAROLE ANNE (COOK), daughter of Leo Bernard

MOLYNEUX

CYRIL EVAN of Radcliffe-on-Trent, Retired Civil Servant and Former Mayor of the Borough

HERBERT KEVIN of New South Wales, Australia, Teacher, son of Cyril Evan
GERALD WILLIAM of Preston, Public House Licensee, another son of Cyril Evan
ELIZABETH BEATRICE of Preston, Clerk, daughter of Gerald William
SEAN DEREK, son of Gerald William
BEATRICE ALICIA of Brussels, Belgium, School Principal, daughter of Cyril Evan

MYRES

MILES TIMOTHY of Jersey, Professor of Zoology, son of John Nowell Linton deceased and grandson of John Linton, Knight, deceased
JOHN ANTONY LOVELL of Oxford, Rear Admiral, Royal Navy, another son of John Nowell Linton deceased and grandson of John Linton, Knight, deceased
DAVID MILES of Oxford, Student, son of John Antony Lovell
PETER JOHN LUKIS of London, Royal Naval Officer, another son of John Antony Lovell
CHARLES CHRISTOPHER LINTON of Oxford, Army Officer, another son of John Antony Lovell
JOHN CHRISTOPHER of Harpenden, Geologist, son of Arthur Thomas Miles deceased
SUZANNE MARIE, daughter of John Christopher
ROSEMARY HELEN, another daughter of John Christopher
MILES PAUL of Oswestry, General Medical Practictioner, another son of Arthur Thomas Miles deceased
DUNCAN STEWART, son of Miles Paul
CATRIONA SIAN, daughter of Miles Paul
THOMAS PAUL, another son of Miles Paul
JOHN MILES of Preston, Retired Draughtsman, son of Miles Yates deceased
JOHN NICHOLAS of Eccleston, Computer Consultant, son of John Miles
ANDREW NICHOLAS, son of John Nicholas
RACHAEL LOUISE, daughter of John Nicholas
KAREN LESLEY (WEBB) of Preston, Nurse, daughter of John Miles
MICHAEL KEITH of Penwortham, Manager, another son of Miles Yates deceased
GRAHAM KEITH of Penwortham, son of Michael Keith
NICOLA JANE, daughter of Graham Keith
JOHN MICHAEL of Penwortham, Salesman, another son of Michael Keith
JOHN DOUGLAS FORSYTH of Queensland, Australia, Pianola Restorer, son of Miles Claude deceased and grandson of John Linton, Knight, deceased
MILES NICHOLAS COTTER of Victoria, Australia, Paramedic, son of John Douglas Forsyth
MELANIE JANE LECLARE, daughter of Miles Nicholas Cotter
JOHN LINTON ALEXANDER, son of Miles Nicholas Cotter
MILES CRISPIN JULIAN, another son of Miles Nicholas Cotter
JONATHON CHARLES SPRAWSON of Western Australia, Teacher, another son of John Douglas Forsyth
DIANA KATHARINE, daughter of Jonathon Charles Sprawson
MILES PATRICK, son of Jonathon Charles Sprawson
KATHARINE JANE of Queensland, Australia, Fashion Designer, daughter of John Douglas Forsyth
ANNE ISOBEL LOUISA of Western Australia, Manager, another daughter of John Douglas Forsyth
JOHN HUGH LINTON of New South Wales, Australia, Electronics Engineer, son of Miles Roderick Whitelocke deceased and grandson of Miles Claude deceased

OWENS

ANTONY of Preston, Solicitor, Town Clerk/Chief Executive of the Borough and Clerk of this Guild
JUDITH CAROLINE of Preston, Student, daughter of Antony, Clerk of this Guild
ALISON JANE of Preston, Student, another daughter of Antony, Clerk of this Guild

PARK

ROGER WULSTAN of Walmer Bridge, Retired Architectural Photographer, son of Francis Joseph deceased

ADRIAN FRANCIS of New Brunswick, Canada, Geologist, son of Roger Wulstan

ANDREW WILLIAM of Penwortham, Electrician, another son of Roger Wulstan

MATTHEW WILLIAM, son of Andrew William

REBECCA LOUISE, daughter of Andrew William

NICHOLAS WULSTAN of Bristol, Film Director, another son of Roger Wulstan

ADAM LOUIS of Longton, Joiner, another son of Roger Wulstan

EMILY JANE, daughter of Adam Louis

ALICE MARY, another daughter of Adam Louis

JANET ELIZABETH (STEFAN) of Longton, daughter of Roger Wulstan

PARKER

HAROLD of Preston, Honorary Freeman, Councillor of the Borough and Mayor of this Guild

GEORGE of Irlam, Retired Newspaper Circulation Director and brother of Harold, Freeman and Mayor of this Guild

GARY of Preston, Civil Servant, son of Harold, Freeman and Mayor of this Guild

DEBORAH of Preston, Journalist, daughter of Harold, Freeman and Mayor of this Guild

HOWARD of Preston, Property Developer, another son of Harold, Freeman and Mayor of this Guild

AMANDA LOUISE of Preston, another daughter of Harold, Freeman and Mayor of this Guild

JOANNA of Preston, another daughter of Harold, Freeman and Mayor of this Guild

PARKER-ROBINSON

HENRY THOMAS of Preston, grandson of Harold Parker, Freeman and Mayor of this Guild

POWNALL

JOSEPH SAUL of Preston, Retired Engineer and former Mayor of the Borough

ANNE CHRISTINE (SHORROCK) of Preston, Teacher, daughter of Joseph Saul, former Mayor of the Borough

JOHN GRAHAM of Preston, Driver, son of Joseph Saul, former Mayor of the Borough

DAVID ANTHONY of Penwortham, Plasterer, another son of Joseph Saul, former Mayor of the Borough

MICHAEL EDWARD of Preston, Machine Operative, another son of Joseph Saul, former Mayor of the Borough

JOSEPH KEVIN of Lostock Hall, Engineer, another son of Joseph Saul, former Mayor of the Borough

CAROLINE SUSAN (BERKLEY) of Penwortham, another daughter of Joseph Saul, former Mayor of the Borough

PHILIP JAMES of Preston, Surveyor, another son of Joseph Saul, former Mayor of the Borough

GEOFFREY CHARLES of Preston, Plasterer, another son of Joseph Saul, former Mayor of the Borough

RATCLIFFE

THOMAS DEREK of Hoghton, son of George deceased

PHILLIP NEIL of Preston, Merchant Seaman, son of Thomas Derek

ALISON JANE (DEWHURST) of Walton-le-Dale, Cook, daughter of Thomas Derek

RAWCLIFFE

MARY of Preston, Retired Teacher, Councillor, former Mayor of the Borough and Deputy
  Mayor of this Guild

RAWSTORNE

MARTIN GWILLYM of Ilminster, Somerset, Solicitor, son of Robert Gwillym deceased
HENRY GWILLYM of Ilminster, Somerset, Student, son of Martin Gwillym
THOMAS LOWRY of Ilminster, Somerset, Student, another son Martin Gwillym
JULIET ROSE, daughter of Martin Gwillym
JULIAN ROBERT of Warwick, Solicitor, another son of Robert Gwillym deceased
GUY THURSTAN, son of Julian Robert
DANIEL RUDDOCK, another son of Julian Robert
HUGO LAWRENCE, another son of Julian Robert
ANDREW FRANCIS of Hereford, Accountant, another son of Robert Gwillym deceased
HELENA MARY, daughter of Andrew Francis
EDWARD CHARLES GLAS, son of Andrew Francis
ANGUS FLEETWOOD LAWRENCE, another son of Andrew Francis

RHODES

ERIC CHRISTOPHER of Farnham, Printer and Paper Merchant, son of George deceased
BARTON JAMES DANIEL of Farnham, Student, son of Eric Christopher
HEIDI JANE, daughter of Eric Christopher
CHARLES RICHARD, another son of Eric Christopher

RICHARDSON

ALBERT JAMES of Preston, Company Director, Councillor and former Mayor of the
  Borough

RIGBY

COLIN ELSTON of Preston, Retired Company Secretary, son of Sidney Elston deceased
COLIN HOWARD of Wrockwardine, Shropshire, Company Director, son of Colin Elston
VICTORIA ANNE, daughter of Colin Howard
ALEXANDER JAMES, son of Colin Howard
GEORGE HOWARD, another son of Colin Howard
TIMOTHY ELSTON of London, Financier, another son of Colin Elston
VANESSA (LIVESEY) of Kirkby Lonsdale, daughter of Colin Elston
JUDITH (WEITZ) of Los Angeles, California, USA, another daughter of Colin Elston
JOHN BRIAN STUART of Preston, Retired Engineer, another son of Sidney Elston deceased
SARAH LOUISE (KOZIARSKA) of Lostock Hall, Civil Servant, daughter of John Brian Stuart

SALTER

ARTHUR of Lostock Hall, Retired Electrical Engineer, son of Charles deceased
ANN CHRISTINE of Lostock Hall, Radiographer, daughter of Arthur
THOMAS of Penwortham, another son of Charles deceased
STEPHEN THOMAS of New Longton, Teacher, (referred to as Stephen in the Guild Roll
  of 1952), son of Thomas
PHILIP RICHARD, son of Stephen Thomas
FREDERICK ARTHUR of Penwortham, Graphic Designer, another son of Thomas

SERGEANT

JOHN EDWARD NORTH of London, Lord of the Manor of Kirkham, son of Edward
  Geoffrey deceased

NICHOLAS JOHN of Victoria, Australia, Computer Programmer, son of John Edward North

REBECCA MARY of South Australia, Secretary, daughter of John Edward North

VIRGINIA JANE (JONES) of South Australia, another daughter of John Edward North

GEORGE FRANCIS of Wrea Green, Company Director, son of Joseph Theodore deceased

STEPHEN GEORGE JOSEPH of Staines, Manager (referred to as Stephen George in the Guild Roll of 1972), son of George Francis

JESSICA MARY, daughter of Stephen George Joseph

CHRISTINE MONICA of Kirkham, Secretary, daughter of George Francis

CAROLE ELIZABETH of Wrea Green, Clerk, another daughter of George Francis

SHARPLES

JOSEPH KENNETH of Preston, Engineer, son of Catherine, former Mayor and Honorary Freeman of the Borough deceased

JACQUELINE ANN (MERTER) of Hoghton, daughter of Joseph Kenneth

PAULINE MARY of Hoghton, Teacher, another daughter of Joseph Kenneth

JOHN WILLIAM of Tunbridge Wells, Teacher, son of John of Exeter deceased

TIMOTHY JOHN DALE of Hastings, Student, son of John William

JEREMY CHARLES of Hastings, Student, another son of John William

NICHOLAS WIILLIAM, another son of John William

BENJAMIN NELSON JAMES, another son of John William

SAMUEL, another son of John William

JONATHAN FREDERICK ADAM HORWOOD, another son of John William

SHERLIKER

FRANCIS RAYMOND of Runcorn, Retired Research Chemist, son of Ignatius deceased

PETER FRANCIS of Runcorn, Company Personnel Manager, son of Francis Raymond

STEPHEN JOHN of Charnock Richard, Chartered Engineer, another son of Francis Raymond

LAURA ANN, daughter of Stephen John

SIMON MARK, son of Stephen John

SUSAN MARGARET of Runcorn, Local Government Officer, daughter of Francis Raymond

SINGLETON

ROBERT WILLIAM of Blackburn, Retired Bank Manager, son of Robert deceased

JANET ANNE of Blackburn, Radiographer, daughter of Robert William

MICHAEL TELFORD of Stevenage, Manager, son of Allan deceased

MATTHEW JAMES of Stevenage, Student, son of Michael Telford

JOANNA LINDY, daughter of Michael Telford

GEOFFREY NEIL of Reading, Printer, another son of Allan deceased

SIMON PAUL, son of Geoffrey Neil

JAMES IAN, another son of Geoffrey Neil

EDWIN WISEMAN of Burnley, Gentleman, son of George Edwin deceased

BERNARD ANTHONY of Burnley, Trades Instructor, son of Edwin Wiseman

ANTHONY of Burnley, Electrician, son of Bernard Anthony

BEN ANTHONY, son of Anthony

JUNE (ZELLY) of Burnley, Office Supervisor, daughter of Bernard Anthony

JEAN MARY (JOHNSON) of Burnley, daughter of Edwin Wiseman

FREDERICK of Bradford, Retired Materials Controller, son of Joseph Wiseman deceased and grandson of George Edwin deceased

PHILIP DANIEL, son of Roderick Michael deceased and grandson of Frederick

RICHARD MARK, another son of Roderick Michael deceased and grandson of Frederick

THOMAS of Great Harwood, Retired Farmer, son of Robert deceased

WILLIAM LESLIE of Longridge, Steel Erector, son of Thomas

LEE DUDLEY of Longridge, Steel Erector, son of William Leslie
JASON THOMAS of Longridge, Steel Erector, another son of William Leslie
ROBERT GEOFFREY of Longridge, Tarpaulin Repairer, another son of Thomas
KIRSTY MARIE, daughter of Robert Geoffrey
ANDREW GEOFFREY, son of Robert Geoffrey
LORNA DUILLIA (KING) of Blackburn, Caterer, daughter of Thomas
MAUREEN (GREENALL) of Longridge, Baker, another daughter of Thomas
ANDREW of Claughton-on-Brock, Farmer, son of Richard deceased and grandson of
    Robert deceased
STUART, son of Andrew
LYNNE, daughter of Andrew
JOHN of Myerscough, Farmer, another son of Richard deceased and grandson of Robert
    deceased
RICHARD WILLIAM of Myerscough, Farmer, son of John
GRAHAM JOHN of Myerscough, Engineer, another son of John
PAUL EDWARD, another son of John
HARRY of Whitechapel, Farm Worker, son of Harry deceased and grandson of Robert
    deceased
ROBERT of Whitechapel, Farmer, another son of Harry deceased and grandson of Robert
    deceased
GEORGE of Penwortham, Quality Assurance, Manager, son of George deceased
JAMES of Broughton, Clinical Psychologist, another son of George deceased
PAUL JAMES, son of James
MARK ALEXANDER, another son of James
ROBERT of Preston, Cost Controller, another son of George deceased
GRAHAM ROBERT of Twickenham, Advertising Executive, son of Robert
PHILIP STEPHEN of Preston, Shop Assistant, another son of Robert
JOHN of Goosnargh, Farmer, son of John deceased and grandson of Thomas deceased
JOHN of Goosnargh, Farmer, son of John
SARAH ELIZABETH, daughter of John
COLIN of Goosnargh, Farmer, another son of John
JAMES ROBERT of Goosnargh, Farmer, another son of John
ANDREW of Goosnargh, Farmer, another son of John
DOREEN MARGARET (WOOD) of Goosnargh, Bank Clerk, daughter of John
BARBARA STELLA (KNOWLES) of Preston, Nurse, another daughter of John

SMIRK

CHARLES EDWARD of Preston, son of Robert Joseph deceased
NIGEL ROBERT of Preston, Engineer, another son of Robert Joseph deceased

SMITH

ARTHUR CHRISTOPHER LLEWLYN of Abilly, France, Retired Solicitor, son of Samuel
    Harold deceased and grandson of John Robert deceased
ELIZABETH HELEN COMSTOCK of London, Literary Agent, daughter of Arthur Christo-
    pher Llewelyn
LEWIS PROCTOR of Skipton, Company Director, son of Lewis Barlow deceased and
    grandson of John Robert deceased
PETER LEWIS PROCTOR of Chulmleigh, Devon, Chartered Civil Engineer, son of Lewis
    Proctor
CHARLOTTE ELIZABETH PROCTOR, daughter of Peter Lewis Proctor
HARRIET LOUISE PROCTOR, another daughter of Peter Lewis Proctor
CHRISTOPHER DAVID PROCTOR of Leeds, Surveyor, another son of Lewis Proctor
RICHARD MICHAEL PROCTOR of Skipton, Student, another son of Lewis Proctor
NICOLA of Leeds, Physiotherapist, daughter of Lewis Proctor

STANLEY BERNARD of Garstang, Retired Company Chairman, son of Stanley Herbert deceased and grandson of John Robert deceased

STANLEY BRIAN RUTHERFORD of Garstang, Textile Agent, son of Stanley Bernard

SIMON MICHAEL RUTHERFORD, son of Stanley Brian Rutherford

SALLY JOANNE, daughter of Stanley Brian Rutherford

PETER ROBERT MILLER of Overijse, Belgium, Manager, another son of Stanley Bernard

GEMMA ANN MILLER, daughter of Peter Robert Miller

SAMUEL PETER RUTHERFORD MILLER, son of Peter Robert Miller

DEIDRE GILLIAN (SWAILES) of Feltham, Middlesex, Civil Servant, daughter of Stanley Bernard

JOHN TATTERSALL of Preston, Consultant, son of John Palmer deceased and grandson of John Robert deceased

ANDREW NICHOLAS of Preston, Gardener, son of John Tattersall

SARAH JANE, daughter of John Tattersall

BRYAN PRESTON of Oxshott, Surrey, Building Contractor, son of Sydney Preston deceased

DAVID PRESTON of Dorking, Surrey, Company Director, another son of Sydney Preston deceased

JANINE LYNN, daughter of David Preston

DAVID PRESTON, son of David Preston

CAROLYN MARY, another daughter of David Preston

FRANCIS ROBERT of Morden, Retired Shop Assistant, son of Frederick Edward deceased

STANLEY

EDWARD JOHN, 18th Earl of Derby, son of Edward Montague Cavendish, Lord Stanley PC MC deceased

EDWARD RICHARD WILLIAM of London, Merchant Banker, son of Hugh Henry Montague deceased and grandson of Edward Montague Cavendish, Lord Stanley PC MC deceased

PETER HUGH CHARLES of Newmarket, Stud Manager, another son of Hugh Henry Montague deceased and grandson of Edward Montague Cavendish Lord Stanley PC MC deceased

NICHOLAS CHARLES of Liverpool, Film Production Accountant, son of Michael Charles deceased

TAYLOR

JOHN JAMES of Preston, Retired Timber Merchant, son of John William, Alderman, former Mayor of the Borough and a Steward of the Guild of 1972 deceased

JOHN DAVID of London, Barrister, son of John James

CHRISTINE MARY (PEACOCK) of Frome, Somerset, daughter of John James

HELEN MARGARET of Taplow, Physiotherapist, another daughter of John James

WILLIAM SIMON of Lytham St. Annes, Accountant, son of Gerald Raymond deceased

ARTHUR CLIFFORD of Preston, Retired Company Director and former Mayor of the Borough

NEIL RAE of Preston, Company Director, son of Arthur Clifford, former Mayor of the Borough

NANCY of Preston, Councillor and former Mayor of the Borough

BARRY RICHARD BYROM of Preston, Engineer, son of Nancy, former Mayor of the Borough

TERENCE WILLIAM HALDREN of Morecambe, Catering Manager, another son of Nancy, former Mayor of the Borough

TEEBAY

PETER FRENCH of Liverpool, General Medical Practitioner, son of George Cyril deceased

PAUL ANTHONY of Runcorn, Dental Practitioner, son of Peter French

RACHAEL JESSICA EVELYN, daughter of Paul Anthony
SARAH ELIZABETH, another daughter of Paul Anthony
LYDIA JANE, another daughter of Paul Anthony
ANDREW PETER of Hayes, Computer Analyst, another son of Peter French
RICHARD GEORGE WILLIAM, son of Andrew Peter
PETER ANTHONY GORDON, another son of Andrew Peter
ANNE MARY (SPENCER) of Falmouth, Teacher, daughter of Peter French
CATHRYN JANE, another daughter of Peter French

TOPPING

FREDERICK JAMES of Burnaby, Canada, Retired Building Contractor, son of John of
Preston deceased
JOHN FREDERICK of Vernon, Canada, Electronics Technician, son of Frederick James
CHRISTOPHER ALLAN, son of John Frederick
KEVIN MICHAEL, another son of John Frederick
BEVERLEY (CRAY) of Richmond, Canada, Clerk, daughter of Frederick James
ALAN DAVID of Bolton, Printer, son of John Richard deceased and grandson of Richard
deceased
CHRISTOPHER ALAN of Bolton, Printer, son of Alan David
CAROLINE CLAIRE of Bolton, Clerk, daughter of Alan David
ANDREW of Poulton-le-Fylde, Soldier, son of Eric deceased and grandson of Richard
deceased
NIGEL of Marton, Garage Manager, another son of Eric deceased and grandson of
Richard deceased
JAMES of Preston, Gentleman, son of James deceased
ALAN of Preston, Electrical Engineer, son of James
GRAHAM, son of Alan
BARBARA (HALLAS) of Preston, daughter of James
JOHN RICHARD CHARLES of Liverpool, Sales Manager, son of Thomas Edward deceased
CHARLES PETER of Ashton, Northants, Company Director, son of Cyril deceased
CHRISTOPHER JAMES of Ashton, Northants, Student, son of Charles Peter
FREDERICK of Preston, Retired Company Director, son of Frederick deceased
RAYMOND LEIGH of Preston, Company Director, son of Frederick
STUART LEIGH of Preston, Bank Clerk, son of Raymond Leigh
MATTHEW RICHARD, another son of Raymond Leigh
DAVID STEWART of Preston, Company Director, another son of Frederick
EMMA CLAIRE, daughter of David Stewart
HANNAH ELIZABETH, another daughter of David Stewart
LUCY FRANCES, another daughter of David Stewart
CLIFFORD of Newark, Methodist Minister, another son of Frederick deceased
PAUL of Sevenoaks, Kent, Operations Director, son of Clifford
CHRISTINE (COLE) of Newark, Teacher, daughter of Clifford
NORMAN of Walton-le-Dale, Retired Postal Worker, another son of Frederick deceased
MARTIN STUART, of Walton-le-Dale, Supervisor, son of Norman
LUENA MARGARET, daughter of Martin Stuart
SAMANTHA JANE, another daughter of Martin Stuart
JOHN of Chester, Retired Bank Manager, son of James deceased
ANNE ELIZABETH (WARD) of Nottingham, Teacher, daughter of John
MARGARET PATRICIA (MADGE) of Nottingham, Local Government Officer, another
daughter of John
BARBARA GRACE (FURNIVAL) of Chester, Local Government Officer, another daughter
of John
CATHERINE CLARE (BROOKES) of Great Sutton, Wirrall, Midwife, another daughter of
John

JOHN ALLAN of Cleveland, U.S.A., Research and Development Manager (described as Frank John Allan in the Guild Roll of 1972), son of Allan deceased

KAREN ELIZABETH, daughter of John Allan

ALLAN GEOFFREY, son of John Allan

TOULMIN

ARTHUR HEATON of Cranleigh, Retired Solicitor, son of John deceased and grandson of John deceased

JOHN KELVIN of London, Queen's Counsel, son of Arthur Heaton

GEOFFREY JOHN DONALD of London, son of John Kelvin

ALISON ELIZABETH, daughter of John Kelvin

HILARY LYDIA, another daughter of John Kelvin

WILLIAM BENNETT of Penwortham, Retired Agricultural Produce Merchant, another son of John deceased and grandson of John deceased

STEPHEN WILLIAM of Preston, Accountant, son of William Bennett

PENELOPE JANE (HEFFERNAN) of Prestwich, Property Manager, daughter of William Bennett

JOHN HEATON of Preston, Retired Solicitor, son of George Fisher deceased and grandson of John deceased

VICKERS

KENNETH WILFRID of Preston, Driver, son of William deceased and grandson of Daniel deceased

IAN STUART of Preston, Labourer, son of Kenneth Wilfrid

LISA MARIE, daughter of Ian Stuart

JENNA LOUISE, another daughter of Ian Stuart

REBECCA JANE, another daughter of Ian Stuart

MICHAEL ANTHONY, son of Ian Stuart

KARL DENNIS of Preston, another son of Kenneth Wilfrid

DARREN BILLY, another son of Kenneth Wilfrid

JADE LOUISE, daughter of Darren Billy

SUSAN CATHRINE, daughter of Kenneth Wilfred

GERARD of Peterborough, Electrician, son of William Joseph deceased and grandson of Daniel deceased

MELISSA ELLEN, daughter of Gerard

LAURA GRACE, another daughter of Gerard

DOMINIC GERARD, son of Gerard

ALBERT EDWARD of Walton-le-Dale, Retired Joiner, son of Albert Edward deceased

GREGORY GEORGE of Preston, Education Officer, (described as Gregory in the Guild Roll of 1972), son of Albert Edward

CLAIRE LOUISE ANN, daughter of Gregory George

PAUL GREGORY, son of Gregory George

JAMES BERNARD of Preston, Sheet Metal Worker, son of James deceased and grandson of Albert Edward deceased

JOSEPH of Preston, Toolmaker, son of Joseph deceased

JAMES of Preston, Taxi Proprietor, another son of Joseph deceased

GARY of Wooloware, New South Wales, Australia, Chemical Engineer, son of James

ZAK NAYLOR, son of Gary

CLAUDIA CHAREL, daughter of Gary

STEPHEN JAMES of Walton-le-Dale, Market Trader, another son of James

JAMIE LEE, son of Stephen James

JODIE ALICE, daughter of Stephen James

DANIEL of London, Retired Security Officer, son of William deceased

DANIEL STEPHEN CHARLES of Ilford, Staff Welfare Officer, son of Daniel

MARK THOMAS of Ilford, Electrician, son of Daniel Stephen Charles

LYNNETTE ANNE KATHERINE (ROCK) of London, Nurse, daughter of Daniel Stephen
Charles

KAREN SUSAN of Ilford, Insurance Broker, another daughter of Daniel Stephen Charles

CHRISTINE JANET (COUSINS) of Hornchurch, Essex, another daughter of Daniel Stephen
Charles

TERENCE JAMES ROY of Ilford, Advertising Executive, another son of Daniel

PAUL FRANCIS of Stratford, Site Supervisor, son of Terence James Roy

ADAM DAVID, son of Paul Francis

STEPHEN PAUL, another son of Paul Francis

VICTORIA ANN, daughter of Paul Francis

TERENCE JOHN of Dagenham, Chef, another son of Terence James Roy

MICHELLE FRANCES, daughter of Terence James Roy

ALAN JAMES of Rainham, Essex, Electrician, (described as Allan James in the Guild Roll
of 1972) another son of Daniel

KELLY LOUISE, daughter of Alan James

MARY ELIZABETH (GROSTATE) of London, Market Trader, daughter of Daniel

VERONICA FRANCES (RYALLS) of Ilford, Care Officer, another daughter of Daniel

TOM ALLENBY of Kirkham, Retired Physiotherapist, son of Thomas of
Bamber Bridge deceased

THOMAS DANIEL of Garlieston, Newton Stewart, Scotland, Retired Engineer, son of
Thomas of Lancaster deceased

MICHAEL JOHN of Whithorn, Wigtownshire, Scotland, Newsagent, son of Thomas Daniel

JOSHUA JAMIE, son of Michael John

KITTY ELIZABETH, daughter of Michael John

MAUREEN JOY (TOMLINSON) of Whauphill, Newton Stewart, Scotland, Teacher, daughter of Thomas Daniel

HENRY ROBERTSON of Lancaster, Retired Joiner, another son of Thomas of Lancaster
deceased

WALMSLEY

JOHN of Preston, Gentleman, son of James deceased

JOAN (KEAN), daughter of John

BASIL of Barnston, Wirrall, Retired Security Controller, son of Benjamine deceased

MICHAEL BENJAMIN FRANCIS of Higher Tranmere, Catering Manager, son of Basil

CHRISTOPHER COLIN of Alberta, Canada, Senior Maintenance Supervisor, another son
of Basil

AMANDA CRYSTAL, daughter of Christopher Colin

SARAH ELAINE, another daughter of Christopher Colin

MAUREEN ISABELLA (MURPHY) of Villa Nova, USA, daughter of Basil

GERARD of Preston, Retired Electrician, Councillor and former Mayor of the Borough

NEIL ALFRED of Preston, Plasterer, son of Gerard, former Mayor of the Borough

JACQUELINE (REID) of Preston, daughter of Gerard, former Mayor of the Borough

ANN LYDIA of Preston, Textile Operative, another daughter of Gerard, former Mayor of
the Borough

JAMES DOMINIC of Preston, Technician, another son of Gerard, former Mayor of the
Borough

WARD

JOHN COULTHURST of Goosnargh, Retired Medical Practitioner, son of John James of
Ashton-on-Ribble, Dental Surgeon, Mayor of the Guild of 1952, deceased

JOHN JAMES of Broughton, Solicitor, son of John Coulthurst

FIONA JANE, daughter of John James

LUCY GEORGINA, another daughter of John James

JOHN CHRISTOPHER, son of John James
SUSAN PENELOPE (PREST) of Blackburn, Accountant, daughter of John Coulthurst
JOSEPH of Preston, Retired Engineer, Councillor and former Mayor of the Borough
COLIN JOSEPH of Preston, Sales Clerk, son of Joseph, former Mayor of the Borough

WEIR

ROBERT of Preston, Retired Sheet Metal Worker, former Mayor of the Borough
ROBERT of Preston, Engineering Designer, son of Robert, former Mayor of the Borough

WHITTLE

RICHARD JOHN of Lightwater, Surrey, Chartered Accountant, son of John deceased and
   grandson of Richard deceased
CHARLES LAURENCE of Leyland, Optician, another son of John deceased and grandson
   of Richard deceased
ELISABETH CLAIRE, daughter of Charles Laurence
MARTIN ANTHONY, son of Charles Laurence
HELEN MARGARET, another daughter of Charles Laurence
JAMES JUDE WORDEN of Chorley, Sales Manager, son of Francis Richard deceased and
   grandson of Richard deceased
JOANNE LOUISE, daughter of James Jude Worden
ALISON KARIN, another daughter of James Jude Worden
ROBERT FRANCIS of Chorley, Accountant, another son of Francis Richard deceased and
   grandson of Richard deceased
JASON DAVID, son of Robert Francis
BEN ROBERT, another son of Robert Francis
THOMAS of Lytham St. Annes, Retired Bank Manager, son of Thomas deceased and
   grandson of William deceased
PETER LAWRENCE of Lytham St Annes, Accounts Manager, son of Thomas
CHRISTOPHER ROY of Bermuda, Chartered Accountant, another son of Thomas
JEREMY RICHARD of Bermuda, Student, son of Christopher Roy
BARBARA MARY (WEATHERBEE) of Denver, Colorado, USA, daughter of Thomas
HENRY GREGORY of Dorchester, (a Burgess of the Guild of 1952), another son of Thomas
   deceased and grandson of William deceased
ANNE (BUTLER) of Market Drayton, daughter of Henry Gregory
SARAH ELIZABETH of Brighton, Computer Programmer, another daughter of Henry
   Gregory
MELANIE ANNE (KINSMAN) of Brighton, another daughter of Henry Gregory
JOHN FREDERICK of Preston, Loom Overlooker, son of Frederick deceased
GARETH JOHN, son of John Frederick
SIMONA, daughter of John Frederick
ALFRED of Preston, Bus Driver, another son of Frederick deceased
PAUL ALFRED, son of Alfred
STEVEN JOHN, another son of Alfred
SARAH LOUISE, daughter of Alfred
DEREK of Preston, Labourer, another son of Frederick deceased
GORDON of Penwortham, Driver, another son of Frederick deceased
CRAIG JOHN FREDERICK, son of Gordon
KATE ANN ELIZABETH, daughter of Gordon

WILLIAMSON

DENNIS of Worthing, West Sussex, Accountant, son of Matthew deceased
SUSAN MARY of London, Teacher, daughter of Dennis
PENELOPE ANN (ROBERTS) of Victoria, Australia, Medical Practitioner, another daughter
   of Dennis

LINDSAY MARY (BLAKELOCK) of London, Social Worker, another daughter of Dennis
PETER of Wimbledon, Chartered Engineer, another son of Matthew deceased
PAUL ERIC DOMINIC of London, Museum Curator, son of Peter
SIMON DENNIS of Wantage, TV News Operations Supervisor, another son of Peter
JAMES ALEXANDER, son of Simon Dennis
KATHRYN HANNAH, daughter of Simon Dennis
NANCY MARY (BOSTON) of Leicester, Journalist, daughter of Peter
MARY TERESA (HOWARTH) of Sheffield, Teacher, another daughter of Peter
CHRISTINE MARGARET of Sheffield, Teacher, another daughter of Peter

WILSON

FRANCIS EDEN of Broughton, Retired Solicitor, son of Albert William deceased
CHARLES EDWARD of Singapore, Chartered Accountant, son of Francis Eden
TAMSIN ANNE, daughter of Charles Edward
KIM ANNE, another daughter of Charles Edward
RICHARD THOMAS HENRY of London, Solicitor, another son of Francis Eden
KATERIN ELIZABETH, daughter of Richard Thomas Henry
SALLY JANE, another daughter of Richard Thomas Henry
THOMAS JAMES PATRICK, son of Richard Thomas Henry
ANDREW JAMES of Broughton, Solicitor, Under Sheriff of Lancashire, another son of Francis Eden
CHARLES ROBERT EDEN, son of Andrew James
EDWARD JAMES THOMAS, another son of Andrew James
JENNIFER MARY (HOPKIN) of St Annes, Teacher, daughter of Francis Eden
ALBERT GERALD of New South Wales, Australia, Grazier, son of Gerald Edward deceased and grandson of Albert William deceased
DAVID HENRY THOMAS of Perth, Australia, RAAF Officer, another son of Gerald Edward deceased and grandson of Albert William deceased
RICHARD THOMAS, son of David Henry Thomas
JOSHUA DAVID, another son of David Henry Thomas
HENRY VALENTINE of New South Wales, Australia, Retired Grazier, son of Charles Valentine deceased
SUSAN JOAN (COOPER) of New South Wales, Australia, daughter of Henry Valentine

WOODCOCK

THOMAS of Hurst Green, Solicitor, son of Thomas deceased
THOMAS of London, Somerset Herald, son of Thomas and grandson of Thomas deceased
CATHERINE (WALKER) of Ribchester, Nursery Garden Proprietor, daughter of Thomas of Hurst Green
GRAHAM of Rossendale, Solicitor, another son of Thomas deceased
BRIAN of Jersey, Retired Solicitor, another son of Thomas deceased
JAMES WILLIAM of Jersey, Student, son of Brian
SARA JANE of Jersey, Wine Merchant, daughter of Brian
SAMUEL GRAHAM of Blackburn, Administrator, son of Samuel Richard deceased and grandson of Thomas deceased
IAN PHILIP of Warminster, Wiltshire, Farmer, son of John Forbes deceased
SARAH JANE (SINCLAIR) of Teddington, daughter of Ian Philip
RACHAEL MARY (AUSTIN) of Twickenham, another daughter of Ian Philip
ANNA RUTH (GENT) of Newbury, another daughter of Ian Philip

WOODS

BARRY THOMAS of Preston, Cashier, son of Barton Neville deceased
MARK JOHN of Preston, Production Manager, son of Barry Thomas
VICTORIA LOUISE, daughter of Mark John

Foreign Burgesses

BLACKHURST

DAVID of Ormskirk, Company Director, son of Robert Whalley deceased
ROBERT RYAN, son of David
JOHN EDWARD, another son of David
MARGARET ELIZABETH, daughter of David
SARAH ALISON, another daughter of David
ROBERT WARD of Lytham St Annes, Machine Operator, another son of Robert Whalley
    deceased
RICHARD MATTHEW of Lytham St. Annes, Sales Agent, another son of Robert Whalley
    deceased
EDWARD, son of Richard Matthew
LAURA ELIZABETH, daughter of Richard Matthew

BRANDWOOD

JOHN of Penwortham, Stockbroker, son of Frank deceased
KAREN JANE (LOWE) of Penwortham, Clerk, daughter of John
ANNA LOUISE (TAYLOR) of Illinois, USA, another daughter of John
GRAHAM ALAN of Lancaster, Administrator, son of Walter Ronald deceased
REBECCA GAIL, daughter of Graham Alan
HELEN KATY, another daughter of Graham Alan
MICHAEL of Lancaster, Sales Manager, another son of Walter Ronald deceased
SARAH LOUISE, daughter of Michael
DAWN ELIZABETH, another daughter of Michael
MALCOLM JOHN of Lichfield, Teacher, another son of Walter Ronald deceased
JASON DAVID, son of Malcolm John
ALEXANDER JOHN, another son of Malcolm John
MARK of Cleveleys, Police Officer, another son of Walter Ronald deceased
DANIEL PAUL RONALD, son of Mark
HEATHER LOUISE, daughter of Mark
CARL MARTIN of Horton-in-Ribblesdale, Soldier, another son of Walter Ronald deceased
CONNOR MATTHEW, son of Carl Martin

BRANDWOOD-SPENCER

DAVID of Penwortham, Chartered Civil Engineer, son of Frank Bertram deceased and
    grandson of Frank Brandwood deceased
MICHAEL DAVID of Penwortham, Salesman, son of David
SARAH, daughter of David

ELLISON

FRANK of Leyland, Architectural Technician, son of James Henry deceased
IAIN STUART of Wyton, RAF Fitter, son of Frank
ELAINE (PRESSLEY) of Euxton, daughter of Frank

HOUGHTON

MAURICE THOMAS of Aylesbury, Financial Consultant, son of Thomas of Reading
    deceased and grandson of Thomas of Hutton deceased
STEVEN ANDREW, son of Maurice Thomas
KATIE SARAH, daughter of Maurice Thomas
THOMAS of Crewe, Retired Farm Manager, son of Thomas of Haslington deceased
THOMAS FREDERICK of Haslington, Farmer, son of Thomas

THOMAS SHAW, son of Thomas Frederick
RACHEAL LEANNE, daughter of Thomas Frederick
NEIL TIMPERLEY of Newbold, Teacher, son of John deceased and grandson of Thomas of Haslington deceased
DOUGLAS GERARD of Preston, Clerk, son of William Thomas deceased and grandson of Thomas deceased
PETER THOMAS of Ulverston, Priest, son of Douglas Gerard
EDWARD JOSEPH of Preston, Student, another son of Douglas Gerard
MARY (DONLAN) of Preston, Careers Officer, daughter of Douglas Gerard
ADRIENNE (WARLEY) of Lytham, another daughter of Douglas Gerard
ANNE (SHAW) of Preston, another daughter of Douglas Gerard
COLETTE (SAUNDERS) of Hitchin, Nurse, another daughter of Douglas Gerard
GEORGE EDWARD of Cheadle Hulme, Retired Buyer, son of Robert Ward deceased
SYDNEY of Birmingham, Retired Accountant, another son of Robert Ward deceased
BRIAN DAVID of Tynemouth, Sales Manager, another son of Robert Arnold deceased and grandson of Robert Ward deceased
PHILIP ROBERT WILLIAM, son of Brian David

SOUTHWORTH

GILBERT of Carlisle, Company Director, son of Gilbert deceased
PETER of Carlisle, Postman, son of Gilbert
JULIE of Carlisle, Air Stewardess, daughter of Gilbert
ANN of Carlisle, Computer Operator, another daughter of Gilbert
CAROL of Carlisle, Sales Office Manager, another daughter of Gilbert

Appendix 6

List of sponsors for the 1992 Guild

Industrial sponsors:

British Aerospace Defence
British Nuclear Fuels plc—Springfields
Lancashire County Council
National Westminster Bank
Norweb plc
Heritage Covers Ltd (Plumbs)

Sponsors:

42 (North West) Brigade
Alliott, Rawkins and Holden—Chartered Accountants
Barclays Bank plc
Baxi
British Tourist Authority
British Telecom plc
British Gas plc
Building Design Partnership
Chris Miller Ltd
CCA Stationery Ltd
Commission for New Towns
Country Landowners Association
Countryside Commission

Daniel Thwaites plc
English Tourist Board
English Nature
Fishers Carpets
Friends of the Harris Museum and Art Gallery
GEC Alsthom Traction Ltd
Harris Charity
Heartbeat
Heineken
Iron Trades Insurance Co Ltd
James Hall and Co (Southport) Ltd
James Starkie and Sons Ltd
KPMG Peat Marwick
Lancashire Evening Post
Legal & Trades Collections
Intercity
Post Office Counters
Leyland DAF plc
Marks and Spencer plc
Matthew Brown plc
McDonalds Restaurants plc
Midland Bank plc
Preston Farmers Ltd
Municipal Mutual Insurance Ltd
Napthen Houghton Craven—solicitors
National Farmers Union
North Western Society of Chartered Accountants
North West Tourist Board
Pennine Telecom Ltd
Preston and District Master Butchers Association
Preston Borough Transport Ltd
Preston Lions
Preston Marine Services
BBC Radio Lancashire
Red Rose Community Trust
Ribble Vintners Ltd
Rockwell Graphics Systems Ltd
Rotarians
Royal Mail
Royal Bank of Scotland plc
Rural Development Commission
J Sainsbury's plc
Speedy Hire Centres Ltd
St Catherine's hospice
St. George's Centre
Standard Life
TSB Bank plc
The Elephant Trust
Royal Navy
Town and County Magazines
UCI Cinemas
Whitbreads Beer Co
Wilkinson's Cameras
Yates' Wine Lodge
The Waterfront (Toby Grill)

Appendix 7

The 1992 Guild Year Calendar

This list includes almost all the Guild events which took place during 1992. It excludes street parties, because these were held in such large numbers, and only a selection of the events and activities of local schools is included.

Part 1: Events spread over several weeks or months:

Feb 91–Mar 92	Four series of Guild lectures at Harris Museum
Mar–Jun	Schools Lunchtime Musical Festival (nine concerts at the Harris Museum)
Apr–May	'A seat at the Guild'—touring performances by the Guild Players
Apr–Aug	County and Regimental Museum lecture series
May–Sep	Street theatre (various locations in the town and adjacent villages)
	Programme of four organ recitals at Parish Church
June–Jul	Best–Kept Garden Competition
	Design a Guild Garden Competition
June–Nov	University of Central Lancashire lecture series
Jul–Aug	Horse and Bamboo Theatre Project (Harris Museum)
Oct–Dec	Guild lectures at Harris Museum

Part 2: Calendar of events and activities

19 Dec 91	Official dispatch of Guild emblem to North America
31 Dec 91	Civic launch of 1992 Guild Year (Flag Market)
	New Year Dance at Guild Hall
4 Jan 92	Viennese Evening with the Halle Orchestra
5 Jan	Guild 10k Road Race/Fun Run
7 Jan	Official dispatch of Guild emblem to Australasia
11 Jan	Higher Walton CE School Guild mural unveiled
18 Jan	Opening of 'Once Every Preston Guild' exhibition at Harris Museum
23 Jan	Mayoral reception for designers of Guild medals (Harris Museum)
3 Feb	Ceremonial opening of Guild window and new building at Our Lady's High School
22 Feb	Opening of 'Guild to Guild' exhibition (Harris Museum)
28 Feb	Preston Drama Club 'Guild Girls' production
9–13 Mar	Guild Arts Week at Carr Hill High School, Kirkham
11–12 Mar	'A Pageant of Music in England' by Penwortham Girls' High School (Guild Hall)
24 Mar	Guild Cover competition award ceremony (Harris Museum)
25–28 Mar	Edge Hill College production of 'Hard Times' (Harris Rotunda)
Apr	Old Tyme Music Hall Revue (Charter Theatre)

3–5 Apr	National Championships of the British Association for Sport in Colleges (Preston)
4 Apr	Lostock Hall High School 'Table Games Tournament' in St George's Centre
10 Apr	Commemorative tree-planting ceremonies
11 Apr	Guild Charity Ball (Guild Hall)
12 Apr	Guild Mountain Bike Race
21 Apr	Easter Sunday United Songs of Praise for Guild Year (parish church)
26 Apr	Olde Tyme Music Hall (Guild Hall)
1 May	Opening of Guild Garden at Penwortham Priory High School
	Age Concern Olde Tyme Champagne Ball
2–4 May	Guild Steam Rally
3 May	Guild Concert by National Band of Church Lads' and Girls' Brigade (Guild Hall)
9 May	Kite-making workshops at Moor Park and Ashton High Schools
13 May	Brigham Young University concert (parish church)
15–16 May	'Once Every Preston Guild' Vintage Motorcycle Club 'Round Lancashire Rally' (starting at Flag Market and ending at Ashton Park)
16 May	Re-naming of Guild locomotive, and Guild Steam
	Special over Settle and Carlisle line
	Guild Ball (Guild Hall)
16–17 May	Aerial Spectacular (Ashton Park)
17 May	Preston Guides Religious Service (Guild Hall)
23 May	Preston Guild Town Criers Competition
23–25 May	Thomas the Tank Engine steam weekend
31 May	Stage 7 of the 1992 Milk Race, finishing in
	Preston after eight town centre laps
	Guild Folk Fiesta (Guildhall and town centre)
1 June	Guild Year Concert by New York Salvation Army Staff Band (Guild Hall)
2 June	Judges Service (parish church)
5 June	Tree-planting ceremony at Fishwick CP School
7 June	State Visit of Guild Mayor to parish church
	Service of reunion for Loyal Regiment (parish church)
	Mammoth open air party for elderly residents (Covered Market)
13 June	First Preston Churches Heritage Walk
13–14 June	'The return of the Vikings' (Avenham Park and the Dock)
	Woodplumpton Parish Guild Event
15–26 June	Guild Bowling Competition
18 June	Guild Night of Magic (Guild Hall)
20 June	Guild Dance Festival for schoolchildren (Avenham Park)
	Lea Parish Council Guild Field Day

Launch of 'Round Preston Walk' booklet and commemorative walk

William Temple High School Guild Summer Fair

Preston Guides Campfire in Avenham Park

20–21 June	Guild Hobbies Fair (Tulketh High School)
21–27 June	Grimsargh Village Guild Festival
21 June	St Pius X School Summer Fete
23 June	Enterprising Technology Exhibition at Moor Park High School
25–26 June	'The Living Newspaper' production by Ashton High School and Framework Community Theatre
25 June	Christ the King High School Guild Reunion Disco at Squires Gate Nightclub
27–28 June	'The Countryside comes to Town' exhibition (Moor Park)
29 June	Ashton High School Guild Summer Fair
30 June	Production of 'Hamlet' at Preston College Open Air Theatre
	Musical evening and photographic competition award ceremony at Broughton High School
1 July	Junior Technical School (Harris Institute) Reunion
4–18 July	Coast to Coast Walk to commemorate Guild (St Bees to Robin Hoods Bay)
3 July	Guild 'Blue and White Disco' at Fishwick CP School
4 July	Broughton High School Guild Fayre
5 July	Preston Guild Golf Trophy (Preston Golf Club, Fulwood)
	Preston Round Table Party for Under-Privileged Children (Covered market)
9 July	Formal naming of part of Penwortham bypass extension as Guild Way
6–13 July	STEEL Fair (University of Central Lancashire)
7 July	Preston Schools Guild Adventure Challenge (West View Leisure Centre)
10 July	Playground 'street party' at Longridge CP school
11 July	Visit to Carey Baptist Church by Czechoslovak Choir
12 July	Christ the King High School Hallé Project performance
23–27 July	Heineken Music Big Top (Avenham Park)
25 July	Longton Children's Guild Party
25 July	Finals of 'Young Musician of the Guild' competition
25–26 July	Grand Northern Archery Meeting
26 July	Preston Guild Budgerigar Society Show
31 July	International Women's Soccer Tournament
1 Aug	Preston Guild Pop Concert
8–9 Aug	Canal and Vintage Festival (Haslam Park)
	Guild Festival of Bridge (Guild Hall)
15 Aug	First Proclamation of the Guild Merchant
	Parade by members of the Sealed Knot
15 Aug	Preston Guild Ceilidh

15–16 Aug	'The Storming of Preston' by Sealed Knot (Avenham Park)
22 Aug	Second Proclamation of the Guild Merchant
	Historic Commercial Vehicle procession
	Preston Opera production of Verdi's 'Nabucco' at the Guild Hall
	Cottam Village Guild Party
22–23 Aug	Guild Triples Blind Bowling Club Tournament (Moor Park)
22–29 Aug	Preston Guild 'Victorian Theatre' in Miller Arcade
23 Aug	Historic Commercial Vehicle Spectacular (Riversway)
	First performance of 'A Georgian Evening with the Horrocks Family' (Lark Hill House)
30 Aug and 2 Sept	'One More Song' barbershop concert at the Guild Hall
	Guild Party for the Blind and Partially Sighted (Canterbury Hall)
27 Aug	'Firefighting through the Ages' display and demonstration by County Fire Brigade (Flag market)
	Luncheon Clubs' Guild Lunch
28–30 Aug	International Caravan Fellowship of Rotarians Guild Rally (Myerscough Hall)
28 Aug	International Police Bands Guild Spectacular Concert (Guild Hall)
	Opening of 'Proud Preston' Exhibition at Moor Park (for Guild Week)
	The 'Walk the Plank' show opens at the Riversway Festival, Preston Dock
29 Aug	Third and Final Proclamation of the Guild Merchant
	Presentation to the Guild Mayor of Guild emblems and scrolls from Australasia and North America
	March past by international police bands
	Open air Salvation Army service in Friargate
	Opening of 'Proud Preston' Exhibition and the Moor Park Spectacular
	Catenian Association Banquet and Ball (Guild Hall) in presence of Cardinal Hume
	Guild Rock Concert
	Firework and Laser Symphony Concert, with Royal Philharmonic Pops Orchestra (Avenham Park)
29–30 Aug	Judging of Best Decorated Street Contest
29–31 Aug	Riversway Festival
30 Aug–4 Sep	'Historical Fayre' in town centre
30 Aug	Guild mayor's civic procession to the parish church
	Divine service in the parish church
	Open air ecumenical service (Avenham Park)
	Special Guild Mass at St Walburge's Church
	Guild Anniversary and Thanksgiving Service at Fishergate Baptist Church

First performance of 'The Old Lamb and Flag' by the Jolly Fine Company Company

Social evening arranged for twin town guests by Preston Twinning Liaison Committee (PNE Stadium)

Guild Golf Tournament Final (Ladies)

Guild 10k Road Race in town centre

Guild Week

Carey Baptist Church partnership mission

Football history exhibition at Our Lady's High School

Flower and Quilt festival at parish church

31 Aug Mayoral civic procession to the Guild Hall

Formal opening of the Guild Court

Religious service at the Guild Hall

First Ecumenical Churches Procession

Live Guild Roadshow (Avenham Park)

Guild Inaugural Ball

Sessions House open to public, with exhibition, for one week

First night of Preston Musical Comedy Society production of 'My Fair Lady'

1 Sept Second Ecumenical Churches Procession

'Jazz on the Park' (Avenham Park)

Official unveiling of new name sign at University of Central Lancashire

2 Sept Trades Procession

'Opera on the Park' (Avenham Park)

Guild Mayoral Ball

3 Sept First-ever Guild Community Procession

First performance of the Guild Schools' Pageant:

A Pageant of Preston: The Story of a Proud Town

Mayoral reception for overseas visitors

4 Sept Guild Mayoress' Church Procession

Second performance of the Guild Schools' Pageant

Carnival Ball

5 Sept Formal adjournment of the Guild Court

Military Open Day and Beating the Retreat (Fulwood Barracks)

Torchlight Procession

Grand Firework Display

Guild Mayor's Farewell to Guild Week

6 Sept Guild Mayor's Church Procession to Service of Thanksgiving

Guild Golf Tournament Final (Men)

Hockey For All Ages event (PNE Stadium)

12 Sept Preston Guild Dog Show (West View)

24 Sept Opening of new hydrotherapy tank at The Elms Special School

26 Sept	Second Preston Churches Heritage Walk
5 Oct	Charity Guild Fashion Show by University fashion students (Charity Theatre)
9 Oct	Launch of GIFT '92
21 Oct	Institution of Electrical Engineers Guild Year Faraday Lecture
7 Nov	'Preston in 1992' photography exhibition (Harris Museum)
24 Nov	Unveiling of Guild tiled panel at Middleforth CE School
4 Dec	Salvation Army Guild Year Carol Concert (Guild Hall)
31 Dec	Farewell to Guild Year event and fireworks (centred on Market Square)

Appendix 8

The advance proclamation of the Preston Guild 1992

The Mayor of this Borough of Preston hereby giveth open knowledge monition and warning to all and every the Free Burgesses of this Borough, as well Inhabitants as Foreigners, that they and every of them do make their repair by themselves or their friends as proxies to this Town, upon Monday, the 31st day of August next coming, being the Monday next after the Feast of Decollation of St. John the Baptist, at which Feast a Guild Merchant within this Town hath heretofore for divers ages last past been held and kept every twenty years. And now likewise upon the day aforementioned a New Guild Merchant is appointed to be holden and kept according to Ancient Custom and of divers Charters and Grants heretofore made, granted, and confirmed to the Mayor, Bailiffs and Burgesses of this Borough; for the solemnisation of which Guild Merchant, here to be holden as aforesaid, the Mayor of this Borough giveth further Notice and Warning that all free Burgesses inhabiting within this Town be ready upon the 31st day of August next by ten o'clock in the morning at the Guild Hall in this Borough, to attend upon the Mayor, and Stewards of the said Guild Merchant in their distinct Companies of Trade, with their Masters and Wardens well ordered and disposed for that purpose, and all those that cannot attend in such order as at that time shall be assigned them, and from the Guild Hall aforesaid to attend Mr Mayor in solemn procession through the several streets in such order, precedence and solemnity as heretofore hath been accustomed.

And moreover the aforesaid Mayor giveth notice and warning that all and every Burgess and Burgesses as well Foreigners as Inhabitants within this Borough claiming any franchises, either by ancestry, prescription, or purchase, within this Borough of Preston, after their repair to this Borough at the day and time aforesaid that then and there they not only claim and entitle themselves to all such Liberties, Privileges and Freedoms as to them or any of them not only shall be due or in any ways belong, but also there and then they likewise may understand and be acquainted with what orders, statutes and ordinances by the Mayor and Stewards of this ensuing Guild, shall and may be thought fit either to be added, altered, abrogated or confirmed, not being repugnant to the known laws of this Realm for the good and welfare of this Borough of Preston according to the tenor of the letters patent of our late Sovereign Lord King Charles the Second and others his Royal Progenitors, Kings and Queens of this Realm, and according to the laudable practice and customs of many Guilds Merchant heretofore held within this Borough.

GOD SAVE THE QUEEN

Appendix 9

The recital of Charters and Account of Declaration of Guilds

WHEREAS King Charles the Second, by his Royal Charter in the thirty-sixth year of his reign did grant and confirm to the Mayor, Bailiffs and Burgesses of this Borough of Preston, That the said Borough as, and is, an Ancient and Free Borough, and did likewise confirm and ratify ALL and EVERY the Ancient Rights, Privileges, Immunities and all other Franchises that at any time theretofore had been granted and confirmed to the Mayor, Bailiffs and Burgesses or to the Burgesses of the Town or Borough of Preston aforesaid by any of his Predecessors or Progenitors, Kings and Queens of the Realm of England and by the said Charter did also grant and confirm to the said Mayor, Bailiffs and Burgesses of the said Borough of Preston, and their Successors, that they and their Successors should have a Guild Merchant in the said Borough, with all privileges and free custom thereto belonging as they had theretofore used and enjoyed the same.

AND WHEREAS King Henry the Second, after the Conquest, granted by his Royal Charter to the said Burgesses of Preston certain liberties and free customs granted to the Burgesses of Newcastle-under-Lyme which were subsequently confirmed in a Charter by Henry III in 1235 and appear to be in these words:

KNOW YE US to have granted and by this Our present Charter to have confirmed for us and for our heirs, to our Burgesses of Newcastle-under-Lyme, that the Town of Newcastle-under-Lyme be a Free Borough, and that the Burgesses of that Borough have a Guild Merchant within the said Borough, with all liberties and free customs to such Guild Merchant appertaining, and that they may go through all our Land with all their Merchandise, buying, selling and trading well and in peace, freely, quietly, and honourably, and that they may be free from toll, Passage, Pontage, Stallage, Lastage, Ulnage, and all other Customs saving in all things our City of London

AND WHEREAS the Ancient and Free Burgesses of this Borough of Preston have many years since obtained from many succeeding Kings and Queens of England full liberty and freedom for all those and many other Privileges, Immunities and Franchises, which stand ratified and confirmed by several Royal Grants and Charters, and have for many ages past held and kept within this Borough a Guild Merchant as appears by the Records and Books belonging to this Incorporation, as for instance:

GUILDS MERCHANT were held in the second year of the Reign of King Edward the Third, in the twentieth year of the Reign of King Richard the Second, in the third year of the Reign of King Henry the Fifth, in the thirty-seventh year of the Reign of King Henry the Sixth, in the sixteenth year of the Reign of King Henry the Seventh, in the thirty-fourth year of the Reign of King Henry the Eighth, in the fourth, twenty-fourth and forty-fourth years of the Reign of Queen Elizabeth the First, in the twentieth year of the Reign of King James the First, in the eighteenth year of the Reign of King Charles the First, in the fourteenth and thirty-fourth years of the Reign of King Charles the Second, in the first year of the Reign of Queen Anne, in the ninth year of the Reign of King George the First, in the sixteenth year of the Reign of King George the Second, in the second, twenty-second and forty-second years of the Reign of King George the Third, in the third year of the Reign of King George the Fourth, in the sixth, twenty-sixth and forty-sixth years of the Reign of Queen Victoria, in the second year of the Reign of King Edward the Seventh, in the thirteenth year of the Reign of King George the Fifth, and in the first and twenty-first years of the Reign of Her present Majesty Queen Elizabeth the Second

AND NOW ANOTHER GUILD MERCHANT according to the Rights, Precedents, Practices and Ancient Customs of this Borough, commences this present Monday, the Thirty-first day of August, in the forty-first year of the Reign of Her present Majesty

Queen Elizabeth the Second, and in the year of Our Lord One thousand nine hundred and ninety-two, before the Right Worshipful Harold Parker, Mayor, and Richard Atkinson, Ian Whyte Hall, Joseph Hood, Dennis Kehoe and Ronald Philip Marshall Stewards, Anthony Charles Jolly, Honorary Recorder, and Antony Owens, Clerk of this Guild, which Mayor, Stewards and Clerk will sit in the Town Hall in this Borough from day to day during the time of this Guild to receive the claims and pretensions of all Free Burgesses of this Borough on behalf of themselves or of their sons and daughters and for the doing and performing of all such other matters and things as by the Mayor and Stewards of this Guild shall be lawfully agreed upon.

Appendix 10

The proclamation in open court of the 1992 Guild

THE RIGHT WORSHIPFUL THE MAYOR OF THIS BOROUGH duly caused to be inserted in appropriate Papers a Notice that a Guild Merchant would be Opened and Held in and for this Borough according to Ancient Custom on this present Monday, the Thirty-first day of August, One thousand nine hundred and ninety-two, being the Monday next after the feast of the Decollation of Saint John the Baptist, and also caused a Proclamation to be duly made and published in this Borough on Saturday, the Fifteenth day of August last and two succeeding Saturdays of the Opening and Holding of the said Guild Merchant, and which said Notice and Proclamation required all and every the Free Burgesses of this Borough as well Inhabitants as Foreigners to appear by themselves or their Proxies at this time and place to attend the Mayor and Stewards of this present Guild, and to give such attendance and service as to them should appertain, and for divers other reasons and purposes therein and thereby specified and set forth

THE MAYOR of this Borough, in pursuance and under and by virtue of the powers and authorities contained in certain Royal Charters granted to this Borough by King Henry the Second and others, his Royal successors, Kings and Queens of this Realm, and according to ancient usage and custom, HEREBY DECLARES that a Guild Merchant for the said Borough is now Opened and Held and will continue to be Open and Held for all the purposes of the said Guild Merchant.

AND THE MAYOR of this Borough hereby requires and commands that all and every Burgess and Burgesses as well Inhabitants as Foreigners within this Borough claiming any Franchises either by Ancestry, Prescription or Purchase within this Borough of Preston do claim and entitle themselves to all such Liberties, Privileges and Freedoms as to them or any of them shall be due or any way belong at the Guild Court now Open and Held before the Mayor and Stewards of the said Guild Merchant, or at the said Court which will be held by adjournment at the office of the Town Clerk/Chief Executive, Town Hall, Preston, aforesaid.

AND THE MAYOR of this Borough hereby giveth Notice that all persons neglecting to claim and entitle themselves to the Freedom of this Borough as aforesaid will lose all Rights Privileges and Immunities connected herewith.

GOD SAVE THE QUEEN

Appendix 11

The four Latin orations of the 1992 Guild

I   By the Principal of Cardinal Newman College

PRAETOR DIGNISSIME: More antiquo semper fuit discipulus e Schola Prestoniensi electus qui Latine orationem habeat apud iudicium hoc ad ferias celebrandas convocatum. Schola illa Prestoniensis iam pridem portas suas clausit, nec multo diutius superfuit quod successit, Conlegium Prestoniense Studiorum Superiorum. Nostris diebus in municipio Prestoniensi sita, duo conlegia habemus, alterum Cardinali illustri Newman dedicatum, civibus Prestoniensibus gloria gaudioque alterum: quae surrexerunt ambo his viginti annis e cineribus scholarum huius oppidi.

Dignitatem igitur habeo tibi introducendi duos horum conlegium discipulos, Cathy Hume et Alex McLaren, qui, si iusseris, orationem more antiquo Latinam habebunt.

RIGHT WORSHIPFUL SIR: By ancient tradition it was always a selected student from Preston Grammar School who gave the Latin Oration before the Guild Court. That school has long since closed its doors, and its successor the Sixth Form College did not survive much longer. Now, in Preston, we have two Colleges, Cardinal Newman College and Preston College, both of which have arisen, within the last twenty years, from the ashes of the Grammar Schools of this town.

I therefore have the honour of introducing to you two students from these Colleges, Cathy Hume and Alex MacLaren who, if you desire, will deliver, according to Custom, the Latin Oration.

II   By Cathy Hume

PRAETOR DIGNISSIME, Iudex venerande, Decuriones amplissimi, Cives Prestoniensis:

Hoc eodem conventu abhinc annos viginto habito, iudex municipii nostri venerandos commemoravit se timore affici ne lingua latina mox omnino perderetur. Pauci vero iam sunt qui linguas antiquas, olim omnia iuvenum nostrorum studia maiestate superantes, adhuc studeant.

Nos tamen, discipuli horum conlegiorum electi dignitatem amplissimam habemus orationis huius habendae. Secundum morem antiquum a maioribus traditum lingua latina utimur. Conlegia nostra non iam similia sunt scholis illis maiorum nostrorum. Tunc quidem totum diem ab anno undecimo discipuli studebant, diebus nostris dimidiam partem diei nonnulli, et aetatis cuislibet: tunc artibus litterarum exercebantur, nunc machinis mirifice adaptis ad quaestiones mathematicas resolvendas utuntur et scientiam naturae rerum hominumque persequuntur: tunc iuvenis solus orationem hanc habebat: iam mihi denique, puellae tantum, dimidia pars honoris huius traditur. O Tempora, O Mores!

Quamvis per multos annos cives huius oppidi suas scholas ipsi curaverint, iam sub potestate Comitatus Lancastrensis submissae sunt. Ei qui tempora illa memoria tenent maximas gratias civibus qui tam bene studia liberorum curabant, libentur agunt.

Multa alia mutata sunt: scholae hae clausae sunt, illae cum aliis coniunctae, nonnullae, vinculis auctoritatis superioris deminuitis, per libertatem res ad aerarium pertinentes ipsi curant: discipuli iam student ut opera utilia per vitam perficere possint: respublica cursus studiorum omnibus imponit et, quod maximi momenti est, discipuli per quaestiones difficiles inspiciuntur num omnia perdidicerint.

Academiam denique habet municipium nostrum, non nomine Prestoniensi guadentum sed certe situ, quae fundamentis clarissimis conlegii Harris erigitur. Quibus feliciter inauguratis, haec civitas cursus studiorum liberis, pueris, pellis, adulescientibus, iuvenibus omnibus denique civibus suis munifice praebere poterit. Deo gratias.

THE MAYOR AND BURGESSES OF PRESTON

At this Guild Court twenty years ago the Recorder of the town said that he was afraid the Latin language would soon completely disappear; and there are few indeed who still study the Classical languages, which were once the mainstay of our young people's studies.

Nevertheless, we two students of the Preston Colleges have the considerable honour of making this speech. According to ancient custom, we are using the Latin language. Our Colleges are very unlike the Grammar schools of former times; then, pupils studied full-time from the age of eleven; now, many are part-time students and of any age; then, they mainly studied literature; now they use computers and study natural and social science; then, a young man used to make this speech, but now, in these modern times, a half of this honour has been given to me, a girl! So changed are things today!

For many years the townspeople of Preston administered their own schools, but now they are under the control of Lancashire County Council. Those who remember those times are pleased to record their gratitude to the people who guided so well the town's education service.

Many other things have changed; some schools have closed, others have been amalgamated, and some look after their own finances now that their links with the education authority have been weakened; students now take vocational courses, the State has introduced the National Curriculum, and the progress and knowledge of pupils are now formally assessed.

Finally, our town now has a University; it is not blessed with the name of Preston, but at least with a Preston site! It is founded on the well-known Harris College. With this institution our town will now be able to offer a full education to all its young people of any age. Thanks be to God.

III   By Alex MacLaren

Quamvis, cives Prestonienses, abhinc viginti annos cum feriae recentissime praeteritae huius municipii concelebrarentur, neque ego neque comes mea adhuc nati essemus, tamen seniores nostri multa, et mirabilia et memorabilia, in municipio nostro viderunt. Imprimis vero, Regina ipsa Britannica octingentesimo anno a municipio hoc condito nos visere dignata est: portus Prestoniensis, quondam navium multitudine frequentissimus, magno labore renovatus, iam tabularia, domus, officinas, tabernas novas, omnibus praebet. Nec iam naves onerarias a terris peregrinis venientes accipit, sed scaphas modo ad otium destinatas: ponte novissimo se supra flumen tollente, vehicula plurima itinere novo et miro commeant. Nec pauci sunt qui conqueruntur se non iam posse itinere recto domum redire! Fines municipii ipsius ad septentriones et orientem extensi sunt: haec ipsa basilica, abhinc viginti paene annos dedicata, in loco stat antiquae illius basilicae qua tot concetus clari, orationes fervidae, saltationes lepidae fuerunt: nomina denique illustria, Horrocks et Cortaulds, non iam praestantia sunt in municipio, et officinae eorum clausae sunt: machinae nostri aevi ad volandum sicut aves adaptae hic iam creantur rarae.

His temporibus, cives Prestonienses neque in finibus municipii sui cohibentur, neque Britanniae totius. Bello isto finito, quod merito 'frigidum' dicitur, iam Respublica Europaea. Quattuor praeterea municipia Europaea. nobis comiter coniuncta, quorum legatos benigne inter nos hodie accipimus, novas spes praebent. Proximis his viginti annis, rebus asperrimis et mutabilibus sine dubio occurremus nos cives Prestonienses, sed periculis, discriminibus, quaestionibus nullis umquam vincemur.

Floreat semper municipium nostrum. Floreat comitatus Lancastrensis. Floreat ecclesia. Viva Regina.

Twenty years ago, fellow citizens, when the last Guild celebrations were held, we two were not yet born. However, older Preston people have witnessed many wonderful events in our town. Most importantly, the Queen visited us in commemoration of the octocentenary of the town's Charter. The Port of Preston which used to bustle with mercantile activity is undergoing the great work of renewal, with shops, houses, offices, and new taverns; it no longer welcomes merchant vessels from foreign ports, but has now a marina for pleasure craft. A new bridge soars across the river and many vehicles use this wonderful new route - although not a few complain that they can now no longer go home by a direct road! The town itself has taken in fresh areas to the north and east. This very Hall, opened almost twenty years ago, has replaced the Public Hall, scene of so many notable concerts, speeches and dances. Famous names, such as Horrocks and Cortauld, are gone from the town and their cotton mills have been closed. The aircraft industry is also shrinking.

As elsewhere in the land, many citizens of Preston now look beyond their borough and beyond England itself. Now that the 'Cold War' is over, the European Community beckons us. And indeed, four towns of Europe, closely linked with us, and represented here today, offer new hope. There will be challenges and changes, without doubt, in the next twenty years for us Prestonians, but we will never be overcome by the dangers, trials and tests that are to come.

May our town always prosper. May the County of Lancaster prosper. May the Church thrive. Long live the Queen.

IV *The reply by the Honorary Recorder, Judge Anthony Jolly*

Annos prope octingentos quidem Gilda Mercatoria huius municipii habita est; minus viginti annos oratores nostri hi nati sunt; inter quos terminos ego denique gradum incertum consecutus sum. Nec minime laetitia me afficit quod ego primus omnium Iudicum Venerandorum huius municipii honorem habeo officii huius cum puellae partiendi, quodque Gilda haec prima civium volunmini filiarum nomina addit. Credo praeterea (nec quisquam tam tugratus erit ut dissentiat) discipulum utrumque pari eloquentia et arte locutum esse. Et eis gratiam ago et Rectori conlegii Cardinali Newman dedicati quod nobis introduxit.

Cum sim rogatus ut brevi loquar, necesse est ut nomen amplissimum Academiae nostrae novae praetermittam. Magistros eius tamen et discipulos gratulor quod leaudem maximam iam adsecuti sunt. Municipium Prestoniense iam pridem viget quod virtutem omnibus scholis et conlegiis intra fines suos auctam laudavit, nec magni interest num huius regionis, nostri cultus, generis virilis, sint. Multum igitur refert quod paucis diebus pompa omnium civium, quod numquam antea accidit, feriis Gildae huius addetur.

Via nostra maxima extensa, ponteque novo et splendido aedificatio, municipium Prestoniense iam pars gravissima omnium viarum huius regionis manifeste fit. Spero attamen, si pons alter olim exstruetur, tam alte trans flumen volaturum esse ut scaphas ad portum Prestoniensem (deminutum vero sed prosperum) commeantes non impediat. Est iam municipium hoc, debebitque, semper esse, caput rerum comitatus administrandarum, et iudiciorum. Nova quidem iudicia decem, tribus annis portas apertura, duobus addentur quae more antiquo ornata maxime amantur.

Cum municipium Prestoniense pars integra Europae esse valde cupiat, legatos municipiorum Almelo, Nimes, Recklinghausen, Kalisz, libenter saluto accipioque. In Europa vero rebus et prosperis et asperis occurrimus et sine dubio occurremus, sed more nostro, constantia, benignitate, sale, obibimus. Gilda Mercantoria haec et cives Prestonienses et amicos nostros Europenses salvos vult. Spero nos omnes, sicut unum corpus agentes, nosmet ipsos labore, exemploque alios servaturos esse.

Viva regina.

Preston Guild is nearly eight hundred years old. The last two speakers are each under twenty years old. I am somewhere in between. I am very conscious of the fact that I am the first recorder who has been privileged to share this occasion with a young female orator and that this is the first Guild to admit the daughters of burgesses to the Guild Roll. In my judgment, from which on this occasion I am sure that no one will dissent, both students have spoken with equal eloquence and excellence. I thank them and thank the Principal of Cardinal Newman College for introducing them to us.

I have been asked to keep my oration reasonably short and that necessarily deters me from referring to Preston's new University by its full name. I nevertheless congratulate its staff and students on the distinguished reputation which it has already achieved. Preston has prospered by saluting merit, fostered by all the admirable educational establishments within its boundaries, and regardless of race, creed or gender. It is noteworthy that next Thursday, for the first time, a Community procession will be part of the Guild Celebrations.

Recent motorway extensions and its elegant new bridge confirm Preston as the hub of communications in the North West. It is, nevertheless, to be hoped that any further new bridge will soar sufficiently high to avoid impeding river traffic to the successful new marina at Riversway. Preston is and must continue to be the administrative and legal centre of the County. Ten new courts, promised to be open in January 1995, are to be added to the two most admired and traditional of the present courts.

Preston intends to play its part in Europe and I warmly welcome the representatives of Almelo in Holland, Nîmes in France, Recklinghausen in Germany and Kalisz in Poland. Here, we have had and will doubtless continue to have our periods of success and our hard times. They will both be met with characteristic Prestonian determination, kindliness and humour. This Guild Court sends its sincere best wishes to all the people of Preston and our friends in Europe. I expect that we shall now continue to act together and that we shall save ourselves by our efforts and others by our example.

God Save The Queen.

Appendix 12

The participants in the 1992 Trades Procession

Mounted police escort
The Band of Her Majesty's Royal Marines, Commandos
Preston Farmers Ltd
Preston Ladies N.F.U.
Barton Grange Garden Centre
E. H. Booth & Co.
W. H. Bowker Ltd.
Royal Mail
The Band of the 14th/20th King's Hussars
Leyland DAF Ltd.
Bottle Van Co.
Lancashire Evening Post
W. Monks (Longridge) Ltd.
D. J. Ryan & Sons Ltd.
Dutton-Forshaw, Preston
Lancashire County Fire Brigade
Lancashire County Council
University of Central Lancashire
Marks and Spencer plc
National Hairdressers' Federation
Bass North West
British Telecom

Banking Insurance and Finance Union
The Band & Corps of Drums of the Queen's Lancashire Regiment
The Royal Electrical & Mechanical Engineers
The Corps of Royal Engineers
C & A
North West Cable Communications
CCA Stationery Ltd.
Conlon Construction Ltd.
Croft Roplasto
Thomas Croft
Edward Dewhurst Ltd.
Alliance and Leicester
Amalgamated Engineering & Electrical Union (Engineering Section)
T. & R. Theakston Ltd.
Gran Sol Properties
The Grommet Group
James Hall & Co. (Southport) Ltd.
GEC Alsthom
Retail Fruit Trade Federation
GMB/APEX Partnership
Carlova School of Dancing
The Chartered Institute of Marketing
Dairy Crest Dairies
Dilworth Brothers
Dorman Smith Switchgear
Preston Trades Union Council
A. J. Evans (Preston) Ltd.
The Preston Forte Crest Hotel
Fulwood Hall Hospital
Central and West Lancashire Chamber of Commerce and Industry
Preston Junior Chamber
HM Prison Service
British Aerospace Defence
Plumbs Heritage Covers Ltd.
John Noye (Tarmacadam) Ltd.
Preston Borough Council
Inland Revenue Staff Federation
T. Jolly (Services) Ltd.
Building Employers Confederation
Employment Service
Dale Farm Dairy Group
Midland Bank plc
Chris Miller Ltd.
Manufacturing, Science and Finance Union
M.F.S.U. (BAe)
MPH Windows
National Westminster Bank plc - Preston Business Centre
NORWEB
National Union of Public Employees (NUPE/NALGO/COHSE)
Peter Craig
British Telecom Union Committee
G. R. & J. Pemberton & Sons
British Nuclear Fuels plc
Pickfords Removals Ltd
Preston Business Venture

Preston and District Fruit and Potato Merchants Association
Preston Licensed Victuallers' Association
Union of Shop, Distributive and Allied Workers
Preston Health Authority
Preston Health Authority – Priority Care Services division
Red Rose Radio
Somic plc.
William Pye Ltd.
Jack Smith (Builders) Ltd.
Spring Grove Services
The Band Detchment of the Lancashire Army Cadet Force
James Starkie and Sons Ltd
A. G. Strachan and Co. Ltd.
Craftsman Roofing
Swan Bearing Factors Ltd.
Thorn Lighting
Thompson Builders Merchants (Preston) Ltd.
Transport and General Workers Union
UCI Cinemas
Vernon-Carus Ltd.
Bernard Watson (incorporating J. Corbishley & Sons Ltd.)
Barclays Bank plc
The Whitbread Beer Co.
Preston Whitbread Football League
Baxi Heating
Dutton-Forshaw Riversway
National Westminster Bank plc
The Vineyard Hotel
J. T. Care Homes Ltd.
Standard Life
William Taylor Pools
GUS Catalogue Order Co.
British Decorators Association
Lanfina Bitumen Ltd.
British Gas plc
Matthew Brown plc
Peter Guy's Period Interiors
ASDA Stores
Cicely Continental
Ashworth's Foods Ltd.
The National Grid Co. plc
James Askew & Son Ltd.
Bainbridge Silencers
British Road Services
British Sugar Craft Guild
Holdens Computer Services
Lancashire Waste Services Ltd.
Mitie Group (Northern) Ltd.

Appendix 13

Resolutions of the Borough Council after the Guild

At the meeting of the Council on 23 September 1992 it was moved by Councillor Ian Whyte Hall and seconded by Councillor Joseph Hood—both Stewards of the Guild and Honorary Freemen of the Borough—and RESOLVED unanimously:

i) That the members of this Council place on record their thanks and appreciation to the officials and staff of this authority for their expertise and dedication to the organisation and operation of the Guild Celebrations which have been an unqualified success due, in the main, to the total commitment of the staff and workforce involved;

ii) that the appreciation of this Council be placed on record for the contribution, both financial and in kind, of other public and private bodies, commercial and industrial organisations, voluntary bodies and private individuals who, together with the general populace, have contributed in no small way to a successful and trouble-free Guild Celebration;

iii) that the sincere thanks of the Council be placed on record for the most able manner in which the Guild Mayor (Councillor Harold Parker) and his Mayoress (Mrs Enid Parker) have carried out their Mayoral duties during the hectic period leading up to, and including, Guild Week.

Appendix 14

The involvement of the Lancashire County Council

Lancashire County Council made a major contribution to the success of the 1992 Preston Guild, and its specific work in this respect is listed below:

§ General help with publicity and promotion;

§ Chairman's reception for Borough and Guild officers and councillors, and Chairman's attendance at many functions;

§ Cataloguing and arrangement of Guild and Borough records by staff of Lancashire Record Office, and assistance with exhibitions of documents;

§ Floats in Guild processions and participation in several major exhibitions;

§ Help and financial assistance with Schools Pageant;

§ Lancashire Schools Symphony Orchestra contribution to Guild Young Musician competition;

§ Close involvement through the work of all Preston schools;

§ 'STEEL' exhibition (Science, Technology and Engineering Education in Lancashire);

§ 'Firefighting Through The Ages' event on Flag Market;

§ Close involvement of libraries in the Preston area;

§ Part-funding of, and publication of, Alan Crosby's *History of Preston Guild;*

§ Involvement of County and Regimental Museum;

§ Work on conservation and tree-planting schemes in the Preston district;

§ Environmental improvement projects, including the landscaping of Pitt Street;

§ Major assistance by Social Services Department with transport and arrangements for the elderly and disabled;

§ Assistance with park and ride schemes;

§ The essential and invaluable role of the County Constabulary in the planning, policing and management of the Guild.

List of Subscribers

in alphabetical order

A F plc, Preston
Rodney Alker, Penwortham
Mr and Mrs J. A. Allsopp, Dewsbury
Alston Lane R. C. Primary School, Longridge
Michael D. Anson, Broughton
Mr M. D. Anson, Ingol
Mrs Ruth Archer, Fulwood
Cyril Milton Ashcroft, Fulwood
Joan T. Ashcroft, Ormskirk
Michael B. Ashcroft, Ormskirk
Thomas Ashcroft, Ormskirk
Thomas J. Ashcroft, Ormskirk
Ashton-on-Ribble High School, Preston
James Ashton, Preston
Mrs Nellie Ashton, Fulwood
David Assheton, Bilton, Rugby
The Hon. Nicholas Assheton, London
Mark Aungier, Fulwood
Mrs D. M. Bagwell, Ashton-on-Ribble
Mrs E. Baines, Walton-le-Dale
Kathleen T. Baines, Penwortham
Mrs Edith Bamber, Broadgate, Preston
Richard Noel Bamber, Garstang
Thomas Bamber, Garstang
William Andrew Bamber, Walmer Bridge
Banking, Insurance and Finance Union,
    Preston Branch
Paul H. Bannister, Broughton
Joyce and Stephen Battarbee, Euxton
Alan Beaumont, South Africa
John Eric Beaumont, Churchtown, Southport
Audrey Beckett, Lostock Hall
Mrs and Mrs A. N. Bennett, Ansdell
D. A. G. Bennett, Ansdell
Mr William Frederick Bennion,
    Ashton-on-Ribble
Mr F. S. Benson, Fulwood
Mr and Mrs P. Benson, Warton
Gillian Benton, Blackpool
Brian Berry, Leyland
Jean and Norman Billington, Preston
Blessed Sacrament R. C. School, Ribbleton,
    Preston
Wing Commdr D. G. Blunden MBE,
    RAFRO, St. Michael's
Rhiannon Booth, Fulwood

Edric and Marjorie Brabbins, Cheadle
Mr A. H. Brandreth and Mr T. J. Brandreth,
    Macclesfield
John Brandwood, TD, JP, Penwortham
Malcolm John Brandwood, Lichfield
David Brandwood-Spencer, Penwortham
Kevin and Jennifer Brennan,
    Ashton-on-Ribble
Broad Oak County Primary School,
    Penwortham
Brookfield County Primary School, Preston
Mary Frances Brown, Ashton-on-Ribble
Philip S. Brown, Penwortham
Ian, Carol and Bridget Buckley
Miss J. Burnett, Ashton-on-Ribble
Mr S. R. Burns, Preston
Thomas Butcher, Ashton-on-Ribble
Mrs Anne Butler (née Whittle), Market
    Drayton
Patricia and Peter Butterworth, Penwortham
Mr Peter Cain, Fulwood
Mr and Mrs W. Campbell, B.C., Canada
Cardinal Newman College Library, Preston
Lilian Carruthers, Woodford Green
Mrs J. C. Carter, Ashton-on-Ribble
Barrie M. Cartmell, Sedgeberrow, Worcs.
Harry Leslie Cartmell, St Annes
Robert James Cartmell, Sedgeberrow, Worcs.
Thomas Chambers, Penwortham
Richard Chapman, Penwortham
Gillian Charnley, Fulwood
Helen Charnley, Fulwood
Jack Clay, Addingham
John Clayton, Preston
Pamela J. Cleator, Walkden, Manchester
Mrs Hilda Clitheroe, Preston
The Lord Clitheroe DL, Downham, Clitheroe
Elizabeth Helen Comstock-Smith, Chipping
    Norton
Councillor Alfred James Coop, Little
    Singleton
Jason and Tanya Cox, Longridge
Joyce Cragg, Preston
E. Cronshaw, Penwortham
Miss Sheila Crook, Fulwood
A. A. Cross, Tiverton

W. J. A. Cross, Huntsham, Tiverton
Mr Gerald William Cutler, Preston
R. M. Danielak, Ashton
Antony Robert John Dark, Penwortham
H. B. Davis, Preston
Arnold Christopher and Mary Applegarth
    Dawes, Penwortham
Mr and Mrs J. B. de Rome, Penwortham
Deepdale County Primary Junior School,
    Preston
Deepdale County Infants School, Deepdale
The Earl of Derby MC, Knowsley
Ian A. R. Derrick, Fulwood
Miss Joyce Dewhirst, Walton-le-Dale
John and Dorothy Dewhurst,
    Ashton-on-Ribble
Thomas Dewhurst, Croft, Warrington
Mr George Dickinson, Fulwood
Peter and June Dix, Ontario, Canada
Christine Elaine Doughty, Melbourne,
    Australia
John Dovey, Preston
Mr and Mrs J. Drage, Preston
Mr Martyn Alan Driver, Fulwood
Mr Robert Alan Driver, Fulwood
George and Kathleen Duck, Fulwood
Jean A. Dyer, Fulwood
Mr J. R. Eastham, Ribbleton
Mary Diane Eaves, Hutton
Harry and Margaret Eccles, Preston
Charles G. Ethrington, Fulwood
George Etoe I.S.M., Ashton on Ribble
A. J. Evans (Preston) Ltd., Preston
Johan and Margaret Fabricius, Cape Town,
    S. Africa
Mrs Dorothy Faraday, Tatham Fells
Farington County Primary School, Farington,
    Leyland
Mrs J. A. Farrington, Leyland
Hilda Mary Feeley, Fulwood
Mrs B. Fenton, Stockport
Miss M. Fenton, Stockport
Mr R. Fenton, Stockport
Gillian and John Ferris, Penwortham
Mr J. L. Finlayson, Fulwood
Lynn Fishwick, Preston
Mr John Paul Fitzsimmons, Preston
I. J. Foden, Fulwood
Austin Ford, Preston
Stephen Foster, Goosnargh
Mr A. P. Fothergill, Fulwood
Karen Mortensen-Fowler (Miss Preston
    Guild, 1972), Fulwood
Barbara Freeman, Preston
Eric and Avis Gates, Goosnargh
GEC Alsthom Traction Ltd., Preston
Michael A. Gee, New Longton

Catherine E. Gee, Birmingham
GMB Lancashire Region
Sam Gorrell, Fulwood
Mr R. S. Gray, Askam-in-Furness, Cumbria
The Green family, Fulwood
Maureen Greenall, Longridge
Susan M. Greenall, Ribbleton
Mr R. J. Grime, Ashton-on-Ribble
Anthony Richard Guest-Gornall, Sunningdale
Alan and Joan Hackett, Fulwood
Marjory and Billy Hall, Longton
Mr and Mrs M. Halsall, Ashton-on-Ribble
Thomas Ernest Hamilton, Preston
Tony Hampson, Hawkshaw, Bury
Benjamin J. Hardman, Fulwood
Thomas Allan Harrison, Ulverston, Cumbria
Mr Paul Anthony Hatton, Fulwood
Mrs B. A. Hayes, Preston
Mr and Mrs R. Hayton, Whittle-le-Woods
Headquarters 42 (NW) Brigade, Fulwood
    Barracks
Mr and Mrs E. J. Heathman, Fulwood
Gladys Emily Heaton, Hawkshaw, Bury
Bob Hempton and Gerald Rawlinson,
    Longridge
Carole Anne Henery, Canada
Peter J. Henery, Lytham
Mr Stanley B. Higginson, Ashton
George Frederick Hind, Birkdale, Southport
Simon Hindle, Ingol
Mr Ralph L. Hinton, Loughborough
Holme Slack County Primary School, Preston
Louise and James Holmes, Freckleton
Michael Peter Hopkinson, Penwortham
Mrs J. M. Hornby, Tarleton Moss, Tarleton
Dr J. Stuart Horner, Samlesbury
Mrs Phyllis Horner, Maldon, Essex
George Edward Houghton, Cheadle Hulme
Maurice Thomas, Steven Andrew and Katie
    Sarah Houghton, Haddenham
Neil Timperley Houghton of Newbold,
    Derbyshire
Thomas Houghton of Crewe, Cheshire
Steven Andrew Houston, Fulwood
Mrs Brenda Graham Howe, Penwortham
Mrs Judith K. Hughes, Fulwood
Bob Hunter, Southport
Philip Robert Hunter, Crossens
Mr Trevor Richard Hunter, Swanage, Dorset
Keith and Pat Hutton, Fulwood
Mrs Linda Hyde, Fulwood
Bernard Iddon, Preston
Mrs Fleetwood Inglefield, Penwortham
Mrs Elsie Jackson, Ashton
Mr J. Alan Jackson, London
Mr John William Jackson, Alton, Hants
Gordon James Jamieson, Nottingham

Wm Jenkinson, Preston

Gerard Johnson, Fulwood

Mrs Pauline Johnson, Walton-le-Dale

Mrs M. Johnson, Hesketh Bank

Mr and Mrs M. R. Johnson, Attleborough

Mr Mark Jolly, Fulwood

T. Jolly (Services) Ltd, Preston

Justine Jury, Penwortham

Julie Kelly, Higher Walton

Terry Kelly, Higher Walton

Mrs Eileen Kenyon, Penwortham

Mrs E. Kershaw, Grimsargh

Mr and Mrs I. D. Kewley, Ramsgreave

Peter Kitchen, Darwen

KPMG Peat Marwick, Preston

Mr Alban Lakeland, Fulwood

Mrs Iris Lilian Lambert and Miss Sherry
Lambert, Preston

Janet Lancaster, Fulwood

Mr and Mrs H. R. Latham, Boddington Pub
Co., Preston

Beryl Lawson and Russell M. Beaumont,
Fulwood

Pat and Bob Lawson, Ashton-on-Ribble

Betty and Mary Leach, Fortrose, Rosshire

Mr Philip H. Lee, Bamber Bridge

Legal & Trade Collections Ltd., Preston

S. Marcus Leigh, Penwortham

Mr J. and Mrs A. Leeming, Ashton-on-Ribble

Mr I. Lewis, Preston

Leyland Methodist Infant School, Leyland

Longridge High School, Longridge

Peter Middleton Lovett, Swanage

Karen Jane Lowe, Penwortham

Frank and Barbara Lupton, Fulwood

Miss S. M. Malinowski, Penwortham

Derek W. Marland, South Queensferry,
Scotland

W. S. Marsden, Netherlands

Mrs Linda Martens, Canada

Andrew Martindale, Fulwood

Mr Harold Martindale, Preston

Mrs E. M. Mason, Hoghton

Terry Mason, Ashton-on-Ribble

Mr and Mrs D. T. May and family, Preston

Nathan McIlwaine, Fulwood

Mr and Mrs P. D. McLinden, Great Sankey,
Warrington

Mr and Mrs J. F. D. McMillan, Croston

George and Joan Mercer, Penwortham

Mr Alexander W. Miller, Fulwood

Hugh Miller, Golborne, Warrington

C. G. Millward, Preston

Martin, Caroline, Matthew and Jill Moore,
Fulwood

Vera and Dennis Moran, Astley Bridge

Mrs Joyce Muir, Fulwood

Mrs M. V. Muncaster and Mr B. S.
Muncaster, Woodplumpton

Jean Murdoch, Preston

Ian, Stephanie, Clare and Benjamin Murray,
Hoghton

Mr William Murray, Hoghton

Rear Admiral J. A. L. Myres CB, Oxford

Katharine Myres

Mr and Mrs James, T. and Joan Nelson,
Walton-le-Dale

George Raymond and Joyce Newman,
Hutton

Gail Newsham, Bispham, Blackpool

Miss M. J. Ogden and Miss S. M. Crooks,
Longridge

Mr and Mrs G. O'Neil, Fulwood

Mrs Elizabeth O'Reilly, Ingol

Our Lady's High School, Fulwood

Our Lady and St Edward's R. C. Primary
School, Fulwood

P. and G. Paccy and family, Fulwood

James Parker, Salwick, Preston

Stephen L. Pearce, Fulwood

Mrs Ann M. Pendlebury, Grimsargh

Mr T. Pothecary and Mrs V. Cochrane,
Blackpool

Mr William Potts, Fulwood

Henry and Irene Preston, Preston

Ingrid and Jeff Price, Walton-le-Dale

William Pye Ltd., Civil Engineering,
Longridge

Brian George Quinn, Lostock Hall

Mr and Mrs R. G. Rawlinson, Fulwood

Patricia Richards, Ashton on Ribble

P. T. and J. Richardson, Penwortham

Mrs D. Rigby, Ingol

Master David Rhys Riley, Cottam

Jean and Frank Riley, Adelaide

D. K. Roberts Textiles, Fulwood

Eric and Celia Roberts, Burghfield

Mr and Mrs J. N. Ruffley, Preston

St Andrews C. E. Primary School, Ashton

Paul and Rosemary Sallis, Penwortham

Arthur Salter, Lostock Hall

Frank W. Salter and Mrs W. Salter, Fulwood

Mrs Brenda Isabell Scholes, Penwortham

Gareth Seal, Bamber Bridge

Bernard Seed, Longridge

Douglas Seed, Fulwood

Mrs Mary Agnes Sefton, Preston

Pat Sefton and Bernadette Sefton, Preston

John Sergeant, Brixton, London

Ruth Sharples, Ingol

Mr and Mrs W. Shaw, Penwortham

F. R. Sherliker, Runcorn

Mr and Mrs S. J. Sherliker and Family,
Chorley

Mr and Mrs E. Shorrock, Rusland, Ulverston
The Lord Shuttleworth, Carnforth
Rokaya, Ismail, Rehana, Imran and Ikram
    Sidat, Preston
Mr and Mrs Frank Sim, Garstang
Paul T. R. Simons, Penwortham
R. W. Singleton, Blackburn
Alice Smith, Canada
Mrs Dorothy Smith, Ingol
Eileen M. Smith, Bamber Bridge
Mrs Joan E. Smith, Bamber Bridge
John and Eileen Smith, Fulwood
Lesley-Anne Smith, Bamber Bridge
Mr Martin B., Mrs Margaret M., Helen and
    Philip Smith, Fulwood
Paul Henry Smith, Preston
Edmund Snailham, Preston
Mary Sontag, Fulwood
Edmund and Kathleen Southworth, Lostock
    Hall
Edward Stanley, London
Adrian Paul Stephenson, Fulwood
Mr and Mrs B. Stevens, Fulwood
Stephen Stirland, Stoke-on-Trent
Alice Stirzaker, aged 2, Longton
Jenny Stirzaker, aged 9, Longton
Louise Stirzaker, aged 6, Longton
Richard James Stirzaker, Longton
Allan and Dorothy Sumner, Preston
Mr and Mrs F. Sutcliffe, Ontario, Canada
Jeff Sutcliffe, Woodplumpton, Preston
R. and W. Sutcliffe, Woodplumpton, Preston
Joseph William Sutton, Penwortham
Deidre G. Swailes, Feltham
I. R. Swarbrick, Brisbane, Australia
J. B. R. Swarbrick, Fulwood
P. A. Swarbrick, York
Olwen and William Swindlehurst, Longton
Roy Tattersall, Fulwood
Ann and Tom Taylor, Penwortham
Clive Taylor, Longton
David and Maureen Thornton and Family,
    Preston
Miss Helen Tomlinson, Fulwood
George Clifford Tootell, Ashton
Alan and Ann Topping, Fulwood
James Topping, Fulwood
John Richard Charles Topping, Childwall
Alison E. G. Toulmin, Burgess, Dulwich
Arthur H. Toulmin, Burgess, Cranleigh
Geoffrey J. D. Toulmin, Burgess, Dulwich
Hilary L. M. Toulmin, Burgess, Dulwich
John Toulmin QC, Burgess, Dulwich
Aidan Turner-Bishop, Frenchwood

The Library, University of Central
    Lancashire, Preston
Mr Daniel Vickers, East Ham, London
T. A. Vickers, Kirkham
Gillian and William Waddilove, Wolston,
    Coventry
Marjorie and William Waddilove (snr),
    Broughton
Mrs Anna Walker, Kirkandrews-on-Esk,
    Longtown
Basil and Constance Isabella Walmsley,
    Barnston, Wirral
William B. Walsh, Preston
Mrs E. Warburton, Preston
Raymond and Marguerite Warburton,
    Preston
Miss J. Ward, Fulwood
J. J. Ward, Broughton
Bernard Watson, Painting Contractor, Preston
Terence E. Whitfield, New Longton
Mr and Mrs J. A. Whittaker, Penwortham
Richard John Whittle, Lightwater, Surrey
C. C. Wilcock, Lostock Hall
Helen Wilcockson, Salisbury
Richard Howson Wilcockson, Plymouth
Mr David S. Wild, Penwortham
John Wilkinson, Fulwood
John and Shelley Maloney, Preston
Mark and Rachel Williams, Accrington
Mr T. J. and Mrs D. A. M. Williams,
    Ashton-on-Ribble
Andrew and Tricia Wilson, Broughton
Deborah A. Wilson, Reading
Francis Eden Wilson, Broughton
Mrs Joan Mounsey, Lostock Hall, Preston
D. Winnard, Inskip
R. G. Winnard, Inskip
Graham Woodcock, CBE, MA, Haslingden
Ian P. Woodcock, Warminster
T. Woodcock, Somerset Herald, College of
    Arms, London
Josh William Worthington, Ashton-on-Ribble
Ryan Francis Worthington, Ashton-on-Ribble
Alison and John Wright, Preston
Amy Victoria Wright, Penwortham
Lucy Jane Wright, Fulwood
Sally Wright, Penwortham
Margaret Woods, Penwortham
Rebecca Dawn Yates, Broadgate, Preston
Susan Yeadon, Preston
J. G. Youll, Preston
Catherine Siran Young, Woodplumpton
Diane Young, Woodplumpton
Norman B. Young, Woodplumpton